# English Alive!

*Nelson Thornes Caribbean English*

Book ③

Alan Etherton
Thelma Baker
Joyce Jonas
Judith Pereira

UNIVERSITY PRESS

Great Clarendon Street, Oxford, OX2 6DP, United Kingdom

Oxford University Press is a department of the University of Oxford.
It furthers the University's objective of excellence in research, scholarship,
and education by publishing worldwide. Oxford is a registered trade mark of
Oxford University Press in the UK and in certain other countries

Text © Alan Etherton 2004
Original illustrations © Oxford University Press 2015

The moral rights of the authors have been asserted

First published by Nelson Thornes Ltd in 2004
This edition published by Oxford University Press in 2015

All rights reserved. No part of this publication may be reproduced,
stored in a retrieval system, or transmitted, in any form or by any
means, without the prior permission in writing of Oxford University
Press, or as expressly permitted by law, by licence or under terms
agreed with the appropriate reprographics rights organization.
Enquiries concerning reproduction outside the scope of the above
should be sent to the Rights Department, Oxford University Press, at
the address above.

You must not circulate this work in any other form and you must
impose this same condition on any acquirer

British Library Cataloguing in Publication Data
Data available

978-0-7487-8534-6

17

Printed and bound by CPI Group (UK) Ltd, Croydon, CR0 4YY

**Acknowledgements**

**Illustrations:** Geoff Jones (Beehive Illustrations), Peter Dennis, Judy Stevens and Avril Turner
**Cartoons:** Rupert Besley
**Page make-up:** Pantek Arts Ltd, Maidstone, Kent

Although we have made every effort to trace and contact all
copyright holders before publication this has not been possible in all
cases. If notified, the publisher will rectify any errors or omissions at
the earliest opportunity.

Links to third party websites are provided by Oxford in good faith
and for information only. Oxford disclaims any responsibility for
the materials contained in any third party website referenced in
this work.

# Contents

Introduction ix

## Unit 1 *Pirates of the Caribbean* page 1

| | | |
|---|---|---|
| 1.1/3 | Reading comprehension | 1 |
| 1.4 | Vocabulary: meaning in context | 4 |
| 1.5 | Expand your vocabulary | 5 |
| 1.6 | Looking ahead | 6 |
| 1.7 | Writing: handwriting | 6 |
| 1.8 | Thinking skills | 7 |
| 1.9/10 | Grammar: using the Simple Present tense | 8 |
| 1.11 | Grammar: 'too' + adjective + infinitive | 10 |
| 1.12 | Punctuation: using a full stop (revision) | 11 |
| 1.13 | Spelling (revision) | 12 |
| 1.14 | Writing: story, narrative or factual | 14 |

## Unit 2 *Trinidad at War* 15

| | | |
|---|---|---|
| 2.1/3 | Reading comprehension | 15 |
| 2.4 | Vocabulary: meaning in context | 17 |
| 2.5 | Expand your vocabulary | 18 |
| 2.6 | Speaking: history | 19 |
| 2.7 | Grammar: using the Simple Past tense (1) | 20 |
| 2.8 | Grammar: using the right preposition | 21 |
| 2.9 | Grammar: using the Simple Past tense (2) | 22 |
| 2.10 | Speaking and listening | 24 |
| 2.11 | Study skills: the parts of a book | 24 |
| 2.12 | Study skills: reference sources | 25 |
| 2.13 | Enjoying poetry: 'If' and 'The Listeners' | 25 |
| 2.14 | Writing: making a summary | 27 |

## Unit 3 *Danger – Bears!* 31

| | | |
|---|---|---|
| 3.1/3 | Reading comprehension | 31 |
| 3.4 | Vocabulary: meaning in context | 33 |
| 3.5 | Speaking: asking for help | 34 |
| 3.6 | Vocabulary: the formation of nouns | 34 |
| 3.7 | Vocabulary: figurative language – metaphors (revision) | 35 |

| 3.8 | Grammar: using the Present Continuous tense (revision) | 36 |
| 3.9 | Grammar: construction shift (re-expression) | 39 |
| 3.10 | Grammar: using 'whose' | 39 |
| 3.11 | Grammar: using 'then', 'therefore' and 'thus' | 40 |
| 3.12 | Reading: In Jasper National Park | 42 |
| 3.13 | Writing a news report (writing and summary) | 44 |

## Unit 4  Tiger Gets an Education  45

| 4.1/3 | Reading comprehension | 45 |
| 4.4 | Punctuation: using the full stop | 47 |
| 4.5 | Study skills: using a dictionary | 48 |
| 4.6 | Vocabulary: dialect and standard English | 49 |
| 4.7 | Grammar: using the Past Continuous tense | 50 |
| 4.8 | Punctuation: using an apostrophe | 52 |
| 4.9 | Enjoying poetry: 'A Tale of Two Tongues' | 54 |
| 4.10 | Writing: argumentative and creative topics | 55 |

## Unit 5  A Foggy Night  56

| 5.1 | Writing skills: stories | 56 |
| 5.2/3 | Reading | 58 |
| 5.4 | Writing: starting a story | 60 |
| 5.5 | Understanding | 61 |
| 5.6 | Vocabulary: meaning in context | 61 |
| 5.7 | Discussion | 62 |
| 5.8 | Writing: using paragraphs | 62 |
| 5.9 | Expand your vocabulary | 63 |
| 5.10 | Writing: completing a report | 64 |
| 5.11 | Vocabulary: figurative language | 65 |
| 5.12 | Listening: understanding a map | 65 |
| 5.13 | Think, discuss, decide | 67 |
| 5.14 | Writing: factual, story or summary/report | 68 |

## Unit 6  The Corn Thief  69

| 6.1–4 | Reading comprehension | 69 |
| 6.5 | Vocabulary: meaning in context | 71 |
| 6.6 | Vocabulary: idioms | 72 |
| 6.7 | Study skills: using a thesaurus | 74 |
| 6.8 | Grammar: agreement of subject and verb (revision) | 75 |
| 6.9/10 | Grammar: relative pronouns | 76 |
| 6.11 | Grammar: 'there is' and 'there are' (revision) | 79 |

| | | |
|---|---|---|
| 6.12 | Grammar: 'there was' and 'there were' (revision) | 80 |
| 6.13 | Punctuation: using capital letters and full stops (revision) | 80 |
| 6.14 | Enjoying poetry: two poems about dawn | 81 |
| 6.15 | Writing: a poem, continuing/writing a story | 83 |

## Unit 7  *Modelling*  84

| | | |
|---|---|---|
| 7.1/3 | Reading comprehension | 84 |
| 7.4 | Vocabulary: meaning in context | 86 |
| 7.5 | Vocabulary: the emotive value of words | 87 |
| 7.6 | Grammar: using the Present Perfect tense (revision) | 89 |
| 7.7 | Grammar: correcting mistakes | 91 |
| 7.8 | Grammar: using 'It's time …' | 92 |
| 7.9 | Writing: making a summary | 93 |
| 7.10 | Enjoying poetry (1): 'On an Afternoon Train from Purley to Victoria' | 93 |
| 7.11 | Writing: addressing an envelope | 94 |
| 7.12 | Enjoying poetry (2): limericks | 95 |
| 7.13 | Writing: narrative, story, expository | 97 |

## Unit 8  *Medical Training?*  98

| | | |
|---|---|---|
| 8.1/3 | Reading comprehension | 98 |
| 8.4 | Vocabulary: meaning in context | 101 |
| 8.5 | Vocabulary: homophones | 102 |
| 8.6 | Vocabulary: synonyms | 102 |
| 8.7/8 | Grammar: questions with tags | 104 |
| 8.9 | Grammar: using the right pronoun (revision) | 106 |
| 8.10 | Spelling: '-ce' and '-se' (revision) | 107 |
| 8.11 | Enjoying poetry: 'Song of the Banana Man' | 108 |
| 8.12 | Writing: story, narrative, expository | 110 |

## Unit 9  *Emigration*  111

| | | |
|---|---|---|
| 9.1 | Enjoying poetry (1): 'Colonisation in Reverse' | 111 |
| 9.2 | Enjoying poetry (2): 'The Emigrants' | 113 |
| 9.3/5 | Reading comprehension | 115 |
| 9.6 | Vocabulary: meaning in context | 117 |
| 9.7 | Writing: making a summary | 118 |
| 9.8 | Spelling | 119 |
| 9.9 | Grammar: making a complaint | 119 |
| 9.10 | Writing: story or expository | 121 |

## Unit 10 *The Treeman* — 122

| | | |
|---|---|---|
| 10.1/3 | Reading comprehension | 122 |
| 10.4 | Speaking: making an oral summary | 124 |
| 10.5 | Speaking: asking questions | 125 |
| 10.6 | Vocabulary: meaning in context | 125 |
| 10.7 | Grammar: compound adjectives | 126 |
| 10.8 | Grammar: reflexive and emphatic pronouns (revision) | 127 |
| 10.9 | Grammar: prepositions | 128 |
| 10.10 | Grammar: articles 'a', 'an', 'the' (revision) | 130 |
| 10.11 | Punctuation practice | 131 |
| 10.12 | Enjoying poetry: 'The Village' | 133 |
| 10.13 | Writing and summarising | 134 |
| 10.14 | Asking questions | 135 |

## Unit 11 *Sherlock Holmes* — 136

| | | |
|---|---|---|
| 11.1/3 | Reading comprehension | 136 |
| 11.4 | Vocabulary: meaning in context | 137 |
| 11.5 | Grammar: making and using adjectives | 138 |
| 11.6 | Vocabulary: occupations | 140 |
| 11.7 | Speaking: finding out somebody's occupation | 141 |
| 11.8/9 | Grammar: using the Past Perfect tense | 142 |
| 11.10 | Grammar: prepositions | 145 |
| 11.11 | Listening practice | 147 |
| 11.12 | Enjoying poetry: epitaphs | 148 |
| 11.13 | Writing: expository or narrative | 150 |
| 11.14 | Using a comma | 150 |

## Unit 12 *Gun Hill* — 151

| | | |
|---|---|---|
| 12.1/3 | Reading comprehension | 151 |
| 12.4 | Vocabulary: meaning in context | 153 |
| 12.5 | Semaphore | 154 |
| 12.6 | Sending a cable or telegram | 154 |
| 12.7 | Vocabulary: problem words | 155 |
| 12.8 | Vocabulary: affixes and roots | 157 |
| 12.9 | Vocabulary: prefixes | 158 |
| 12.10 | Punctuation: using a question mark | 159 |
| 12.11 | Grammar: reporting orders | 160 |
| 12.12 | Grammar: reporting statements | 161 |
| 12.13 | Enjoying poetry: 'Look Closer'; 'I Look Into My Glass' | 163 |
| 12.14 | Writing: descriptive, factual or argumentative | 165 |

## Unit 13  *The Best Sugar Boiler* — 166

| | | |
|---|---|---|
| 13.1/3 | Reading comprehension | 166 |
| 13.4 | Vocabulary: meaning in context | 168 |
| 13.5 | Vocabulary: idioms | 169 |
| 13.6 | Vocabulary: proverbs | 170 |
| 13.7 | Grammar: using adjectives | 171 |
| 13.8 | Writing: the structure of a story | 172 |
| 13.9 | Writing: starting a story | 173 |
| 13.10 | Punctuation: using inverted commas (revision) | 174 |
| 13.11 | Listening practice | 175 |
| 13.12 | Grammar: comparison of adjectives (revision) | 175 |
| 13.13 | Enjoying poetry: 'In the Gentle Afternoon' | 177 |
| 13.14 | Writing: narrative, descriptive or imaginative | 178 |

## Unit 14  *Bite-marks* — 180

| | | |
|---|---|---|
| 14.1/3 | Reading comprehension | 180 |
| 14.4 | Vocabulary: meaning in context | 182 |
| 14.5 | Writing: making a summary | 184 |
| 14.6 | Vocabulary: idioms | 185 |
| 14.7 | Grammar: indirect (reported) speech | 185 |
| 14.8 | Punctuation: using a question mark (revision) | 187 |
| 14.9 | Grammar: showing the purpose of an action | 187 |
| 14.10 | Enjoying poetry: 'Ana' | 188 |
| 14.11 | Writing: making up a story | 190 |
| 14.12 | Writing a story | 191 |

## Unit 15  *Black Bart* — 192

| | | |
|---|---|---|
| 15.1/3 | Reading comprehension | 192 |
| 15.4 | Vocabulary: meaning in context | 194 |
| 15.5 | Vocabulary: a cloze passage | 196 |
| 15.6 | Grammar: using 'as' | 197 |
| 15.7 | Grammar: indirect questions (1) | 198 |
| 15.8 | Pronunciation: syllable stress | 200 |
| 15.9 | Pronunciation: the letter 'h' | 200 |
| 15.10 | Grammar: indirect questions (2) | 201 |
| 15.11 | Grammar: using 'used to' | 202 |
| 15.12 | Enjoying poetry: 'For My Mother' | 203 |
| 15.13 | Writing: narrative, speech or expository | 204 |
| 15.14 | Uncountable nouns (revision) | 205 |

| **Unit 16** | *Tantie's Tooth* | 206 |
|---|---|---|
| **16.1/3** | Reading comprehension | 206 |
| **16.4** | Vocabulary: meaning in context | 208 |
| **16.5** | Punctuation: using an exclamation mark | 209 |
| **16.6** | Writing: developing character in a story | 210 |
| **16.7** | Discussion: would you like to be an author? | 210 |
| **16.8** | Vocabulary: changing dialect to standard English | 210 |
| **16.9** | Grammar: correcting common errors | 211 |
| **16.10** | Understanding: comparing pie charts | 213 |
| **16.11** | Grammar: adjective or adverb? (revision) | 214 |
| **16.12** | Grammar: using the right preposition | 215 |
| **16.13** | Enjoying poetry: 'Letter to England' | 216 |
| **16.14** | Writing: descriptive or narrative | 217 |

| **Appendix 1:** | Learning About Verbs | 218 |
|---|---|---|
| **Appendix 2:** | The Main Uses of Tenses | 222 |
| **Appendix 3:** | Irregular Verbs – Principal Parts | 227 |
| **Appendix 4:** | Glossary of Language Words | 232 |
| **Appendix 5:** | Glossary of Literary Terms | 238 |

| **Index** | 243 |
|---|---|
| **Acknowledgements** | 246 |

# Introduction

This **English Alive!** course has been written with three main aims:

- to help students to do well in their school and CSEC examination
- to enable students to become increasingly accurate, perceptive and sensitive when they make or receive communications in English, and
- to present a moral purpose common to all major religions where that is possible.

The course is meant to be student-friendly and teacher-friendly. It has been developed as a pan-Caribbean series and supports English-learning across the region, leading to the CSEC examination.

In Book 3 the main emphases are on the following basic areas.

## Reading comprehension

In addition to a variety of prose passages, this section includes the understanding and appreciation of poetry. The poems have been chosen to encourage students to develop a positive attitude to the appreciation of poetry and to illustrate a wide range of styles and topics. As in previous books in this series, the emphasis is firmly on enjoying poetry but greater attention is paid to the various stylistic devices which poets can use.

Questions on reading passages include ones set in multiple-choice and free-response form and cover a number of reading skills listed in the various syllabuses. When possible, the skills of writers are studied to see how a particular effect is achieved by an author.

## Vocabulary

The emphasis here is not only on understanding meaning in context but on the development of vocabulary and on the way in which individual words contribute to the enjoyment of the reader and/or to the fulfilment of the author's aim. In addition, there is considerable work on such areas as antonyms, synonyms, idioms, proverbs, affixes and words known to cause problems at this level.

## Grammar

Teachers are free to decide how much formal grammar they feel is appropriate for their students and helpful to them. The aim throughout the series is to provide students with an understanding of the basics of grammar, e.g. the parts of speech, sentence construction and the correct use of tenses, pronouns, etc. These elements should provide a foundation for subsequent work on correct usage. A great deal of the work on grammar is based on error analysis at this level, i.e. in addition to providing a clear guide to usage, the grammar sections deal with problems which are known to exist at Form 3 (or Grade 9) level.

## Writing

This area includes work on paragraphs, informal and formal summaries, reports, statements, spelling and punctuation. It also provides a wide range of composition topics (often related to a theme or passage in the unit) to give students practice in various types of written work. As far as possible, interesting topics have been chosen to act as a stimulus for the writer.

Throughout the book, students are introduced to specific writing skills and there is particular emphasis on the techniques involved in writing a short story.

A **Teacher's Guide** is available on the Internet at www.oxfordsecondary.co.uk/english-alive or in hard copy form from your local agent. The Guide contains answers, helpful suggestions and scripts for use in listening practice work.

# 1  Pirates of the Caribbean

### 1.1
## Pre-reading

In the seventeenth century, pirates attacked Spanish ships and towns in the Caribbean. At one time, a pirate (Henry Morgan) even became governor of Jamaica. In modern times, pirates still exist in S.E. Asia and the South China Sea but they are not as successful as the seventeenth-century pirates were.

In Disneyworld and Disneyland, 'Pirates of the Caribbean' is one of the most popular attractions. Visitors travel in small boats along a 'river' which takes them into the world of pirates and even through a town being burnt and looted by pirates.

### 1.2
## Reading

## Pirates of the Caribbean

If you visit Disneyworld (in Florida) or Disneyland (in California), make sure that you go into one of the star attractions: 'Pirates of the Caribbean'. Don't be deterred if there is a long queue. Each small boat inside the attraction takes over 20 people at a time, and there is a non-stop chain of boats ready to take visitors.

5   When you venture inside, you soon reach the embarkation point on the bank of a miniature artificial river. There you will see a number of parallel white lines on the ground, and an attendant dressed as a pirate will usher you into a pair of the lines. The purpose of the lines is to indicate which row of seats you must sit in when your boat arrives. Within a few seconds, a small boat appears out of the
10  semi-darkness and you step into it. Adventurous (or foolhardy?) passengers sit in the first or second row, unaware of what awaits them. More experienced or timid passengers sit farther back.

When our turn comes, we get into the last row of a boat which soon moves forward, fastened to an unseen track below the surface. We pass an old man
15  rocking peacefully in his chair on the verandah of his wooden house. Fireflies flit around him, creating the illusion of a tropical Caribbean forest.

Almost immediately, the voice of a seventeenth-century pirate booms out above us. It tells us to beware. We are approaching unseen dangers!

'Hm,' you think to yourself. 'You can't scare me. It's only a boat ride. I'm not
20  frightened!'

You soon will be! A few seconds later, our boat falls straight down a waterfall, throwing up spray which drenches passengers in the first two rows. From our vantage point in the last row, we look back and watch the following boat shoot down the waterfall.

25  'Oh! So there ARE dangers in this place,' you think. 'I wasn't expecting that.'
Our boat sails peacefully along the underground river. Then 'Whoosh! Here we go again!' and the boat drops down a second waterfall, soaking the unlucky people in the prow. 'Serves them right for sitting there!'
By this time, you may begin to feel a little apprehensive, not knowing exactly
30  what comes next. But there are no more waterfalls to come. The boat sails serenely past spacious caves in which the figures of pirates (and some skeletons) sit amidst treasure chests and piles of jewellery and gold coins.
After a few leisurely minutes, the river opens out into a harbour. We see a pirate ship anchored off-shore and exchanging shots with a fort on land. The path of our
35  boat takes us between the ship and the fort. Cannon balls splash into the sea close to the boat.
Luck is with us. We manage to get past the fort unscathed and enter a burning town. Outside one house, a group of pirates have a rope round the neck of a wealthy landowner and are lowering him into a well to encourage him to disclose where
40  his savings are.
Our boat goes deeper and deeper into the burning town. Pirates shoot at us and we hear the ping of bullets hitting metal.
Then we pause at the foot of a 45 degree upwards slope. The boat ahead of us climbs up the slope and disappears round a bend at the top. Now it is our turn. The
45  submarine track hoists us safely up the slope and delivers us to the embarkation point at which the voyage started.
We get out and run off to rejoin the queue, anxious to have another encounter with the pirates. This time we must sit in the front row of our boat.

## 1.3
## Understanding

**A**  Choose the best answer each time.
1.  The first paragraph implies that ____.
    A. people should not bother to go into 'Pirates of the Caribbean' if the queue is long
    B. the queue moves forward quite swiftly
    C. you can see 'Pirates of the Caribbean' in Florida or California but not at both places
    D. the boats are chained together so that they cannot move

2.  By using 'venture' instead of 'go' in line 5, the author ____.
    A. shows that he does not enjoy the 'Pirates of the Caribbean' attraction
    B. warns readers not to go into 'Pirates of the Caribbean'
    C. shows his disapproval
    D. suggests that some risk is involved

3.  The white lines at the embarkation point are meant to ____.
    A. reduce the length of the queue

B. show which way the boats are going
   C. make passengers get on the boats in an orderly way
   D. show passengers where to get off

4. Some passengers prefer to sit at the back of a boat ____.
   A. to get a better view
   B. to keep dry
   C. because it is safer there
   D. because there is more space there

5. What apparently makes the boat move along the river?
   A. A moving track in the water.
   B. An engine in the back of the boat.
   C. Sails in the middle of each boat.
   D. The passengers have to row.

6. The old man, his house and the fireflies are meant to ____.
   A. warn passengers to expect dangers
   B. make passengers forget a possible danger
   C. scare passengers in the boats
   D. create a suitable background atmosphere

7. In line 28, what word has been omitted before 'Serves'?
   A. He    B. It    C. They    D. Waterfall

8. What might cause the concern mentioned in line 29?
   A. The old man's warning.
   B. The noise of ship's guns.
   C. The unexpected waterfalls.
   D. Their fear of pirates.

9. It is likely that the jewellery and gold coins mentioned in line 32 were ____.
   A. genuine
   B. imitations
   C. stolen
   D. on loan

10. In line 37, the sentence 'Luck is with us' is ____ because luck was not involved.
    A. misleading
    B. a warning
    C. a simile
    D. ungrammatical

**B** Answer these questions about the passage.

1. If you saw this passage in a travel magazine, what do you think its purpose would be?

2. At what point does the author start to use short paragraphs and why does he use them?

3. Why does the author often use 'we' and 'our' in the passage?

4. A euphemism is a deliberate understatement. (See Appendix 5.) Which verb is used as a euphemism in line 39?

## 1.4 Vocabulary: meaning in context

**A** Choose the word(s) which best show(s) the meaning of the underlined words as they are used in the passage in 1.2.

1. go into one of the <u>star</u> attractions (line 2)
   A. shining   B. rare   C. best   D. biggest

2. Don't be <u>deterred</u> if there is a long queue. (line 3)
   A. put off   B. surprised   C. impatient   D. made out

3. When you <u>venture</u> inside (line 5)
   A. look   B. enquire   C. remain   D. take the risk of going

4. you soon reach the <u>embarkation</u> point (line 5)
   A. end of the queue   C. getting on
   B. place where you pay   D. most important

5. on the bank of a <u>miniature</u> artificial river (line 6)
   A. unnatural   B. very small   C. slow-moving   D. attractive

6. on the bank of a miniature <u>artificial</u> river (line 6)
   A. attractive   B. diverted   C. man-made   D. peaceful

7. a number of <u>parallel</u> white lines (line 6)
   A. pointing in the same direction   C. brightly painted
   B. of roughly similar length   D. having the same width

8. an attendant … will <u>usher</u> you into a pair of the lines (line 7)
   A. force   B. escort   C. push   D. enclose

**B** Match the underlined words with the meanings which they have in the passage.

| Words from the passage | Meanings |
|---|---|
| 1. Adventurous (or <u>foolhardy</u>?) (line 10) | a) not hurt or damaged |
| 2. creating the <u>illusion</u> (line 16) | b) front (of a boat) |
| 3. which <u>drenches</u> passengers (line 22) | c) fearful, concerned |
| 4. in the <u>prow</u> (line 28) | d) wide, large |
| 5. feel a little <u>apprehensive</u> (line 29) | e) reveal |
| 6. The boat sails <u>serenely</u> (line 31) | f) lifts |
| 7. <u>spacious</u> caves (line 31) | g) false impression |
| 8. <u>unscathed</u> (line 37) | h) taking foolish risks |
| 9. <u>disclose</u> where (line 39) | i) calmly |
| 10. <u>hoists</u> us safely (line 45) | j) makes very wet |

English Alive!

## 1.5 Expand your vocabulary

Expand your vocabulary by completing Exercises 1 and 2 below. All the underlined words are taken from past CSEC examination papers.

### Exercise 1

Give antonyms (words of opposite meaning) for the underlined words *as they are used in these sentences.*

1. The bus stopped <u>abruptly</u> when a cow wandered across the road.
2. Our neighbours have a very <u>docile</u> dog.
3. It is <u>dangerous</u> to attempt to cross the river here.
4. Mr Williams is well known in our neighbourhood for his <u>generosity</u>.
5. The referee proved to be <u>impartial</u> and did an excellent job of controlling the game.
6. In some countries, the number of <u>literate</u> people is not very high.
7. Some students show a very <u>mature</u> approach to their studies.
8. Our bus service has proved to be very <u>reliable</u> for several years.
9. The manager of the football club became more and more <u>irate</u> as the game progressed.
10. When you go hiking, take only <u>essential</u> items with you to reduce the weight of your back-pack.
11. The soldiers marched <u>briskly</u> back to their barracks.
12. When the candidate announced his plans to the crowd, most people appeared to be rather <u>apathetic</u>.

### Exercise 2

Give brief explanations of the underlined words in the following sentences. Try to use no more than 10 words in each explanation. Your answers need not be complete sentences.

1. This field has not been <u>cultivated</u> for several years.
2. There are <u>predators</u> in both forests and towns.
3. Complete honesty is <u>priceless</u> in business and politics but is not very common.
4. If the police decide that the driver of the lorry was <u>negligent</u>, he may be charged with manslaughter.

5. There is an old saying in the Army: 'Never <u>volunteer</u> for anything'.

6. <u>Rowdy</u> members of the public were quickly ejected by stewards at the meeting.

7. Scientists say that it has taken millions of years for mankind to <u>evolve</u>.

8. Hyberna <u>glared</u> at the shop assistant and then walked out.

9. Stray animals are a constant <u>hazard</u> in many areas but most drivers try to avoid harming them.

10. Your plan seems quite reasonable but it does have one <u>flaw</u>: who is going to provide the necessary finance?

11. Make sure that you check your work <u>thoroughly</u> before you hand it in.

12. Who is <u>responsible</u> for keeping this lift in good working order?

## 1.6
## Looking ahead

The next 2½ years may decide the quality of your life for the next 50–60 years. The better your examination results are, the more chance you have of developing a successful career.

In the CSEC English examination, your result will depend upon several factors. These are the most important ones, and we will focus on them for the next 2½ years:

- the quality of your handwriting – if it is poor, the examiner may not be able to understand your ideas, no matter how clever they are

- the quality and accuracy of your language

- the quality of your thoughts, ideas and arguments

- your ability to arrange points in a logical order

- the range and quality of your vocabulary.

## 1.7
## Handwriting

### Exercise 3

Copy out the list above in the style of handwriting you will use in an examination. Show your work to at least two classmates and ask them to comment on it. Learn from their criticisms.

Avoid these errors:
- Don't make your handwriting too small. Take your time and make your words easy to read.

- Form each letter clearly:
  - Don't make 'd' look like 'cl'.
  - Don't make 'e' look like 'i'.
  - Put a dot (and *not* a small circle) above the letter 'i' and not above the next letter.
  - Cross the letter 't'.
  - Don't put long tails on letters such as 'g', 'j' and 'y'.
  - Make capital letters about twice as tall as small letters.
- If possible, use black or dark blue ink.
- Make your full stops clear. Use dots and not small circles.
- Don't start a new line with a comma. Put it after the preceding word.
- Don't squeeze up the letters in each word. Leave sufficient space between words.

If your handwriting is easy to read, and your classmates are satisfied with it, that's fine. You have made a good start. Now we will start to consider thinking skills.

## 1.8
## Thinking skills

Think about the following situations and answer the questions.

1. Amelia Smith was arrested outside a store, taken to a police station and charged with shoplifting. When her case is reported in a newspaper, which of the following descriptions of her can be used before her trial?
   a) a thief   b) a shoplifter   c) the suspect   d) an alleged shoplifter   e) a robber

2. When her case went to trial, Ms Smith was found not guilty. She saw the descriptions above in five different newspapers which gave an account of her arrest. Which of the newspapers can she sue for defamation of character?

3. Sheep have four legs. Cows have four legs. Therefore sheep are cows. What is wrong with this argument?

### Exercise 4

The following sentences were written by students. Comment on the faulty reasoning and/or faulty expression in the statements. Change them to make sense, if possible.

1. Some airlines are beginning to expand after the recession, so there will be more vacancies in them for pirates and cabin crew.

2. We must follow successful leaders because if we do not follow them who else will?

3. There has been an explosion at a local factory. All hospitals have been alerted. We are not sure how bad the situation is, but we are treating it as a major indecent.

4. In filling in particulars of your health, it is very important to mention any case of tubercular affection.

5. In the fight last night, Referee Tommy Little disqualified the challenger for disuse of his head after repeated warnings.

6. Rain falls in the form of water. Rain often supplies water.

7. We need books which can increase our knowledge. Such books and articles should not be written by any author at all.

8. It is well known that men have larger heads than women do. It follows that men are more intelligent than women.

9. Bob Marley's music is very different from other composers.

10. In your compositions, try to avoid as few mistakes as possible.

11. The distance between the moon and Earth is very far apart.

12. Rich people are to blame for the recession because if there were no rich people there would be more money for the poor.

## 1.9
## Grammar: using the Simple Present tense (1)
### Active forms

|  | Statements | Negatives | Questions |
|---|---|---|---|
| I, you, we, they | walk | do not walk | Do … walk? |
| he, she, it | walk**s** | does not walk | Does … walk? |

### Exercise 5

Make short sentences. Use the Simple Present tense of the verbs in brackets.

1. This torch (work) properly now.
2. Grandma (seem) to be better.
3. Everybody (look) happy now.
4. Miss Lee (speak) very quickly.
5. We (grow) many vegetables.
6. Auntie (hope) to come here tomorrow.
7. The furniture (look) new.
8. We (stay) at home during a hurricane.
9. Letitia (know) where Deena (live).
10. Everything (appear) to be in order now.

### Exercise 6

Complete these questions about present events.

1. ____ you like yams?
2. ____ anybody live in that house?
3. Where ____ your mother work?
4. How often ____ Earl write to you?

8  English Alive!

5. ____ the rain come through the roof?
6. ____ many tourists come here?
7. ____ your right arm still hurt?
8. What ____ the police officers want?
9. Why ____ Grandpa get up so early?
10. How much ____ computers cost?

### 1.10
# Grammar: using the Simple Present tense (2)
## Passive forms

|  | Statements | Negatives | Questions |
| --- | --- | --- | --- |
| I | am invited | am not invited | Am I invited …? |
| he, she, it | is invited | is not invited | Is he invited …? |
| you, we, they | are invited | are not invited | Are we invited …? |

### Exercise 7

Put in the passive Simple Present tense of the verbs in brackets.

1. A large part of the revenue of Trinidad and Tobago (derive) from oil.
2. A considerable amount of bauxite (export) from Jamaica every year.
3. High quality coffee (grow) in the Blue Mountains area of Jamaica.
4. However, sometimes inferior quality beans (mix) with high quality beans.
5. Then independent producers complain that their superior beans (degrade) and poor beans (sell) as 'Blue Mountain coffee'.
6. At the airport, the passengers' luggage (search) by security officers. This (do) as a safety precaution.
7. Passengers arriving in the USA or UK from the Caribbean (sometimes search) by Customs officials if they (suspect) of carrying drugs. If necessary, they (detain) and an X-ray (take) to check on the contents of their stomach.
8. In Singapore, anybody who (find) to be in possession of more than a small quantity of illegal drugs (hang), regardless of race or sex. As a result, Singapore (avoid) by drug smugglers because they (frighten) of being caught.
9. In Barbados there is an enormous underground labyrinth of caves and streams. It (call) Harrison's Cave. Visitors (take) underground in an electric tram, so they (not expect) to do any exploring by themselves.
10. Another attraction in Barbados (name) Orchid World. About 20,000 orchids (display) on a site which (surround) by sugar cane fields.

## 1.11
# Grammar: using 'too' + adjective + infinitive

We often use the pattern 'too' + an adjective + an infinitive, e.g.
   He is **too old to enter** the competition.

We can use a passive infinitive when necessary, e.g.
   She is much **too clever to be deceived** by that trick.

Sometimes the 'subject' of an infinitive is omitted. Compare these sentences:
   This coffee is too hot for me to drink.
   This coffee is too hot to drink.

 *Over to you!*

### Exercise 8

Join each pair of sentences below to make one sentence containing 'too' + an adjective + an infinitive. Leave out any unnecessary words.
1. Donnaree is young. She cannot apply for the job.
2. Mrs Harris is very busy. She cannot come to the phone now.
3. Those shoes are quite small. They will not fit Michelle.
4. The stream is wide. We cannot jump across it.
5. This vase is fragile. It can't be sent by post.
6. Those crabs are expensive. We can't buy them.

### Exercise 9

Make sentences using 'too' + an infinitive. Use 'for' + a noun or pronoun as well. Leave out any words which are unnecessary, e.g.
   That television set is rather expensive. My uncle cannot buy it.
   That television set is too expensive for my uncle to buy.

1. The water is muddy. We cannot swim in it.
2. The rent is very high. Miss Taylor cannot pay it.
3. This problem is extremely difficult. You cannot solve it by yourself.
4. The table is very big and heavy. I can't carry it by myself.
5. Some modern homes are very expensive. Ordinary people cannot afford them.
6. The water in this part of the river is very deep. Young children should not swim in it.
7. The experiment was very complicated. The scientist could not perform it alone.
8. This report is very long. I can't read all of it tonight.

**1.12**

# Punctuation: using a full stop (revision)

- Use a full stop to separate two main clauses *or* join them with a conjunction, e.g.
    Guyana is much bigger than Trinidad. It has fewer people.
    Guyana is much bigger than Trinidad **but** it has fewer people.

- Don't punctuate a subordinate clause as if it is a main clause, e.g.
    *wrong*: Tina noticed a wallet. Lying on the ground outside the store.
    *right*: Tina noticed a wallet lying on the ground outside the store.
    *wrong*: When Spanish slave-traders arrived at Barbados, the Caribs fled to St Lucia. Because they could hide in the mountains there.
    *right*: When Spanish slave-traders arrived at Barbados, the Caribs fled to St Lucia because they could hide in the mountains there.

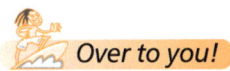

### Exercise 10

Punctuate these sentences and correct any mistakes in them. You may have to put in words or make other alterations.

1. Friendship is very important to us without it we would feel lonely.

2. Mr Buchanan decided not to buy a new car, he did not want to get into debt, anyway he felt sure that his old car was still reliable.

Unit 1 · *Pirates of the Caribbean*

3. Tourists tend to look for cheap goods. Examples radios, cameras, mobile phones.

4. We waited patiently for half an hour the sun set and it grew dark. So we decided to go home.

5. Fashions change. Sleeveless dresses one year, jeans and T-shirts the next.

6. I have finished my account of the problem of production. Next, the question of transport.

7. I remember my first visit to a big town, our village had no more than a hundred people in it at that time. Most of them working on the land.

8. In Guyana rivers are a very important means of transport, in some areas a river is the only highway for people. Because it is too expensive to build and maintain roads.

9. Some people are in favour of tourism and want to expand it. Whereas others do not wish to encourage it.

10. It is not easy for me to concentrate on my homework. While the rest of the family are watching television.

## 1.13

# Spelling (revision)

## 'ei' and 'ie'

When 'ei' and 'ie' are spoken with the sound of 'ee' (as in 'thief' and 'receive'), we usually put 'i' before 'e' except after 'c'. The principal exception is 'seize'.

Notice that this rule does *not* apply when 'ei' and 'ie' are spoken with a sound which is not 'ee'. Thus the rule does not apply to words such as 'foreign' and 'neighbour'.

*ie:* relief, believe, achieve, chief, fiend, field, grieve, briefly, siege, piece, species

*ei:* ceiling, conceited, received, deceive, receipt, perceive, conceive, seize

### Exercise 11

Put in 'ie' or 'ei'.

1. our n__ghbour
2. we rec__ved it
3. his h__ght
4. accused of dec__t
5. a for__gner
6. the c__ling
7. r__gn
8. the cash__r
9. perc__ved
10. n__ce
11. the ch__f obstacle
12. ach__ved
13. conc__ved
14. we bel__ved her
15. sover__gn

## Some problem words

Check that you can spell the words in these lists:

| List 1 | | List 2 | |
|---|---|---|---|
| Wednesday | describe | society | benefits |
| competition | description | journey | until |
| occurred | occasionally | peculiar | scene |
| scenery | behaviour | probably | thieves |
| modern | marriage | properly | library |

## '-ing' and '-ed'

Double the final consonant when you add '-ing' or '-ed' to a word of one syllable which ends in a consonant preceded by a *short* vowel, e.g.

    stop: stopping    clap: clapped    get: getting
    grab: grabbed    shop: shopping    cut: cutting
    skip: skipped    drop: dropped    win: winning
    run: running    hop: hopping    hit: hitting

If the vowel sound is long, the consonant is *not* doubled, e.g.
    hoping    writing    shooting    hiding    raining

Make sure that you can spell these words:
    refer: referred    begin: beginning    admit: admitted
    prefer: preferring    occur: occurred    permit: permitted
    transfer: transferred    remit: remitted    commit: committed

Learn the spelling of these words in standard English:
    travel: travelling    quarrel: quarrelled
    cancel: cancelled    signal: signalled

## Test

Work in pairs or as a class. Write down 10 words ending in –ed or –ing. Use your list to test a classmate or the class.

## 1.14
## Writing

Write about *one* of the following topics. Your teacher will tell you how long your composition should be.

1. Write a story or report in which one or more of the men in the picture below plays a part.

*or*

2. Describe a time when you visited a theme park or place of amusement in your own country or in another country.

*or*

3. If you have a computer, there are hundreds of games which you can play on the Internet. Describe one or more of the games. Can people learn anything by playing the games or are they just a pleasant waste of time?

*or*

4. Are there any pirates in modern times? If so, where are they and what do they do?

# 2 Trinidad at War

### 2.1
## Pre-reading

The Second World War lasted from 1939 to 1945. Soon after war was declared, thousands of young men and women left the Caribbean to enlist in the British Armed Forces. In the following extracts from Sam Selvon's *A Brighter Sun*, we can see how the war affected Trinidad in 1942 and then in 1945 when Germany and Japan were defeated.

### 2.2
## Reading

## Trinidad at War

### 1942

The nearest Trinidad ever got to actual warfare was one dark night in 1942. An enemy submarine sneaked into the harbour and blasted two ships at anchor. The explosions shook the city [Port of Spain]. No one knew what it was about, but terror remained for a few days. A compulsory service bill was never proclaimed because there
5   were sufficient volunteers. Later that year the western coast of the island was mined, and entrances to the harbour closed to shipping, and night sailings by coastal steamers stopped. By this time 15,000 people formerly engaged in food production had either joined the forces or were working with the Yanks. Foodstuffs were subsidised by the government to keep down prices. In a queue for bread
10  at a baker's in George Street a fight broke out between two men and one ran for the cutlass which a coconut vendor had stuck in his donkey cart. At least three marriages were hastened because the girls were pregnant. Tentative programmes of essential works were drawn up in anticipation of unemployment when work on the bases ceased. American authorities agreed to a methodical release of
15  labour so as not to disturb the economic system. The sugar crop dropped to a low level because no one wanted to work in the fields again, but shipping difficulties prevented the export of the reduced quantity and the population was urged to consume more sugar. Steps were being taken to introduce rationing.

### 1945

Precensorship of papers of passengers travelling to England from Trinidad ceased
20  in January 1945, and it was announced by the government that identity cards were no longer necessary. The next month the Home Guard was disbanded, and those

who were in it held parties in the restaurants and got drunk, and one man was run over by an American truck in Park Street. Gradually restrictive legislation slackened. V-E and V-J celebrations were marked by patriotic demonstrations and wild
25 merriment; steel bands, growing in the war years, took to the streets for the first time, and pandemonium reigned as Trinidadians were allowed to indulge in two days of Carnival, an annual festival which was held up when war broke out. There were fights between civilians and service personnel, and steel bands clashed, pelting bottles and stones and wielding sticks. Later on in the year censorship was stopped altogether,
30 motorcar zoning abolished, and restaurants were allowed to serve meals late in the evening. In the sugar and oil industries wage agreements were signed, but many people were still out of work, and labourers marched in the streets with placards, and a delegation visited the Governor, seeking relief. The legislature adopted a motion providing for increased benefits under the workmen's compensation
35 ordinance. In San Fernando a man appeared in court and registered his one hundred and forty-fifth conviction in three years. He had jacked up a car parked in front of a cinema and stolen the tyres. A Pan-American seaplane crashed and twenty-three out of thirty passengers were drowned. The report of the West Indies Royal Commission was released for publication; the demand for copies was five times
40 greater than the quantity available. The cost of living rose to 200 points, and it was a difficult thing to get butter and saltfish in the shops.

## 2.3
## Understanding

**A** Choose the best answer each time.

1. The submarine mentioned in line 2 was probably ____.
   A. American or British        C. French or Swiss
   B. German or Japanese         D. Russian or Chinese

2. The use of 'sneaked' in line 2 tells us that the submarine commander ____.
   A. was not familiar with the harbour   C. wished to be undetected
   B. was afraid of the ships at anchor   D. was not a good sportsman

3. In line 3, 'it' refers to ____.
   A. the attack by the submarine   C. two ships at anchor
   B. an enemy submarine            D. the second explosion

4. It seems very likely that the bill mentioned in line 4 was ____.
   A. to pay for damage to the ships   C. a proposal by the colonial government
   B. never completely paid            D. first approved in 1939

5. As far as we can tell, the purpose of the mining mentioned in lines 5–6 was to ____.
   A. obtain more building materials    C. protect Trinidad
   B. prevent fishermen from working    D. stop ships from sailing at night

*English Alive!*

**B** Answer these questions about the passage.

1. What was the main reason why many small farmers and labourers ceased to produce food?
2. Why did the government start to consider 'essential works' (line 13)?
3. Why did the government want people to eat more sugar although sugar production had fallen?
4. What do you understand by the expression 'precensorship of papers' in line 19?
5. How did (a) the people and (b) the government react to the Allies' victory?
6. Censorship is mentioned in lines 19 and 29. What was the purpose of censorship?
7. What is the connection between the San Fernando criminal and the Pan-American plane?

## 2.4
# Vocabulary: meaning in context

**A** Choose the word(s) which best show(s) the meaning of the underlined words as they are used in the passage in 2.2.

1. A <u>compulsory</u> service bill was never proclaimed (line 4)
   A. severe   B. obligatory   C. involuntary   D. military

2. A compulsory service bill was never <u>proclaimed</u> (line 4)
   A. approved and announced   C. even considered
   B. debated by law-makers   D. considered but defeated

3. there were <u>sufficient</u> volunteers (line 5)
   A. too many   B. not enough   C. enough   D. excellent

4. people formerly <u>engaged</u> in food production (line 7)
   A. forced to work   C. working as slaves
   B. indentured   D. taking part

5. Foodstuffs were <u>subsidised</u> (line 9)
   A. quality-controlled   C. given financial support
   B. rationed   D. imported

6. <u>Tentative</u> programmes of essential works were drawn up (line 12)
   A. not yet definite   C. containing great detail
   B. meant to help the public   D. involving new jobs

7. Steps were being taken to introduce <u>rationing</u> (line 18)
   A. the prevention of the prices of various types of food from increasing
   B. the restriction of the number or amount of something which each person can have
   C. the control of where people are allowed to travel, especially in wartime
   D. the build-up of stocks of food in warehouses

Unit 2 · Trinidad at War   17

**B** Match the underlined words with the meanings which they have in the passage.

| Words from the passage | Meanings |
|---|---|
| 1. the Home Guard was <u>disbanded</u> (line 21)<br>2. <u>restrictive</u> legislation (line 23)<br>3. restrictive <u>legislation</u> (line 23)<br>4. <u>pandemonium</u> reigned (line 26)<br>5. <u>indulge</u> in two days of Carnival (line 26)<br>6. was stopped <u>altogether</u> (line 29)<br>7. motorcar zoning <u>abolished</u> (line 30)<br>8. a <u>delegation</u> visited the Governor (line 33)<br>9. <u>adopted</u> a motion (line 33)<br>10. workmen's compensation <u>ordinance</u> (line 35) | a) chaos<br>b) law<br>c) terminated<br>d) approved and passed into law<br>e) laws<br>f) take part<br>g) closed down and dispersed<br>h) completely<br>i) a representative group of people wanting something<br>j) not allowing people to do certain things |

## 2.5

# Expand your vocabulary

Expand your vocabulary by completing Exercises 1 and 2 below. Some of the underlined words are taken from past CSEC examination papers.

### Exercise 1

Give antonyms (words of opposite meaning) for the underlined words *as they are used in these sentences*.

1. An <u>affluent</u> person is not likely to worry about the cost of a pair of shoes.

2. When a tourist asked the way to the airport, she was <u>disconcerted</u> to be given directions in Creole.

3. There has been a <u>decline</u> in our sales recently.

4. That man is well known for his <u>arrogance</u>.

5. Yesterday a <u>famous</u> composer came to talk to us about music.

6. <u>Prosperity</u> has had quite an effect on some regions of the island.

7. In the past year, the increase in the cost of living has been <u>insignificant</u>.

8. Please have a look at this plan for a trip to Belize and let me know if you think it is <u>feasible</u>.

18  English Alive!

9. Is that building meant to be a <u>permanent</u> structure?

10. Francine's dress looks rather <u>flamboyant</u>.

11. My cousin belongs to a <u>militant</u> party which seeks to gain power.

12. Some animals are well known for their <u>bravery</u> in the face of danger.

### Exercise 2

Give brief explanations of the underlined words in the following sentences. Try not to use more than 10 words in each explanation. Your answers need not be complete sentences.

1. Traffic will flow more easily when this road has been <u>widened</u>.

2. A cat usually moves <u>stealthily</u> when it is stalking a mouse or bird.

3. The results of the competition will be <u>posted</u> on the school notice-board on Monday morning.

4. Arguing with him is <u>pointless</u> because nothing will get him to change his mind.

5. Sometimes politicians seek to <u>manipulate</u> the media in their favour.

6. His motive is <u>transparent</u>; he is trying to make a profit out of your troubles.

7. The Koran is the <u>sacred</u> book of Islam.

8. When Anna obtained a job as a reporter, her first <u>assignment</u> was to watch a match between two female soccer teams and write a report of it.

9. It often happens that people are <u>biased</u> against members of a different race.

10. A major aim of nearly every newspaper is to increase its <u>circulation</u> because then it can increase its charges to advertisers.

11. Don't use the water from that well. It has been <u>contaminated</u> by chemicals used by farmers to kill harmful insects.

12. When the company closed down unexpectedly, the management were unable to pay money due to workers, so several of them were left <u>destitute</u> and dependent on help from relatives and friends.

## 2.6
## Speaking: history

Do you know anybody at least 75 years old? *If possible*, talk to a relative who can remember conditions in your country during the Second World War. Make notes. Then come to school and tell the rest of the class what you have found out.

## 2.7
# Grammar: using the Simple Past tense (1)

See Appendix 3 for a list of the Simple Past forms of common irregular verbs.

## Active forms

|  | Statements | Negatives | Questions |
| --- | --- | --- | --- |
| Regular | stopped<br>rained | did not stop<br>did not rain | Did it stop?<br>Did it rain? |
| Irregular | went<br>saw | did not go<br>did not see | Did … go?<br>Did … see? |

Exercise 3

Answer these sentences. Use complete sentences in your answers.

1. When did the Second World War start?
2. When did the Second World War finish?
3. When were you born?
4. When did you first go to your present school?
5. What time did you go to bed last night? (An approximate time will do.)
6. What time did you get out of bed this morning?
7. When did you leave home this morning?
8. When did you last go to a dentist?

Exercise 4

Complete the following by putting in the question form (Simple Past tense) of the verbs in brackets.

1. ____ you ____ (walk) to school yesterday?
2. ____ it ____ (rain) last night?
3. ____ Germany ____ (win) the Second World War?
4. ____ you ____ (watch) TV yesterday?
5. For how long ____ you ____ (have) the television set on yesterday?

6. What homework ____ you ____ (have) yesterday?

7. ____ you ____ (do) it by yourself?

8. In which century ____ Norman Manley ____ (die)?

9. How much ____ your brother ____ (pay) for his new mountain bike?

10. ____ you ____ (lock) the door properly?

11. ____ Uncle's plane ____ (arrive) safely?

12. ____ you ____ (give) Anna my note?

## 2.8
# Grammar: using the right preposition

Some students have trouble with pairs of words like those shown below. We use a **preposition** after one verb but not after another which has a similar meaning:

| Word | Example |
|---|---|
| answer (no preposition)<br>reply to | Have you answered Tony's letter yet?<br>Have you replied **to** Vimala's letter yet? |
| reach (no preposition)<br>arrive at | When did Lorraine reach Miami?<br>When did Mitzie arrive **at** Orlando? |
| attend (no preposition with this meaning)<br>go to | Lana attends Camperdown High School.<br><br>My friend goes **to** Camperdown High School. |
| accompany (no preposition)<br>go with | The receptionist accompanied us to Miss Lee's office.<br>The receptionist went **with** us to Miss Lee's office. |
| discuss (no preposition)<br>have a discussion about | We discussed ways of fighting crime.<br>We had a discussion **about** ways of reducing crime. |
| demand (no preposition)<br>ask for | The workers demanded a 10% increase in their pay.<br>The workers asked **for** a 20% increase in their pay. |
| enter (no preposition with this meaning)<br>go in(to) | We entered the room cautiously.<br><br>We went **in(to)** the room cautiously. |
| visit (no preposition)<br>go to | Yesterday I visited some relatives in Georgetown.<br>Yesterday I went **to** some relatives in Georgetown. |

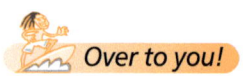 **Over to you!**

### Exercise 5

Complete the sentences below by choosing the right words from the brackets. The symbol (-) means that *no preposition is needed*.

1. If you have good qualifications, you can go (to, -) almost anywhere and get a good job.

2. Have you ever been to St Lucia? We went (to, -) there last month.

3. Children have to obey (-, to) their parents or get (-, into) serious trouble.

4. Owen could not sleep, so he just lay on the bed (during, -) the whole night.

5. If you want to ask a question, raise (up, -) your hand.

6. When you have asked your question, lower (-, down) your hand.

7. If you are not in favour of a proposal at a committee meeting, vote (against, for) it.

8. Lorna has just applied (to, -, for) a job in a bank.

9. My brother likes to listen (-, to) the radio (at, in) bed (in, at) night.

10. Sometimes people come to a Caribbean island to search (-, for) buried treasure.

11. Newspapers rely very heavily (at, on, to) the income (of, from, - ) advertisements, so they are not enthusiastic (for, about, at) printing news which may seem to be harmful (-, to) or critical (at, of) a major advertiser.

12. Is there any difference (at, of, between) these two words? Which of them is the better to use (at, in) this situation?

 ## 2.9
# Grammar: using the Simple Past tense (2)
### Passive forms

The passive form of the Simple Past tense is made with 'was' or 'were' + a past participle.

| Statements | I, he, she, it<br>you, we, they | was (not)<br>were (not) | injured in the accident.<br>insured against accidents. |
| --- | --- | --- | --- |
| Questions | Was<br>Were | I, he, she, it<br>you, we, they | expected to reply immediately?<br>given the correct form? |

English Alive!

## Uses

We use this form of the verb for a past (completed) action when the action is done *to* the subject and not *by* the subject. We often use the passive form of the verb when we do not know who did the action or are more interested in what was done than who did it.

### Over to you!

### Exercise 6

Put in 'was' or 'were'.

1. Our island ____ badly affected by the recent hurricane.

2. More than a hundred buildings ____ destroyed or badly damaged. In some cases, the roof of a home ____ blown off and the contents ____ damaged by heavy rain.

3. Luckily for us, our school ____ not much affected. Part of a fence ____ knocked down and a few windows ____ broken but the damage ____ quickly repaired.

4. Bradley Road is low-lying, so it ____ flooded and several motorists ____ forced to abandon their cars. A lot of mud ____ brought down from the hills and this made the road impassable.

5. A number of people ____ obliged to leave their homes. A community centre ____ opened to provide temporary accommodation for people who ____ made homeless by the storm.

6. Nobody ____ killed as a direct result of the storm but six people ____ taken to hospital. Five of them ____ given treatment and then discharged. One person ____ detained for observation.

### Exercise 7

Put in the passive Simple Past form of the verbs in brackets.

A few days ago, there was a serious fire in a luxury hotel a few miles from my home. According to the newspapers, police and fire officers believe that the fire ____ (start) deliberately. They believe that petrol ____ (use) to start a fire in a restaurant on the ground floor. Although the fire ____ (bring) under control eventually, extensive damage ____ (cause) to the hotel. Guests ____ (evacuate) to other hotels and some of the furniture ____ (save) by members of staff. The police are now searching for an employee who ____ (dismiss) two days before the fire started. The man ____ (allege) to have threatened guests. When he ____ (interview) about complaints which ____ (make) by two guests, he became angry and threatened to burn the hotel down.

## 2.10

## Speaking and listening

### The 'th' sound in 'that' and 'mother'

Listen and then say these words correctly. When you pronounce the /th/ sound in 'that' and 'mother', the tip of your tongue should be between your teeth at the front of your mouth.

1. they are
2. there is
3. this is
4. these are
5. that is
6. the rhythm
7. a fathom
8. the southern area
9. the northern area
10. a smooth skin
11. my mother
12. her father
13. his brother
14. the weather
15. another

### The 'th' sound in 'thick' and 'method'

Listen and then say these words correctly. When you pronounce this /th/ sound, put the tip of your tongue between your teeth but not as far out as for the 'th' sound in 'that' and 'mother' above.

1. a thick skin
2. a thin slice
3. a good theme
4. throw it
5. a lot of thunder
6. a healthy diet
7. a wealthy person
8. breathless
9. catholic
10. a new method
11. open your mouth
12. a small moth
13. an old myth
14. the right path
15. in the south

## 2.11

## Study skills: the parts of a book

Where can we find these parts of a book? What are they used for or what is in them? (Some books do not have all of these things.)

1. the dust jacket
2. the list of contents
3. a glossary
4. the spine
5. a preface
6. an index
7. an appendix
8. a foreword
9. a blurb

## 2.12
## Study skills: reference sources

What information can we obtain from each of the following?

1. a dictionary
2. a thesaurus
3. an almanac
4. a catalogue
5. a cookery book
6. an itinerary
7. a brochure
8. an atlas
9. a schedule (to a law)
10. an anthology
11. an owner's manual
12. a telephone directory

## 2.13
## Enjoying poetry

Read this poem and see if you agree with the advice in it. Does it apply to females as well as to males?

### If

If you can keep your head when all about you
Are losing theirs and blaming it on you,
If you can trust yourself when all men doubt you,
But make allowance for their doubting too;
5  If you can wait and not be tired by waiting,
Or being lied about, don't deal in lies,
Or being hated, don't give way to hating,
And yet don't look too good, nor talk too wise:

If you can dream – and not make dreams your master;
10  If you can think – and not make thoughts your aim;
If you can meet with Triumph and Disaster
And treat those two impostors just the same;
If you can bear to hear the truth you've spoken
Twisted by <u>knaves</u> to make a trap for fools,    **rogues, dishonest people**
15  Or watch the things you gave your life to, broken,
And stoop and build <u>'em</u> up with worn-out tools:    **them**

If you can make one heap of all your winnings
And risk it on one turn of pitch-and-toss,
And lose, and start again at your beginnings

20    And never breathe a word about your loss;
      If you can force your heart and nerve and sinew
      To serve your turn long after they are gone,
      And so hold on when there is nothing in you
      Except the Will which says to them: 'Hold on!'

25    If you can talk with crowds and keep your virtue,
      Or walk with Kings – nor lose the common touch,
      If neither foes nor loving friends can hurt you,
      If all men count with you, but none too much;
      If you can fill the unforgiving minute
30    With sixty seconds' worth of distance run,
      Yours is the Earth and everything that's in it,
      And – which is more – you'll be a Man, my son!

                                        *Rudyard Kipling*

## Questions

1. What is the meaning of 'keep your head' in line 1?
2. In what sense can it be true to call Triumph and Disaster 'impostors'?
3. Are lines 17 and 18 intended to encourage betting on horses?
4. In line 29, what does the poet mean by saying that a minute is 'unforgiving'?

Now read the poem below.

## The Listeners

'Is there anybody there?' said the Traveller,
    Knocking on the moonlit door;
And his horse in the silence champed on the grasses
    Of the forest's ferny floor;
And a bird flew up out of the turret,
    Above the Traveller's head;
And he smote upon the door again a second time;
    'Is there anybody there?' he said.
But no one descended to the Traveller;
    No head from the leaf-fringed sill
Leaned over and looked into his grey eyes,
    Where he stood perplexed and still.
But only a host of phantom listeners
    That dwelt in the lone house then
Stood listening in the quiet of the moonlight
    To that voice from the world of men;
Stood thronging the faint moonbeams on the dark stair,
    That goes down to the empty hall,

Hearkening in an air stirred and shaken
   By the lonely Traveller's call.
And he felt in his heart their strangeness,
   Their stillness answering his cry,
While his horse moved, cropping the dark turf,
   'Neath the starred and leafy sky;
For he suddenly smote on the door, even
   Louder, and lifter his head: -
'Tell them I came, and no on answered,
   That I kept my word!' he said
Never the least stir made the listeners,
   Though every word he spake
Fell echoing through the shadowiness of the still house
   From the one man left awake;
Ay, they heard his voice upon the stirrup,
   And the sound of iron on stone,
And how the silence surged softly backward,
   When the plunging hoofs were gone.

*Walter De La Mare*

### Questions

1. Which two expressions does the poet use for 'ate the grass'?

2. Find an example of alliteration near the start of the poem and another near the end.

3. Suggest a reason why the poet gave the Traveller grey eyes and not brown or blue ones.

4. Who were the listeners?

5. What made the 'sound of iron on stone'?

## 2.14

## Writing: making a summary

### Summaries in daily life

You probably make several informal **summaries** nearly every day. For example, your mother may speak to you when you come home from school:

    **Mother:**   Did you have a good day at school?
    **You:**      Yes, thanks. (You have just made a summary.)

*or*

    **Mother:**   What did you do in Maths today?
    **You:**      Algebra – quadratic equations. (You have made another summary.)

An informal summary can be short or long. You could have used two, three or ten sentences in each of the answers above. The length of your summary depends upon the situation.

Police Sergeant Warren has come to speak to your class about road safety. Read this conversation between him and a student named Marcia.

| | |
|---|---|
| **Marcia:** | Sgt Warren, can you tell us what the most common causes of traffic accidents are? |
| **Sgt Warren:** | By far the most frequent cause is simply lack of care. Motorists may go round a bend on the wrong side of the road. They may fail to watch the traffic or look ahead. Pedestrians sometimes step into the road without bothering to glance at the traffic. |
| **Marcia:** | What would you say is the next most common cause? |
| **Sgt Warren:** | That's hard to say without checking the statistics but I should think it's excessive speed. We get a lot of impatient drivers. They may be late for an appointment or hope to save time. They can't wait, so off they go - straight into the side of a lorry or the back of a taxi. |
| **Marcia:** | They don't do that deliberately, do they? |
| **Sgt Warren:** | No, they just can't stand waiting a few moments. But sometimes we get what I call 'deliberate fools'. They take risks going round a bend or overtaking. They're really reckless and sometimes we arrest them for dangerous driving. They can kill innocent people. |
| **Marcia:** | An uncle told me that alcohol causes many fatal accidents in the States. Is it as bad as that here? There was a bad case in the newspaper yesterday. The accident happened late at night. |
| **Sgt Warren:** | Yes, that's the time when drink takes its toll - usually from about 10 p.m. up to about 2.30 a.m. It's definitely a source of trouble. The guilty parties are almost always young men. They can't drive after they've been drinking, and they haven't got enough sense to let somebody else drive them home. As a result, some of them never see their homes again. Quite frankly, I don't worry much about them but they often involve innocent people, so they have to be stopped. |

| | |
|---|---|
| **Marcia:** | How about vehicles in a poor mechanical condition? And what about bad weather and poor visibility? |
| **Sgt Warren:** | Congratulations! I see you've prepared well. Those things do lead to accidents at times but I wouldn't say they're common causes. We don't check the mechanical condition of most vehicles unless the accident is serious, so we can't be sure of this point. If the weather changes unexpectedly, it can produce a rash of minor skids and bumps but most drivers are careful when the weather is bad. I would say that arrogant drivers are more of a menace than bad weather or faulty brakes. They hate being overtaken. You can guess what happens. |
| **Marcia:** | Well, thanks very much. I guess you've covered about everything. |
| **Sgt Warren:** | Just a minute. I ought to add that very young and very old people are often both the victim and cause of an accident. They shouldn't be on busy roads and they don't know when it's safe to cross. They get caught on corners too. They look both ways but forget about vehicles coming round the corner. |

## Summaries in examinations

In the CSEC examination, you may have to make a summary using a given number of words, e.g. 90–150. Follow these guidelines:

- Study the question carefully. You might have to make a summary of the whole of the passage or about one part or topic only.
- Find the main points.
- Omit details, illustrations/examples and negative information.
- Omit repetition.
- Try not to copy long expressions or sentences from the original. Use your own words whenever possible.
- Use suitable connectives to link your points so that they read smoothly.
- Use as many paragraphs as may be necessary (unless you are told to use one paragraph only).

We will study and practise these skills later in this book.

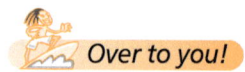 **Over to you!**

### Exercise 8

1. Re-read the conversation on pages 28 and 29. Make a numbered list of eight causes of traffic accidents mentioned by Sgt Warren. Put each cause on a separate line. Do not use more than *three* words for each cause. Make notes, not sentences.

2. Now use your notes to write a summary of the causes of traffic accidents mentioned by Sgt Warren. Use linking and other words to make complete sentences which read smoothly. Your summary can be between 50 and 100 words. Start in this way and include these words in your total number:
    *Sgt Warren spoke to Marcia about the causes of traffic accidents. He said that …*

# 3 Danger – Bears!

### 3.1
### Pre-reading

What chance would a boy aged 5 have in a fight with a fully-grown bear? Would his chance be greater or less if the fight took place mainly in the water of a remote lake? Read on and find out.

### 3.2
### Reading

## Danger – Bears!

This is a true story of Hughie Rosenberg, aged 5, and his sister, Barbie, aged 3. They lived in an isolated house by West Mark Lake in a rural part of the Canadian province of Manitoba.

5    One morning they were playing on a small jetty owned by the family and used by them when they went fishing in the lake. Their mother had ensured that they were wearing life-jackets although both children could swim. Normally, the remoteness of their home was adequate protection against robbers and other dangers, so they could play outside safely.

   However, on this occasion they had a nasty surprise. An adult black bear suddenly
10 appeared from the surrounding forest. Bad weather had deprived it of its normal food, so the bear was hungry. It ambled straight towards the children, probably intending to kill and eat them. As soon as the children saw it, Hughie realised that they were trapped. The bear stood between them and the safety of their home. When the bear approached the jetty, Hughie looked round in desperation. Realising that
15 there was no alternative, he said to his sister, 'Quickly! Let's jump in the lake. Maybe the bear will go away.'

   The children jumped off the jetty and started to swim away from the shore, hoping that the bear would abandon the chase. To their dismay, it followed them into the water and started to swim towards them.

20    'Get to the land!' Hughie shouted to his sister. 'Head for the house!'

   The children began to swim as fast as they could but they were no match for the bear. It soon overtook them and seized the collar of Barbie's life-jacket. Hughie tried to pull her away but the bear would not release its grip. There was only one thing left for Hughie to do. He snarled and growled angrily at the bear. This took the bear
25 by surprise. It let go of Barbie and hesitated for a moment, uncertain how dangerous Hughie was.

'Swim for your life!' Hughie gasped to his sister. 'Get to the house!'

The two children managed to reach the shore a few yards ahead of the bear. With the huge animal lumbering behind them, the children raced round the house, trying to find an unlocked door. Twice the bear caught up with them. Each time, Hughie stopped and snarled at the bear, making it stop in its tracks. After a few frantic moments, they managed to open a door and get into the house.

Mrs Rosenberg heard the children rush into the house. Hughie blurted out, 'There's a bear outside! It tried to kill us!'

With no gun in the house, Mrs Rosenberg telephoned the nearest forest ranger, about five miles away. He alerted the police and forty minutes later two men came in a fast launch. They saw the bear still prowling round the house. Unable to drive it away, they shot the animal. Then they inspected Barbie's life-jacket and saw bite marks and scratches where the bear had tried to get the little girl. They congratulated the children on their escape and praised Hughie for his bravery and quick thinking.

## 3.3
# Understanding

**A** Choose the best answer in each of the following.

1. How did the location of Hughie's home make an attack by a bear not unexpected?
   A. It was in Manitoba, which is a Canadian province.
   B. It was next to an isolated lake.
   C. The area was surrounded by forest.
   D. Bad weather had made the bear very hungry.

2. The main purpose of a jetty is to ____.
   A. allow people to get into and out of boats
   B. provide safe amusement for young children
   C. attract fish so that they can be caught easily
   D. provide shelter from wild animals

3. Mrs Rosenberg made her children wear life-jackets to ____.
   A. keep them warm in chilly weather
   B. give them protection against robbers and wild animals
   C. teach them how to swim
   D. prevent them from drowning

4. What made Hughie think that they were trapped?
   A. There was no boat at the jetty.
   B. The bear was determined and hungry.
   C. The bear blocked their path to their home.
   D. He knew that they could not move as swiftly as the bear.

5. The hope mentioned in line 17 ____.
   A. was soon fulfilled   C. led to their escape
   B. proved to be false   D. was not shared by Barbie

**B** Answer these questions about the passage.

1. What was nasty (line 9) about the surprise which the children had?
2. What is the meaning of 'they were no match for' in line 21?
3. In line 31, why are the moments called 'frantic'?
4. In line 36, what do you think the forest ranger said to the police?
5. If it took the two men ten minutes to get into the launch and start it, what was the speed of the launch in miles per hour?

## 3.4
## Vocabulary: meaning in context

**A** Choose the word(s) which best show(s) the meaning of the underlined words as they are used in the passage in 3.2.

1. They lived in an <u>isolated</u> house (line 2)
   A. single storey   B. temporary   C. remote   D. traditional

2. in a rural part of the Canadian <u>province</u> (line 3)
   A. city   B. town   C. county   D. state

3. Their mother had <u>ensured</u> that they were wearing life-jackets (line 5)
   A. asked   B. made certain   C. expected   D. known

4. the <u>remoteness</u> of their home (line 7)
   A. seclusion   B. size   C. location   D. privacy

5. their home was <u>adequate</u> protection (line 7)
   A. excellent   B. sufficient   C. foolproof   D. good

6. An <u>adult</u> black bear suddenly appeared (line 9)
   A. mature   B. old   C. large   D. male

7. Bad weather had <u>deprived</u> it of its normal food (line 10)
   A. robbed   B. removed   C. reduced   D. lessened

8. It <u>ambled</u> straight towards the children (line 11)
   A. rushed   B. sauntered   C. limped   D. hastened

**B** Match the underlined words with the meanings which they have in the passage.

| Words from the passage | Meanings |
|---|---|
| 1. looked round in desperation (line 14) | a) made aware |
| 2. there was no alternative (line 15) | b) desperate |
| 3. would abandon the chase (line 18) | c) moving heavily and not quickly |
| 4. To their dismay (line 18) | d) said hurriedly |
| 5. and hesitated for a moment (line 25) | e) on the watch for a victim or opportunity |
| 6. lumbering behind them (line 29) | f) did nothing |
| 7. a few frantic moments (line 31) | g) alarm and sorrow |
| 8. Hughie blurted out (line 33) | h) give up |
| 9. alerted the police (line 36) | i) other thing to do |
| 10. prowling around (line 37) | j) ready to act recklessly because of danger |

## 3.5
## Speaking: asking for help

Imagine that you are Mrs Rosenberg in 3.2. Look at line 35 of the passage. With a partner, act out the conversation which you had with the forest ranger.
You can either make notes and write out the dialogue first or give an impromptu performance based on the facts in the passage. Make sure that the forest ranger receives all the necessary information.

## 3.6
## Vocabulary: the formation of nouns

The exercises below show common noun endings. Make **nouns** from the words in brackets using the endings given. Check that you know the meaning of each word and how to use it.

### Exercise 1

1. **-age**: *e.g. damage, baggage* (leak, wreck, post, marry, pack, waste, pass)

2. **-al**: *e.g. arrival, burial* (dismiss, refuse, approve, deny, propose, remove)

3. **-ant**: *e.g. claimant, applicant* (account, depend, descend, inhabit, attend, inform)

4. **-bility**: *e.g. possibility, mobility* (access, soluble, responsible, able, capable)

5. **-ce, -ance, -ence**: *e.g. practice, licence* (insure, interfere, attend, ally, refer, defy)

6. **-cy**: *e.g. secrecy, presidency* (agent, efficient, tenant, democrat, depend, redundant)

*English Alive!*

7. **-dom**: *e.g. kingdom, wisdom* (official, bore, free, martyr)

8. **-ment**: *e.g. government, payment* (develop, entitle, refresh, advertise, acknowledge)

## Exercise 2

1. **-ee**: *e.g. fiancée, guarantee* (employ, absent, license, refuge, pay, refer)

2. **-er, -ar, -or**: *e.g. driver, beggar, actor* (swim, lie, burgle, inspect, invest, conquer)

3. **-ery**: *e.g. bravery, scenery* (machine, slave, bribe, nurse, rob, discover)

4. **-ess**: *e.g. kindness, actress* (lion, host, steward, prince, god, useful, calm)

5. **-hood**: *e.g. childhood, boyhood* (neighbour, man, false, priest)

6. **-ian**: *e.g. Christian, musician* (vegetable, library, electricity, history, mathematics)

7. **-ice**: *e.g. novice, justice* (coward, serve, advise, pre-judge)

8. **-ing**: *e.g. swimming, ending* (begin, cover, offer, fill, warn, travel, quarrel)

9. **-tion**: *e.g. action, application* (compete, combine, despair, accelerate, abbreviate)

## 3.7 Vocabulary: figurative language – metaphors (revision)

Many words can be used **literally** or **figuratively**, e.g.

*literally:* We **dug** a hole and **buried** some rubbish in it.

*figuratively:* When the police **dug** into the case, they made some startling discoveries which forced Inspector Williams to **bury** his early theories.

When a word is used in a non-literal sense, as in a metaphor, it is said to be used **in a figurative sense** or **figuratively**. If it is used as a metaphor, we say that it is used **metaphorically** and is not meant literally.

### Exercise 3

Find any words which are used metaphorically in these sentences.

1. Because of her wealth, she was a fountain of generosity to her relatives and friends.

2. Mohan washed his hands of the whole matter when he discovered that dishonesty was involved.

3. I decided to turn over a new leaf and start with a clean slate.

4. The bear turned the tables on the hunters and began to stalk them while they were still combing the forest for it.

5. The suspect's mind raced furiously as he tried to think of answers to the questions.

6. Don't waste your time banging your head against a brick wall. You're bound to fail because the manager will never change his mind.

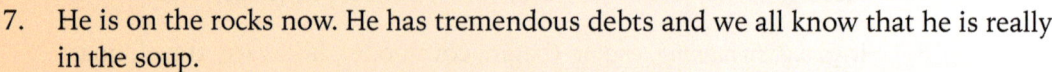

7. He is on the rocks now. He has tremendous debts and we all know that he is really in the soup.

8. She flared up angrily when Paul asked her to drop her plan. She told Paul that he was living in the clouds and ought to get down to earth.

## Exercise 4

Use each of these expressions metaphorically in separate sentences.

1. break the ice
2. lost his head
3. a free hand
4. toe the line
5. pay through the nose
6. be under (somebody's) thumb

## Exercise 5

Use at least five of these words metaphorically.

1. root
2. comb
3. boil
4. cat
5. dog
6. dig
7. snake
8. bite
9. hit
10. heart

### 3.8

# Grammar: using the Present Continuous tense (revision)
## Active forms

| | | |
|---:|---|---|
| I am | (not) | sitting down now. |
| He/She is | (not) | waiting for a bus now. |
| It is | (not) | looking for something to eat. |
| We/You/They are | (not) | trying to climb up a tree. |

## Uses

The main uses of the Present Continuous tense are:

- **for temporary actions** which are happening at the time of speaking and may stop soon, e.g.

   You can't go out now. It**'s raining** heavily.
   Those men **are repairing** a broken electricity cable.

- **for planned future action** (often about travel or movement), e.g.

   When **is** Uncle **returning** from Venezuela?
   Susila **is having** a birthday party next Saturday.

- **with 'always'** to express an action which is frequently repeated. This often suggests that the speaker is irritated by the action or thinks it is unreasonable, e.g.

   Don't pay any attention to him. He**'s always complaining** about something.
   What's the matter with you two? Why **are** you **always arguing** or **fighting**?

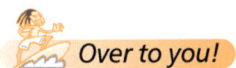 Over to you!

### Exercise 6

Put in 'am', 'is' or 'are'.

1. I wonder what he ____ doing in England now and where he ____ living.
2. Turn the radio down. It ____ making too much noise.
3. How ____ you going into town: by bus or by taxi?
4. Which way ____ the current going?
5. Where ____ those men going at this time of night?
6. What crops ____ you growing now?
7. I can't chat now. I ____ concentrating on my homework.
8. What ____ you doing tomorrow evening?
9. Go out and see why the dog ____ barking like that.
10. When ____ you leaving for the airport?

### Exercise 7

Put in 'Am', 'Is' or 'Are'.

1. ____ I turning this the right way?
2. ____ any of your friends entering the competition?
3. ____ any of the meat showing signs of going bad?

4. ____ anybody waiting for you now?
5. ____ all the players travelling on the same coach tomorrow?
6. ____ all the water from the flood flowing away now?
7. ____ that girl waving to you or to me?
8. ____ I sitting in the wrong place?
9. ____ everybody in the class taking part in the play?
10. ____ Kedeshia and Nakiesha sitting together in that photo?

## Passive forms

| | | |
|---|---|---|
| I am | (not) | being promoted at the end of the year. |
| He/She is | (not) | being invited to Michelle's wedding. |
| It is | (not) | being reopened until the end of next month. |
| We/You/They are | (not) | being followed at the moment. |

### Exercise 8

Put in the *passive* form of the Present Continuous tense of the verbs in brackets.

1. Look at that man. His luggage ____ (search) by two Customs officers.
2. The new swimming pool ____ (open) on Saturday morning.
3. You can't use the computer at the moment. It ____ (repair).
4. According to Uncle, that old house ____ (pull) down next week.
5. The new furniture ____ (deliver) tomorrow morning.
6. That fence ____ (repair) early next week.
7. My brother ____ (transfer) to another branch at the end of the month.
8. We can't use the car at the moment. It ____ (service).
9. The baby is crying. He ____ (bath) and he does not like it.
10. Those old machines ____ (replace) at the end of the year.

## 3.9

## Grammar: construction shift (re-expression)

### Exercise 9

Express these sentences in a different way, using the words in brackets. Retain the meaning of the original sentences but make any changes which are necessary.

1. She prefers tea to coffee. (likes)
2. I do not want to discuss the accident. (prefer)
3. Michelle likes watching television more than going to the cinema. (prefers)
4. Tony was full of confidence that we would win. (felt)
5. Leela lengthened her dress. (longer)
6. I must go home now. (It's time)
7. The film should start now. (time)
8. It's time you went to bed now. (ought)
9. Uncle went home but he did not say goodbye to me. (without)
10. I discussed your proposal with him for ten minutes. (spent)
11. You have left a letter out of this word. (omitted)
12. We agreed to play in spite of the rain. (despite)
13. He drove very fast and could not stop in time. (too)
14. The camera was very expensive, so I did not buy it. (too)
15. There were many CDs, so Trevor did not know which one to buy. (so … that)

## 3.10

## Grammar: using 'whose'

We can use the **relative pronoun** 'whose' to link two statements about a person, animal or (more rarely) a thing. A common pattern is noun/pronoun + 'whose' + a noun, e.g.
    That is the man **whose** car was damaged.
    I have a friend **whose** brother plays cricket for Antigua.

We can combine two sentences by using 'whose', e.g.
    That's the girl. Her sister won the 100 metres.
    That's the girl **whose** sister won the 100 metres.

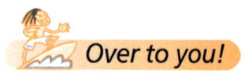 **Over to you!**

### Exercise 10

Combine each pair of sentences to make one sentence containing 'whose'.

1. I feel sorry for the family. Their house was flooded.
2. What happened to the fishermen? Their boat sank during the storm.
3. What's the name of the people? Their dog tried to bite you.
4. We used a stretcher to carry off the player. His left leg was injured.
5. A police officer spoke to the woman. Her car was stolen during the night.
6. What happened to the cat? Its leg was hurt.
7. We have a neighbour. Her daughter hopes to become a pop star.
8. Sometimes I have lunch with a friend. Her home is very near our school.
9. The police are looking for the driver. His car is blocking the road.
10. Several people helped the old woman. Her house was badly damaged during the night.

## 3.11

# Grammar: using 'then', 'therefore' and 'thus'

'Then', 'therefore' and 'thus' cannot be used to link two main clauses, so we must either use a conjunction, such as 'and', before the word or start a new sentence. Look at the examples below:

| Word | Examples |
| --- | --- |
| then (as an adverb meaning 'next', 'after that', 'afterwards', 'at that time') | *wrong:* We ate the food, then we had a rest. <br> *right:* We ate the food, **and then** we had a rest. <br> (We can omit the comma.) <br> *right:* We ate the food. **Then** we had a rest. |
| therefore (as an adverb meaning 'so', 'as a result') | *wrong:* There was a shortage of fresh fish, therefore the price increased. |

40 English Alive!

| Word | Examples |
|---|---|
| | *right:* There was a shortage of fresh fish. **Therefore** the price increased. |
| | *right:* There was a shortage of fresh fish, **and therefore** the price increased. (We can omit the comma after 'fish'.) |
| thus (an adverb, meaning 'in this way', 'as a result') | *wrong:* We were late, thus we missed the first part of the film. |
| | *right:* We were late. **Thus** we missed the first part of the film. |
| | *right:* We were late, **and thus** we missed the first part of the film |

 *Over to you!*

### Exercise 11

Correct these sentences. Insert a full stop or a conjunction.

1. He was lazy, therefore he failed.

2. I opened the door of the taxi, then she got in.

3. We usually play until half past six, then we go home.

4. I get up in the morning, then I go to school.

5. There are not many roads in parts of Guyana, therefore rivers are an important means of transport.

6. Everybody liked Durai, therefore there was no reason for him to leave home.

7. I completed the application form, then I gave it to the clerk.

8. He took the money, then he gave me a receipt.

9. Cattle are often kept in an enclosure called a pen, therefore the man in charge of them became known as the penman.

10. In these two triangles, two sides and an included angle are equal, therefore the triangles are congruent.

11. Tobago is surrounded by water, thus it is an island.

12. The witness for the prosecution failed to attend the court, thus the police had to drop the case.

## 3.12 Reading

In 3.2 we read about an encounter between a bear and two children. Thanks to their bravery and determination, the children escaped. Now read another true bear story. This time the bear is the victim. Read the passage carefully because you will have to write about it later.

## *In Jasper National Park*

Not long ago, a young couple went camping in Jasper National Park in Canada. Wayne Roberts, 24, and his girl-friend, Tanya Johnson, 21, were on their first visit to Canada. They were fond of outdoor life and were enthusiastic conservationists. As far as they knew, the area in which they were camping
5 was perfectly safe, so they took no weapons with them when they set off for their daily walk through the forested hills. However, purely as a matter of habit, Tanya Johnson took her mobile phone with her.

'We weren't anticipating any trouble,' she said later. 'I've got so accustomed to my mobile phone that I feel lost without it.'

10 Subsequent events showed that Tanya's mobile phone proved to be instrumental in saving the life of large female bear.

The couple had walked about two miles from their camp when they heard an unusual scuffling noise some distance from the path they were following. Out of curiosity, they made their way through dense undergrowth, moving steadily nearer
15 to the strange noise. About eighty yards from the path, it became clear that the noise was coming from a large animal but they moved forward cautiously.

Suddenly they came to an abrupt halt. The scuffling noise was accompanied by angry roars.

'We nearly turned back,' Wayne said. 'We guessed that there was a wounded
20 animal ahead of us but we thought we might be able to help. With hindsight, that was a rather ridiculous idea but that's the way it was.'

The couple moved forward a few yards and gasped when they saw a large bear with its rear left leg caught in an illegal wire trap. The bear saw or smelt them and lunged angrily towards them but was checked by the trap.

25 'It would be suicide to try to free it from the trap,' Tanya said. 'Ah! I know!' She took her phone out of her pack and asked the operator for the number of the nearest ranger post. Then she dialled again and spoke to a game ranger. She explained what the couple had seen and asked for help. She gave the ranger directions and then told Wayne that help was on its way.

30 The couple returned to the path and waited nearly an hour before two armed rangers arrived.

'We'll have to tranquilise the bear before we can get it free,' Ranger Carter said. 'We might even have to put it down if its injuries are too bad. Can you lead us to the site?'

35  Wayne and Tanya led the rangers to the trapped bear. The rangers studied the situation and shot the bear in the side with a tranquilising dart. They waited for the bear to collapse. Then they cut it free from the trap and put a dressing on its wound.

'All done! Thanks very much for letting us know. We'd better get out of here. The bear will be all right but she'll not be in a happy mood when she wakes up. Let's
40  make sure we're not around then.'

During the following month, the rangers intensified their patrols in the district, hoping to catch or deter whoever had set the trap.

## Exercise 12

1. What is the meaning of (a) conservationists (line 4) and (b) With hindsight (line 20)?
2. Match these words with the meanings which they have in the passage.

| | |
|---|---|
| 1. purely (6) | (a) increased, strengthened |
| 2. anticipating (8) | (b) very foolish |
| 3. accustomed (8) | (c) make unconscious |
| 4. Subsequent (10) | (d) discourage, keep away |
| 5. abrupt (17) | (e) simply, only |
| 6. ridiculous (21) | (f) kill it |
| 7. tranquilise (32) | (g) later |
| 8. put it down (33) | (h) expecting |
| 9. intensified (41) | (i) used |
| 10. deter (42) | (j) sudden |

## 3.13
## Writing a news report

One of the meanings of 'an intern' is 'a person who is working to gain practical experience'. Most newspapers will accept a few young men and women who hope to become reporters or staff writers. One of the things they have to do is write reports of events like the one described in 3.12.

The format of a news report often follows this outline:

- **start:** one or two sentences which summarise the whole event
- **an account of the event**, using:
  - short paragraphs
  - some dialogue if possible
  - a time sequence
  - accurate information: names, ages, etc.

- **ending:** information about any action taken by the authorities, i.e. the police, military, park rangers, etc.

 *Over to you!*

Imagine that you are working at your local newspaper as an intern. The story in 3.12 has come to your news department by email from a Canadian press agency, i.e. a company which supplies information to the media.

The News Editor says to you, 'Here, this has just come in but it's too long to be used as it is. Cut it down to a report of about 100–150 words. Stick to the facts but – if you like – you can use your imagination and quote one of the campers if you need dialogue, but that's not really essential.'

Prepare the report.

# 4 Tiger Gets an Education

### 4.1
## Pre-reading

In his amusing book *A Brighter Sun*, Sam Selvon describes what happens when a young man, Tiger, decides to get an education. He is working as an assistant to some American land surveyors at the time. His main job is to carry a theodolite for them. The theodolite is used for surveying the land. Tiger starts his education by copying out words from a dictionary. In this extract, he demonstrates his growing knowledge to his wife, Urmilla.

### 4.2
## Reading

## Tiger Gets an Education

Tiger wrote down everything in his copybook. When he read over what he had written he realised that he didn't know any big words at all, except the names of the equipment they were working with. This was a bad thing. All the books he read had big words, and he had to use a dictionary to see what they meant. He
5  could understand some and could spell them, but he couldn't use them. He would have to practise while talking to people. He memorised a few words from the dictionary every night. But while he was learning words he ignored grammar.

'Urmilla,' he said, 'you know what this thing I telling you about is for? I mean the theodolite.'

10  'Ain't you say is that they does use to survey the land?'
'Yes, but I was wrong.' He swallowed and tried to remember. 'Is a surveying instrument for measuring horizontal and vertical angles by means of telescope.'
'Oh – ho, so is that! So they don't measure the land with it then?'
'No. So you see is a important thing that I does have to carry! Now, I will try
15  you out with a little word. What it is "to buy"?'
'Oh, that easy, man. That is when you go in the shop and buy anything, and you pay for it. That mean you buy it.'
'Well, you have the idea, but you still not correct! To buy is to obtain by paying a price!'
20  'But ain't is the same thing I say, Tiger?'
'How is the same thing? You must learn to express yourself good, girl, like me. I will catch you with a easy one now! Every day people passing selling fish – look we just eat some for dinner. You know what a fish is?'
'But how? Is a thing that does live in the sea, and in river and pond too. It does
25  swim, and people does eat it for food. Some of them have scale on them.'
'I know I would catch you! You really wrong this time! The dictionary ain't say

anything like that! It says is a animal living in water, is a vertebrate, cold-blooded animal having gills throughout life and limbs, if any, modified into fins. You see!'

30 'But man, Tiger, why you want to find out all of that for? I don' know what all them big word mean, man. It getting me puzzle up.'

'Is the same thing I tell you. If you don't have education, people could always tie you up. All the time I did think a fish was just like what you say, but now I find out for truth what it really is! Look, hand me my small cylinders of narcotic rolled in paper.'

35 'Cylinder? What is that? Is what you mean at all?'

Tiger chuckled, self-contented. 'Just extend the terminal part of your arm, the extent of space between where you is and what part it is is not remote.'

'I beg your pardon, Tiger, but I really don't know what you mean. This time you really tie me up!'

40 Tiger chuckled again. 'All right, girl. Reach the cigarettes for me, then.'

'Well,' Urmilla said, 'if you did say so all the time, now so you smoking already! Man,' she said, handing him the pack, 'I don't like this business. Too much thing coming between we. If you go on so, I won't understand anything you say.'

## 4.3
# Understanding

**A** Choose the best answer each time.

1. A theodolite (4.1, line 3) is clearly ____.
   A. an intern or an apprentice    C. an experienced surveyor
   B. some kind of instrument    D. a long stick like a spirit level

2. From Urmilla's point of view, the demonstration mentioned in the last line of 4.1 was apparently ____.
   A. disconcerting    B. persuasive    C. impressive    D. admirable

3. Tiger soon came to the conclusion that big words were ____.
   A. to be avoided    B. of value    C. not worth knowing    D. rarely used

4. Which words in the first paragraph best show why Tiger asked his wife about 'buy' and 'fish'?
   A. He realised that he didn't know any big words at all
   B. This was a bad thing.
   C. He would have to practise while talking to people.
   D. But while he was learning words he ignored grammar.

5. Which word has Urmilla left out in line 10?
   A. that    B. all    C. it    D. across

**B** Answer these questions about the passage.

1. What is the attitude of the author (Sam Selvon) to Tiger?

2. In line 11, why does the author put in 'swallowed and'? (What does he seek to achieve by using those words here?)

46    English Alive!

3. How would you describe Tiger's attitude to his wife? What is the evidence for your answer?

4. What did Tiger say to justify his use of dictionary definitions?

5. What do these words mean as they are used in the passage?
   a) except (line 2)    c) ignored (line 7)    e) modified (line 28)
   b) memorised (line 6) d) vertical (line 12)  f) terminal (line 36)

## 4.4
# Punctuation: using the full stop

### Exercise 1

Punctuate or express these sentences correctly, making any changes which are necessary. There are alternative methods in many cases. All the sentences illustrate errors in the use of the full stop or a failure to use one.

1. The road was very busy. People walking about like ants.

2. Derrick could not solve the problem. Because it was very difficult. Involved a knowledge of algebra which was beyond him.

3. There have been many changes in fishing methods during recent years. Except, of course, for the traditional use of the fishing-rod.

4. One type of food that contains an extract of fish is margarine. The subject, oil.

5. Joseph walked all the way home last night. Although it was raining very hard and he had to go at least five miles.

6. Outside the temple we saw many interesting sights. People busily taking photos of each other. Men trying to sell cooked food. Women with all sorts of things for sale. And many families coming and going in their best clothes.

7. In the past six months, thousands of people have died in East Africa. Either because of lack of food or water or because of fighting between rival tribes.

8. The train went very quickly. So I did not have a chance to see very much.

9. We liked the play for a variety of reasons. First because the acting was very good.

10. A man sat in front of Dionne on the bus, he was smoking a pipe, the smoke made Dionne cough.

11. Once I was on a crowded bus, when the bus arrived at a stop, a woman about fifty years old got on the bus.

12. Make sure you return the book by Saturday, otherwise there will be trouble, you will probably have to pay a fine.

## 4.5 Study skills: using a dictionary

Study this extract from a dictionary and then answer the questions about it.

| journal | jurisprudence |
|---|---|
| **journal** ('jœnəl) *n* account of what has happened in a day; diary or other form in which these happenings are recorded; name sometimes used in the title of a newspaper or magazine<br>**journalism** ('jœnəlizm) *n* [U] profession of reporting for newspapers, radio, TV etc —**'journalist** *n* person whose profession is journalism —**journa'listic** *adj*<br>**journey** ('jœni) *n* excursion, trip, occasion of travelling (esp a long way); distance travelled in a given time —*vi* to travel, make a journey —**'journeyman** *n* (*old*) person who has completed an apprenticeship<br>**joust** (jowst) *vi* (of knights) to ride at each other with spears and lances, trying to knock each other off —*n* fight fought in this way<br>**'jovial** *adj* cheerful, merry —**jovi'ality** *n* [U] —**'jovially** *adv*<br>**jowl** *n* area of flesh on the jaw below the chin<br>**joy** *n* [U] feeling of gladness or happiness; [C] anything that gives this feeling; [U] (*infml*) success —**'joyful, 'joyous** *adj* —**'joyfully** *adv* —**'joyfulness, joyousness** *n* [U] —**'joyless** *adj* —**'joyride** *vi* to steal a car and ride around in it for fun —*n* this illegal act —**'joystick** *n* flexible control for an aircraft or similar device for a computer<br>**JP** *abbrev* Justice of the Peace<br>**Jr** *abbrev* (in names) junior<br>**'jubilant** *adj* (*fml*) extremely pleased or happy —**'jubilantly** *adv* —**jubi'lation** *n* [U] great joy or rejoicing<br>**jubi'lee** *n* 25th, 50th or 60th anniversary<br>**'judder** *vi* to shake violently —**'juddering** *n* [U]<br>**judge** *n* person who hears cases and makes decisions in a court of law; person who decides the result of a contest etc; person skilled (**good judge**) or poor (**bad judge**) at making decisions —*vt* to make a decision, eg in a legal case or a contest; to form an opinion on —**'judg(e)ment** *n* [U] power or skill of judging; [C] decision made; [C,U] opinion —**judg(e)'mental** *adj* quick to make decisions or form (esp bad) opinions about others<br>**judicial** (jōō'dishəl) *adj* of or concerning a judge or court; showing good judgement —**ju'diciary** *n* [U] (with **the**) judges as a whole —**ju'dicious** *adj* showing good judgement; careful —**ju'diciously** *adv*<br>**'judo** *n* [U] sport where two contestants try to wrestle each other to the ground<br>**jug** *n* container with a handle, for holding liquids<br>**'juggernaut** *n* huge articulated lorry; anything huge that overwhelms and is difficult to stop<br>**'juggle** *v* [T,I] to perform the trick of keeping (several objects) in the air at once while throwing them from hand to hand; [T,I] to manage to | do (several things) at once; [T] to re-order (various activities, events etc) —**'juggler** *n* person who entertains by juggling<br>**'jugular** *n* (also **jugular vein**) large vein on each side of the neck<br>**juice** *n* [U] liquid drink made from fruits or vegetables; (*infml*) fuel, energy; liquid fat from meat —**'juiciness** *n* [U] —**'juicy** *adj* full of juice; (*infml*; of secrets etc) particularly interesting<br>**ju-'jitsu** *n* [U] sport derived from Japanese self-defence<br>**'jujube** *n* sweet made from gelatine and sugar<br>**July** (jōō'lī) seventh month of the year<br>**'jumble** *vt* to mix up (the order of) —*n* [C] muddled mixture; [U] useless or unwanted articles often sold in a **jumble sale**<br>**jump** *v* [T,I] to spring upwards or forwards (over); [I] to make a sudden nervous movement when surprised or frightened; [I] to move quickly upwards, increase suddenly —*n* act of jumping; sudden increase or rise; distance covered by jumping —**'jumper** *n* person or thing that jumps; loose usu knitted garment covering the top half of the body —**'jumpy** *adj* nervous, frightened —**jump-'start** *vt* to start (a car) by rolling it forwards and letting out the clutch while it is in gear<br>**'junction** *n* place where two or more roads, railway tracks, electrical cables etc meet and join<br>**'juncture** *n* (*fml*) point in time<br>**June** sixth month of the year<br>**'jungle** *n* [C,U] (area of) thick vegetation in a tropical climate; [C] (*fig*) situation which is very difficult to get through or out of —**'jungly** *adj*<br>**junior** ('joonyə) *adj* younger; lower in rank; (of a school) for children of approx 7 to 11 years old —*n* person who is junior to another; child who is at junior school; (in names) indicating a son who has the same name as his father<br>**'juniper** *n* [U] type of evergreen shrub used in making gin<br>**junk** *n* [U] rubbish, unwanted things; [U] (*infml*) nonsense; [C] type of small Chinese sailing boat —**junk mail** leaflets sent by post advertising things one mostly does not want<br>**'junket** *n* trip made supposedly for business reasons but actually more for enjoyment than anything else, and not paid for by those going<br>**'junkie** *n* person addicted to hard drugs<br>**'junta** *n* military government by officers not elected by a country's people<br>**'Jupiter** *n* chief of the Roman gods; largest of the planets, fifth from the sun<br>**juris'diction** *n* [U] (esp legal) authority; [C] area over which this authority is held<br>**juris'prudence** *n* [U] science of law and its principles |

135

1. In this dictionary, the symbol ´ is put _____ a stressed syllable.
   A. under   B. on   C. before   D. after

2. If we use 'stick' after 'joy', we have _____.
   A. two separate words   B. a hyphenated word   C. one word

English Alive!

3. People taking part in a joust are liable to get ____.
   A. obese    B. hurt    C. cholera    D. promoted

4. Both 'jurisdiction' and 'jurisprudence' are concerned with ____.
   A. science    B. area    C. the law    D. principals

5. Sometimes a boxer is referred to as a journeyman. One implication of this is that the man ____.
   A. is very experienced    C. is a novice
   B. is an apprentice    D. has come from overseas

6. We would expect things sold at a jumble sale to be ____.
   A. expensive    C. comparatively rare
   B. very fashionable    D. quite cheap

7. Going for a joyride is a ____ offence.
   A. old fashioned    C. criminal
   B. illegal    D. capital

8. A juggler is usually a type of ____.
   A. vein    B. trick    C. woman    D. entertainer

## 4.6
## Vocabulary: dialect and standard English

Do you agree or disagree with each of these statements? If you disagree, say why you disagree.

1. Dialect and standard English share one factor in common: they both contain words or parts of words from many languages. For example, standard English contains words from German, Latin, Greek, French, Spanish and several other languages. Jamaican Creole, or dialect, shows the influence of West African languages as well as Spanish, Portuguese, French, Dutch, Amerindian and old forms of English.

2. In the CSEC examination, candidates can use dialect when writing conversation. At other times, they have to use standard English.

3. Jamaican dialect is not exactly the same as the dialects of some other Caribbean countries. At a meeting of representatives of several Caribbean countries, there may be difficulties if each representative uses only the dialect of his/her own country.

4. There are several dialects in modern Britain but speakers who use dialect outside their own region may find that they are not understood, so their effectiveness is limited. Similarly, people from the Caribbean will have difficulty communicating with people of other countries if they use dialect only.

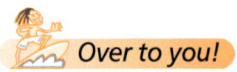 **Over to you!**

### Exercise 2

The following lines are taken from the passage in 4.2. How can we say the same thing in standard English? E.g.

you know what this thing I telling you about is for? (line 8)
*Do you know what this thing I was telling you about is for?*

1. Ain't you say is that they does use to survey the land? (line 10)

2. Oh – ho, so is that! (line 13)

3. So you see is a important thing that I does have to carry! (line 14)

4. But ain't is the same thing I say, Tiger? (line 20)

5. Every day people passing selling fish. (line 22)

6. I know I would catch you! You really wrong this time! (line 26)

7. It getting me puzzle up. (line 30)

8. Is what you mean at all? (line 35)

9. if you did say so all the time, now so you smoking already! (line 41)

10. Too much thing coming between we. (line 42)

## 4.7
## Grammar: using the Past Continuous tense
### Active forms

|  | Statements | Questions |
|---|---|---|
| I, he, she, it | **was** (not) waiting for you. | **Was** he waiting for you? |
| we, you, they | **were** (not) waiting for him. | **Were** they waiting for him? |

### Uses

The main uses of the Past Continuous tense are:
- to show what was happening at some past time, e.g.
    At 7 p.m. last night, we **were watching** a film on TV.
    What **was** your brother **doing** when the fire started?
- to report direct speech; a verb in the **Present** Continuous tense is usually changed into one in the **Past** Continuous tense, e.g.
    *direct:* The lady asked me, "Are you waiting for a bus?"
    *indirect:* The lady asked me if I **was waiting** for a bus.

English Alive!

- in time clauses introduced by 'when', 'while' or 'as' when we want to show the progressive (continuing) aspect of an action, e.g.
    When we **were climbing** up a steep slope, Barry slipped and sprained an ankle.
    This use is similar to the first one discussed.

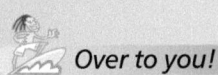 Over to you!

Exercise 3

Put in 'was' or 'were'.

1. Our bus had a puncture when we ____ approaching Sabina Park.
2. What ____ you doing when the lights went out last night?
3. I ____ reading a newspaper when I heard an unusual noise outside.
4. What ____ you and Michael arguing about at the party yesterday evening?
5. Michelle ____ doing her homework when her friend phoned her.
6. Who ____ waiting for you when you reached the cinema?
7. How many people ____ swimming when somebody saw a shark near the beach?
8. Why ____ the dog barking just now?
9. Where ____ your friends standing when the tree fell down?
10. Which car ____ going towards town when the accident happened?

## Passive forms

The passive forms of the Past Continuous tense are made with 'was being/were being' + a past participle, e.g.
    When we reached the scene of the accident, an elderly man **was being carried** to an ambulance. Traffic **was being diverted** round the wrecked cars by a traffic policeman.
    I couldn't do the ironing yesterday because the iron **was being repaired.**
    When the two suspects **were being questioned** by police officers, one of them tried to run away but he was soon caught.

Over to you!

Exercise 4

Put the verb in brackets into the passive form of the Past Continuous tense.

1. When the soldiers ____ (inspect) yesterday, one of them fainted.
2. Two men rushed into the office and tried to snatch some money just as it ____ (count).

3. We noticed several Customs' launches round one of the ships, and my uncle told us that it ___ (search) for drugs.

4. Tiger suspected that he ___ (follow), so he turned round suddenly but saw nothing unusual.

5. While oil ___ (transfer) to a lighter, some of it leaked into the harbour. It ___ (clear) up when we last saw it.

6. We had to squeeze into one room of our house while the rest of it ___ (redecorate) and the wiring ___ (renew).

7. Unfortunately, one of the injured men died when he ___ (take) to hospital.

8. We had to take a different route home because traffic ___ (divert) as a result of an accident.

9. The dentist gave Yvonne an injection, so she didn't feel any pain when her tooth ___ (pull) out.

10. Carts stacked with cane lumbered along the path when the crop ___ (harvest).

## 4.8
# Punctuation: using an apostrophe
## In contractions

We can use an **apostrophe** to show that a letter (or more than one) has been left out of a word, e.g. 'don't', 'I'll', 'shan't', 'I'm'. Notice that we *never* put an apostrophe on 'its' unless it means 'it is' or 'it has'.

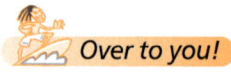

### Exercise 5

Put an apostrophe in the correct place in each of these speech forms. Make sure that the apostrophe is *between* two letters and not above one.

| | | | |
|---|---|---|---|
| 1. didnt | 4. wont | 7. youre | 10. Ive |
| 2. hed | 5. cant | 8. oclock | 11. shell |
| 3. weve | 6. theyve | 9. hes | 12. its |

## To show possession

When an apostrophe is used to show possession, it means 'of', 'of the' or 'belonging to'. We do *not* put an apostrophe on verbs, or on nouns when no possession is involved. The main rules are:

- Add **'s** to a singular noun, or a plural noun which does *not* end in 's', e.g.
    my mother**'s** name   Mary**'s** ring   a children**'s** park
    the woman**'s** hat    Anna**'s** shoes  the women**'s** voices
    Charles**'s** friend *or* Charles**'** friend

- When you need to show possession, put an apostrophe after a plural noun which ends with 's', e.g.
    a girl**s'** school   my friend**s'** bicycles   the ladie**s'** voices

After a lesson on using the apostrophe, a few students put an apostrophe on nearly every word which ends with 's'. Of course, this is wrong. If you are one of those few students, go back and study the rules above again.

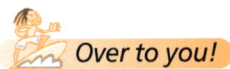 **Over to you!**

### Exercise 6

When necessary, insert an apostrophe in the following sentences. Altogether, you must insert *ten* apostrophes and no more.

1. Cows often wave their tails to drive away the flies.

2. This is not Roys bicycle. It is Delroys.

3. The Old Boys race came just before the inter-house relays.

4. Elaines brother looked at the cat which had hurt both its front paws.

5. Those shoes belong to the two boys who are playing football. Yours are over there – by the girls bicycles.

6. We saw Owens two brothers in the childrens park.

7. My friends brother stopped me and said, 'Francine asked me to say that she can't play netball tomorrow. She has a very bad cold.'

8. One of those doors opens the wrong way, so mind your fingers.

9. The noise of the airplanes frightened my sisters cat.

10. Errol hopes to write to you in two or three days time.

## 4.9 Enjoying poetry

### A Tale of Two Tongues

Miss Ida speaks only English to God.
Scholars cannot fault the diction
of her graces and prayers;
to her, it is the language of holy things;
5   and the giver of commandments
deserves a grammar of respectability
as firm and as polished
as his tablets of stone.

But to fellow mortals she speaks Creole,
10  the tongue of the markets and the fields,
the language of <u>labrish</u>,          gossip
<u>su-su</u>, proverbs and stories,    whispering about people
hot-words, <u>tracings</u> and <u>preckeh</u>;  abuse; quarrels
it is the way to get
15  hard-ears <u>pickney</u> to listen     children
and <u>facety</u> men to keep off;     impudent, bold
it is the tongue of belly laughs
and sweet body action.

And to Miss Ida it is no bother
20  to laugh and suffer in one language
and worship in another.

*Earl McKenzie*

### Questions

1. What does 'graces' refer to in line 3?

2. What does 'tablets of stone' refer to in line 8?

3. In line 8, which word might some people start with a capital letter?

4. In this poem, 'tongue' (line 10) and 'language' (line 11) have more or less the same meaning. Think of a reason why the poet chose to use 'tongue' in line 10 but 'language' in line 11.

5. In line 9, why does the poet use 'mortals' instead of 'people'?

6. As far as we can tell, what is the poet's attitude to Miss Ida and her use of two languages?

## 4.10
## Writing

Write about *one* of these topics:
1. What do you think the future role of dialect will be in your country? Give reasons for your opinions.

or

2. If you were in charge of education, what subjects would you want teenagers to study in school, and why?

or

3. (This is for creative writers only.) Read the passage in 4.2 again. Then try to imitate the author's style. Start at line 8 and change the things and words Tiger is talking about. Do *not* mention a theodolite or the words 'buy', 'fish' or 'cigarette'. Use a dictionary to help you find suitable definitions. If you are a girl, you can change the roles and make Urmilla teach her husband. The choice is yours.

# 5 A Foggy Night

## 5.1
## Writing skills: stories

In the CSEC examination, you may have to write a story of 400–450 words, i.e. 2–4 pages (depending on the size of your handwriting). That is not even half the length of published short stories. For example:

- *The Pearl* (described by its author as a short story) has at least 25,000 words.
- The short stories of Michael Anthony contain from 1200–3000 words.
- The stories of Olive Senior contain 2000–4000–11,000 words.

This means that in an examination you will *not* have the time or space in which to develop all the skills normally used in writing a story. Study the skills and practise using them but accept the fact that you cannot develop all of them fully in the CSEC examination.

### What are the skills needed?

When writing a story we need:
- a plot
- a setting or background
- characters
- language and dialogue.

### Plot

A plot is the result of **conflict**. Common sources of conflict include:
- conflict *with another person*, e.g. two people who want to lead a political party; two men who want to marry the same girl; two people who want the same job; two people who disagree because of their personalities, etc.
- conflict *with external events*, e.g. caused by a storm, an earthquake, a puncture, a loss of a job, success or failure in sport or singing, a faulty machine, etc.
- conflict *caused by a person's character*, e.g. too ambitious, too mean, too generous and trusting, unusually shy, too easily led by others, etc.

### Setting or background

It *may* be possible to set the story in an interesting background. In *The Pearl*, for example, John Steinbeck sets his story in a country where we learn about how poor fishermen live and how people are affected when a fisherman finds a valuable pearl. It is interesting to watch the pearl-buyers at work.

Sometimes it is possible to set a story in a hospital or in a sugar cane factory or (as in *Annie John* and *To Sir with Love*) largely in a school. Other possible settings for a story include a fishing trawler, a prison, a rubbish dump, an orphanage, the offices of a property developer, a dentist's waiting-room.

If your setting is good, the reader gets two things at the same time: the story shown by your plot, and information shown by your setting. Unfortunately, you may not have much time in which to develop a good setting in the CSEC examination but you can try. Perhaps one day you will write your own short stories with well-developed settings.

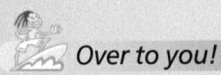 Over to you!

### Exercise 1

In one or two sentences (in each case), give the outline of a plot for each of the following:
1. A teenage girl gradually discovers that she has a marvellous singing voice. How will this affect her?
2. A boy has no confidence in himself. Then a new neighbour starts to teach him to rely on himself. What may happen?
3. A motorist stops his car outside a shop to go in and buy something. He forgets to put on his handbrake, and he leaves the engine running. What happens as a result?

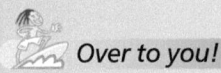 Over to you!

### Exercise 2

Follow the instructions for Exercise 1 but this time use two or three sentences to show how we could develop a plot.
1. Somebody did not believe in ghosts until something happened. What happened?
2. An honest business person or politician was offered a bribe of US $5 million. What did he or she do?
3. A teenager disappears for 24 hours and then is found safe and well. What happened?

## Characters

You may be able to base your characters on people you have met or read about. You may be able to remember a character you have seen in a film or on television. Then you may be able to re-create that person in your story.

If you have time and space, you can develop some of your characters by using one or more of these methods:
- Describe what the person looks like.
- Describe the person's clothes.
- Show how the person moves and speaks.
- Show what other people think of a character and how he/she reacts with them.

- Put words into a character's mouth to reveal his/her character and motives.
- Let the character's actions reveal his/her personality.

### Language and dialogue

Your language must be correct (with no grammatical errors). No publisher or examiner will value your stories if they contain elementary mistakes.

The dialogue should suit your characters. It can contain dialect. If you use standard English, it should contain speech forms such as 'don't' and 'I'm'.

Don't try to impress your reader by using long or unusual words. That will annoy your reader. Keep it simple.

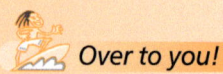 **Over to you!**

### Exercise 3

Choose a topic and follow the instructions.

1. You have just arrived at the home of somebody you like very much and greatly respect. In not more than *five* lines, describe the character and clothes of the person.

2. An old man or woman (whom you know) walked slowly past you towards a shop. In not more than *five* lines, describe how the person walked and what he/she said to you.

### Exercise 4

Choose a topic and in not more than *ten* lines, write a brief conversation. You can use playscript or continuous prose.

1. A woman is praising you for something which you have done.

2. (On the telephone) a listener is complaining to the presenter of a programme called 'Your Views' about a programme or incident which he/she did not like.

## 5.2
# Pre-reading

In 5.3 we can read about what happened when a motorist accidentally blew the horn on his car but …
- Where do we start the story: at the beginning, in the middle or at the end?
- There is no room for a detailed setting.
- Shall we include the man's wife? No, there is no room for her this time. We will have to find a reason for leaving her out. Or perhaps we can put her in at the end?

The story is based on a true incident but the name of the motorist has been changed to protect his identity.

## 5.3 Reading

## A Foggy Night

Not long ago, Jason Walker, 32, decided to go to the Harbour Cinema to see a film called 'Daredevil'. He had offered to take his wife but she had preferred to stay at home to watch her favourite programme on television.

Jason parked his car in the yard at the shipping office where he worked. He preferred to do that rather than park outside and risk vandals damaging his precious car. The walk to the cinema took only a couple of minutes, and he thoroughly enjoyed the film. In his mind, he was the hero performing all manner of daring feats.

When Jason came out of the cinema, he was annoyed to see that a dense mist was rolling into the harbour and across the docks. With some difficulty, he found his car, got in it and prepared to leave. He leaned forward to peer through the mist. As he did so, he accidentally sounded the horn on his car. To his surprise, he heard an echoing horn from somewhere in the vicinity. He pressed the horn again to see whether the echo was caused by the mist, by another car or by something else. A few seconds later, an echoing noise filtered through the mist.

Jason was puzzled. He scratched his head thoughtfully and concluded that a sailor on a ship out in the harbour must be trying to outdo him. He pressed his horn again and held it down for a few seconds.

'That will teach him!' he thought to himself. To his surprise and annoyance, there was an even louder and longer blast in reply.

'All right. You win!' he thought. 'I'm going home.'

Jason gave one final blast on his horn and backed his car out of the parking space. Then he had the biggest shock of his life. As he turned the steering-wheel, he heard a deafening grinding and crashing noise. The bow of a large freighter loomed up through the mist ahead of him and became firmly embedded in the quay.

Jason turned white with shock and then red with embarrassment when he realised what had probably happened. The captain of a ship had mistaken the sound of his car horn for some kind of signal guiding him into the docks. He wondered if the freighter had risked the mist to pick up a perishable cargo. Sometimes ships tried to get away with entering or leaving the harbour without a pilot. An experienced local pilot would never have tried to dock in mist and darkness. A dozen thoughts raced through his mind as he wondered what to do. He realised that the security guard at the company yard had seen and recognised him.

Men shouted down at him from the ship, and Jason attempted to explain what had happened. Then a thought struck him, so he drove off and sped home.

'I wonder … I wonder …' he thought as he neared his home. 'If I'm wrong, I'm in deep trouble …'

Jason parked his car outside his house, opened the door and rushed in. His wife moved to greet him but all he said was, 'Hi! Urgent!' and rushed to his desk. He fumbled through piles of paper until he found what he wanted: the insurance policy for his car. He scanned the policy and then sighed with relief.

The policy included the words: *the Company shall pay all such sums as the insured shall become legally obligated to pay as damages, compensation, legal expenses or for any other means arising out of ownership, maintenance or use of the designated automobile.*

Later, the owners of the ship and dock sued Jason for over five million dollars – the cost of hiring tugs, repairing the ship and repairing the quay – and his insurance company had to pay. Not surprisingly, the insurance company declined to renew his policy for the following year.

## 5.4
## Writing: starting a story

The story in 5.3 started at the beginning (in terms of time). We could have started it at the end in this way:

> For a moment, Diana Walker wondered whether her husband was drunk. He rushed in, brushed her aside, and sat down, searching feverishly through the papers at his desk …

Then we could give details of the insurance policy and Jason Walker could explain to his wife what happened down at the docks. One problem with this method is that the punctuation of direct speech may be tricky, and we may have to use the Past Perfect tense many times.

We could also have started the story by having Diana Walker chatting with a neighbour and explaining what had happened the night before.

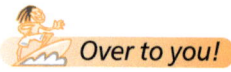

### Exercise 5

Suggest other ways in which we could have started the story of Jason Walker and the ship.

### 5.5
## Understanding

1. Jason Walker offered to take his wife to the cinema. What did she say to him? (Use direct speech to show her answer to his offer.)

2. How might vandals damage Walker's car?

3. What does the word 'precious' in line 5 tell us about Walker's attitude to his car?

4. Explain the meaning of 'all manner of daring feats' without using the words 'manner' and 'feats'. (line 7)

5. In line 8, suggest a reason why the fog annoyed Walker.

6. What one word can we use to replace 'in the vicinity' in line 12 without changing the meaning of the sentence?

7. In line 16, how could a sailor be trying to 'outdo' Walker?

8. In line 18, what does 'That' refer to?

9. What made Walker think that there was no pilot on the freighter? (line 30)

10. If you can, explain what the 'thought' was in line 34.

### 5.6
## Vocabulary: meaning in context

Match the underlined words with the meanings which they have in the story.

| Words used in the story | Meanings |
|---|---|
| 1. risk <u>vandals</u> damaging his … car (line 5) | a) fixed in something |
| 2. The <u>bow</u> of a large freighter (line 23) | b) read quickly |
| 3. <u>embedded</u> in the quay (line 24) | c) responsible |
| 4. a <u>perishable</u> cargo (line 28) | d) appointed, nominated |
| 5. <u>fumbled</u> through piles of paper (line 39) | e) took legal action against |
| 6. He <u>scanned</u> the policy (line 40) | f) refused |
| 7. legally <u>obligated</u> to pay (line 42) | g) hooligans who damage things |
| 8. the <u>designated</u> automobile (line 43) | h) front end of a ship |
| 9. the owners … <u>sued</u> Jason (line 44) | i) liable to rot or go bad quickly |
| 10. the company … <u>declined</u> to (line 46) | j) searched in a clumsy way |

### 5.7
## Discussion

1. What is an insurance policy?
2. What is an insurance premium?
3. Why must motorists have their cars insured?
4. What work do you think an insurance investigator does?
5. Mr X bought an old fishing trawler and insured it heavily. Then he took it out to sea and sank it deliberately. He claimed on his insurance company.
   a) Has Mr X committed a crime?
   b) Must the insurance company pay Mr X the amount for which the trawler was insured?
   c) What can the insurance company do if it thinks that the claim is suspicious?

### 5.8
## Writing: using paragraphs

We met these points in Book 2:

- **Short paragraphs are better than long ones.** If a paragraph is longer than about 6–8 lines, the reader may become bored, so **keep your paragraphs reasonably short.**
- **There should be a link (of ideas) between successive paragraphs.** A new paragraph often shows one of these:
   – a change of time (a step forward or back)
   – a change of place
   – a link of similarity or contrast
   – an extension or expansion of an idea already mentioned.
- **When you use dialogue, each new speaker starts a new paragraph.**
- **Sometimes there is a topic sentence at the start of a new paragraph.** A topic sentence shows what the whole paragraph will be about. However, in many cases paragraphs do not start with a topic sentence.

The type of paragraph you use will depend on whether you are telling a story, describing an experiment, writing a report, discussing the pros and cons of a proposed law, etc.

- **Narrative/story writing:** A new paragraph will often show a change of time or place, or it may show the next thing that happens.
- **Argumentative writing:** We might want to discuss all the advantages and then the disadvantages before giving a conclusion.
- **Reporting a game:** We might start with a summary, use two new paragraphs for the two halves of the game, and then sum up in a final paragraph.

- **Reporting an experiment:** We might start with the aim, describe the experiment step-by-step, and then give a conclusion showing what we proved.

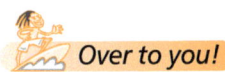 Over to you!

### Exercise 6

Not counting the first paragraph, the writer of the passage in 5.3 starts a new paragraph on twelve occasions. Study the passage and say, each time, why the writer started a new paragraph.

### Exercise 7

Look at the passage in Unit 3, 'Danger – Bears!'. Find the places where the writer has started a new paragraph. Say why he has done this.

## 5.9 Expand your vocabulary

### Exercise 8

Give antonyms (words of opposite meaning) for the underlined words.

1. Mr Nathan thinks this is a <u>cautious</u> way of tackling the problem.
2. In the debate, Pauline proved to be one of our <u>opponents</u>.
3. As far as fashion is concerned, Tina is rather <u>naïve</u>.
4. If you want to use the equipment, membership of the club is <u>optional</u>.
5. Some people find that type of music quite <u>repulsive</u>.
6. Do you think that notice will <u>deter</u> people or not?
7. Many West Indians will find that custom <u>alien</u>.
8. The living-room in their house is quite <u>spacious</u>.
9. When Dennis looked at his test results, he felt rather <u>inferior</u>.
10. A few critics <u>denounced</u> their leader at the annual conference.

### Exercise 9

Give brief explanations of the underlined words in the following sentences. Do not use more than *eight* words in each explanation. Your answers need not be in complete sentences.

1. Frogs are mainly <u>aquatic</u> creatures.
2. The proposed tax is likely to become a very <u>controversial</u> issue.

3. When you heat this chemical, it will <u>emit</u> a gas with an unpleasant smell.

4. That man is <u>notorious</u> for the way in which he conducts his business.

5. The <u>symptoms</u> of influenza include a fever, weakness and a tired feeling.

6. If a tenant does not pay his or her rent, the landlord may take action to <u>evict</u> the person concerned.

7. When my father got in the car, he said, "Oh, what a <u>nuisance</u>! I've left my keys on the table in the kitchen."

8. For centuries, the compass has been a very important <u>navigation</u> aid.

9. If a factory in country A is more <u>productive</u> than a similar one in country B, it is easy to see which factory will get more orders and be able to expand.

10. Some people like to live in a <u>secluded</u> place, away from urban noise and bustle.

11. When a boxer visited a school, the children stared at him in <u>awe</u>.

12. The Minister toured the devastated area and said that he was <u>appalled</u> at the extent of the damage caused by the hurricane.

## 5.10
## Writing: completing a report

Jason Walker (in 5.3) had to fill in a report to his insurance company about the 'accident' when a ship ran into the quay near his office. He wrote down his name, address, car number, policy number and the date of the accident. Then he had to explain briefly what happened. This is what he prepared on a piece of rough paper:

*I blew my horn once or twice and then I heard a ship blowing its horn, so I thought that somebody was playing a game with me. Somebody was trying to make more noise than me, so I blew my horn long and loud. Then suddenly a ship came and hit the quay. It wasn't my fault.*

Mr Walker's wife saw what her husband had written. She said, 'What are you trying to do – make us bankrupt? If you say that you were playing a game, the accident will be your fault, and you'll have to pay the bill for the repairs. You can say goodbye to our house, the car and your job. Think again!'

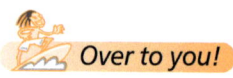 **Over to you!**

Imagine that you are Mr Walker *or* Mrs Walker. Write an explanation of how the accident happened but don't make it seem as if Mr Walker was to blame. Use 50–100 words.

### 5.11
## Vocabulary: figurative language

Find the figurative words or expressions in the following sentences. Explain (a) their figurative and (b) their literal meanings.

1. The suspect claimed that he had a cast-iron alibi but the police managed to break it.
2. You'd better brush up your Science before the test on Monday.
3. Robert got into hot water because he skipped his homework to go and play football.
4. When a property company collapsed, a wave of rumours swept through the town.
5. The question of nuclear weapons is a burning issue in some countries.
6. Hard work is the only reliable path to success but it is one which some people do not have the stamina to take.
7. Mitzie used to be such a sweet person but now she has a really sharp tongue, so be careful that she doesn't cut you up into little pieces.
8. If there is no improvement in the order book, we'll have to axe some of our employees and slash our overheads at the same time.
9. As far as we can tell, the finger of suspicion seems to be pointing at one of the sales staff at the moment.
10. There is a bottleneck on this road not far from our village, so the Government is going to widen the road.
11. You agreed to join us in the protest, so don't get cold feet and back out just when the going gets tough.
12. His story about having something wrong with the horn on his car is simply a red herring, so don't believe it.

### 5.12
## Listening: understanding a map

**A** Look at the map on page 66.

1. Find the post office opposite 21 and 22 City Road. Is it east or west of the book shop? Is it north or south of the coffee shop?
2. What is north-east of the bank?
3. What is south of the park?

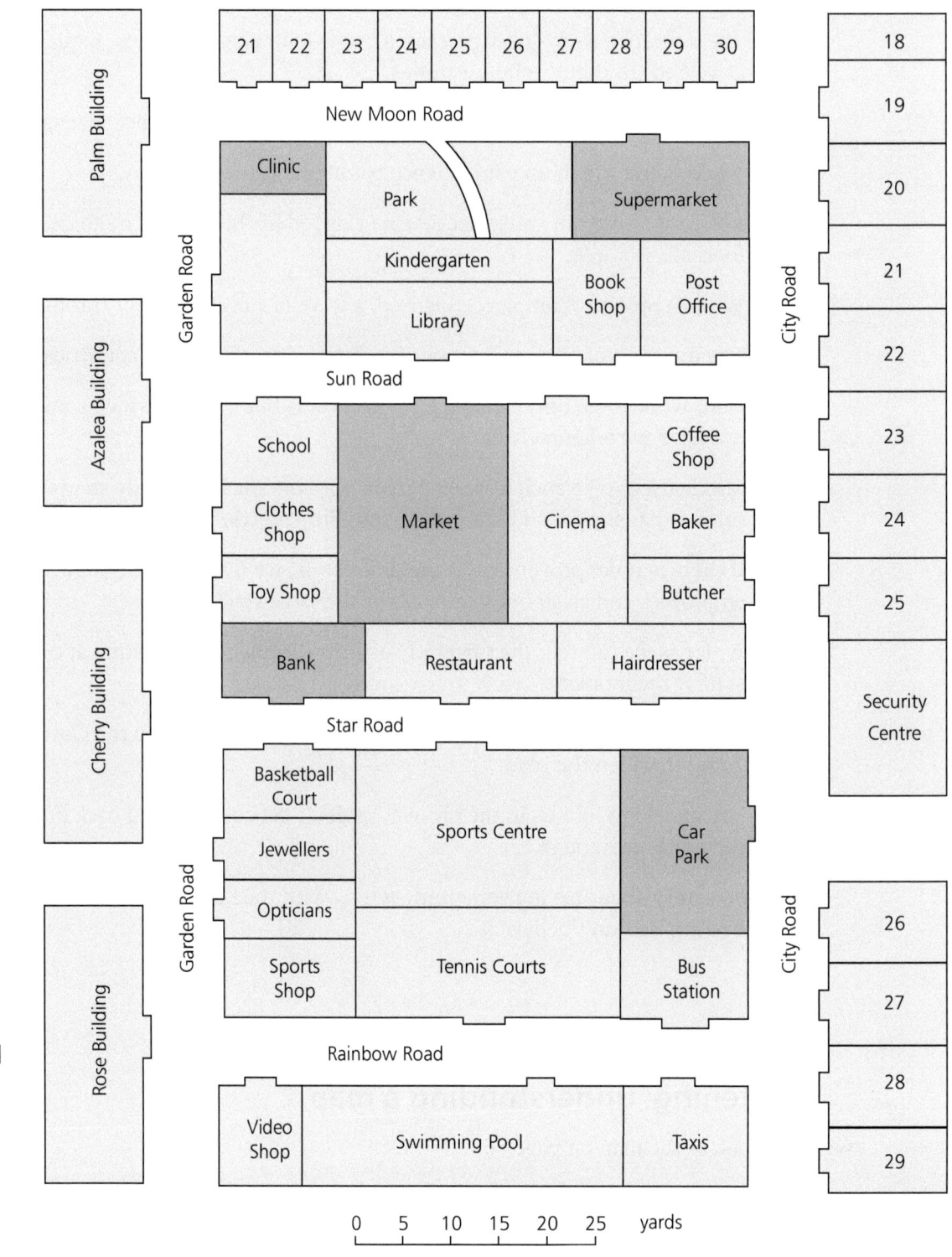

4. Sharma lives in Azalea Building in Garden Road. From the front window of her flat she can see the school. Will her front room get the sun in the morning or in the afternoon?

5. How far is it from Rose Building to Azalea Building?

6. Roughly, what is the area of the sports centre in Star Road?

**B** Now listen to your teacher and answer these questions about the map.
**Questions 1–6** Listen and choose the best answer from A–D in each case.

1.  A. the tennis courts
    B. the restaurant
    C. the car park
    D. the basketball court

2.  A. the post office
    B. the market
    C. the baker
    D. the cinema

3.  A. the park
    B. the library
    C. New Moon Road
    D. the school

4.  A. in Rainbow Road
    B. in Star Road
    C. in City Road
    D. in Garden Road

5.  A. into 30 New Moon Road
    B. into the clinic
    C. into the supermarket
    D. into the school

6.  A. the clinic
    B. the bank
    C. into the coffee shop
    D. into the pharmacy

**Questions 7–10** Listen, follow the directions and answer the questions.
**Questions 11 and 12** Listen and give the necessary directions.

## 5.13
# Think, discuss, decide

If necessary, read the story of Jason Walker (in 5.3) again.

Imagine that the companies which insured (a) Walker's car and (b) the ship which hit the quay could not decide who should pay the $5.6 million needed for repairs to the ship and quay. Because of the expense of taking legal action, they decided to refer the case to an arbitrator. They employed a retired judge to review the case and decide how much (if any) should be paid by the two insurance companies and by Walker himself.

These were the main points which the judge considered:

- **Walker** – irresponsible by blowing the horn but not done maliciously; could not be sure in the fog where the other noise was coming from
- **Walker's insurance company** – responsible unless Walker was negligent or acted maliciously
- **ship's owners** – responsible because the ship came in at night, in dense fog and without a pilot, against local rules for shipping.

 **Over to you!**

Discuss this case. Suggest what percentage of the repair bill should be paid by each of the three parties: Walker and the two insurance companies. See (2) in 5.14 on page 68.

## 5.14 Writing

Write about 250–350 words about *one* of these topics:

1. Write a story or a factual account based on *one* of the people in the photographs on this page. Make up a name and any other necessary details.

*or*

2. The arbitrator in 5.13 has given his decision. (You must decide what it was.) Write a summary of the decision, giving reasons for the various points made by the arbitrator. Your summary will be given to the press for publication. You can write as if you were the arbitrator *or* as somebody summarising what the arbitrator decided.

*or*

3. Make up a story in which a coincidence was either lucky or unlucky for somebody.

# 6 The Corn Thief

### 6.1
### Pre-reading

The passage in 6.2 is an extract from 'The Precious Corn' a short story by Michael Anthony. The story is about a dedicated watchman. By day, he labours on a vast field of corn: digging, manuring, planting, weeding and looking after the plants (called 'trees'):

> In his line, experience was a key thing. You had to have experience and you had to love working with corn. After every crop he manured and forked up every inch of this field. Then he let the soil rest a little. And when he knew the soil was ready he put the very best seeds in. Then, with a little rain and a little care, the shoots sprouted to his hands and grew up like his own children. He could not have loved his own children as he loved this corn.

During the night, a strong wind blew down some of the corn 'trees'. In the extract below, the watchman has gone out to inspect the field and repair any damage – but something (or, rather, someone) is worrying him …

### 6.2
### Reading

## The Corn Thief

On the whole, the wind was no enemy. It had very seldom struck. He couldn't even recall the last time it had damaged his corn. He never feared the wind.

It was corn thieves he feared. Or, the corn thief, rather. He didn't know if there were others but he was sure of this one. The man who lived at the far end of the
5   cornfield was the real dagger in his side. The trees near the house were always stripped of corn. Whenever he passed nearby, there was always the smell of roasting corn in the air. But this man had never put a grain in the soil. This was the real enemy he had to contend with. Day and night he had planned to catch the man. But not one of his traps worked. So he consoled himself by walking with the little stick. The little
10  stick had a big knot at one end. That was the only trap he had left. If he caught the man red-handed, he wouldn't lose his corn any more.

He was scraping earth now around another tree. About half a dozen trees were already out erect. There was a long line of blown down ones stretching into the distance. The watchman stood up again and surveyed the task. It was a tremendous
15  one and not one to brood over. He pulled a deep breath in and clenched his teeth.

It was true that the back of the man's house opened onto the cornfields. Or, as the man regarded it, the cornfield stretched up to his house. By nature he was far from being a thief, but the hard times and the asthma, and the plenty that flourished beside him, would have tested even stronger men.

20  Especially if they liked corn as he did. Often, breathing heavily with the sickness which kept him from work, he crept out among those trees, hastily breaking the ears of corn and dropping them into the little bag. And he crept back into his house again on hands and knees, looking uneasily about him and thanking heaven that he wasn't seen. For he was jealous of his good name and even as he lit the coal fire his
25  conscience would trouble him a little. But the vastness of the plantation reassured him. A few ears of corn would not make the slightest difference to that abundant harvest.

### 6.3
## Post-reading

Most of 6.1 and the first part of 6.2 are concerned with developing the character of the watchman. In the second part of 6.2, we meet the thief. In his story, the writer gives us much more information about each man, knowing that – like the gladiators of old – they will eventually meet. Characterisation is a vital part of this short story.

If possible, read the full story of 'The Precious Corn' in *Cricket in the Road and Other Stories* by Michael Anthony and find out what happened when the two men met. The story is a tragedy.

### 6.4
## Understanding

1. In 6.1, line 4, what does 'line' refer to?

2. Find two expressions in 6.1 which justify the use of 'dedicated' in line 2.

3. In line 5 of 6.2, what figure of speech is 'the real dagger in his side'? What does the expression mean? Why does the author use it here?

4. Why does the author make a big effort to stress the love which the watchman has for the corn?

5. How does the author make the reader somewhat sympathetic towards the thief? Why does he do this?

6. In line 9, how could the watchman console himself by carrying a little stick?

7. In line 21, why did the man work 'hastily'?

8. In line 24, what word can we use instead of 'name' without changing the meaning of the sentence?

### 6.5
## Vocabulary: meaning in context

**A** Choose the word(s) which best show(s) the meaning of the underlined words as they are used in 6.1 and 6.2.

1. We can read about a <u>dedicated</u> watchman (6.1, line 2)
   A. very experienced
   B. devoted to his job
   C. clever and skilful
   D. not always very healthy

2. <u>manuring</u>, planting, weeding (line 3)
   A. removing stones
   B. letting air into the soil
   C. applying animal fertiliser
   D. keeping the soil damp

3. experience was a <u>key</u> thing (line 4)
   A. vital    B. necessary    C. helpful    D. useful

4. It had very <u>seldom</u> struck. (6.2, line l)
   A. slightly    B. lightly    C. rarely    D. frequently

5. He couldn't even <u>recall</u> the last time (line 2)
   A. bear to think about
   B. remember
   C. discuss with anybody
   D. forget

6. he had to <u>contend</u> with (line 8)
   A. bargain    B. deal    C. struggle    D. argue

7. So he consoled himself by walking with the little stick (line 9)
   A. assured   B. comforted   C. contented   D. satisfied

8. If he caught the man red-handed (line 11)
   A. in the act of stealing
   B. in the presence of a policeman
   C. without help from anybody
   D. with mud or earth on his hands

**B** Match the underlined words with the meanings which they have in the passage.

| Words from the passage | Meanings |
| --- | --- |
| 1. The watchman … surveyed the task. (line 14) | a) viewed |
| 2. not one to brood over (line 15) | b) brought him confidence |
| 3. He … clenched his teeth (line 15) | c) a disease affecting breathing |
| 4. as the man regarded it (line 17) | d) anxious to protect |
| 5. the hard times and the asthma (line 18) | e) closed tightly |
| 6. the plenty that flourished (line 18) | f) inner feeling of right and wrong |
| 7. he was jealous of his good name (line 24) | g) looked at and thought about |
| 8. his conscience would trouble him (line 25) | h) plentiful |
| 9. the vastness … reassured him (line 25) | i) grew well |
| 10. that abundant harvest (line 26) | j) waste time by thinking too long |

## 6.6
# Vocabulary: idioms

In line 5 of the passage, the watchman felt that the thief was a 'real dagger in his side'. There are many idioms which refer to parts of the body. Check that you know the ones below.

### Exercise 1

Match the expressions in *italics* with the meanings given below. The meanings are not in any special order.

1. The thief *took to his heels* when he saw a police officer coming.

2. That girl's *Achilles heel* is her pride.

3. Be careful what you say. Don't *tread on his toes* if you can avoid it.

4. The new manager is very strict, so make sure that all the staff are *on their toes* when she arrives.

English Alive!

5. Don't worry about him. Leela can easily *twist him round her little finger*.

6. He has all the information which you need *at his fingertips*.

7. Don't ask him to buy land. He *burnt his fingers* two years ago when he bought a plot of land which turned out to be useless swamp.

8. Miss Saville has just bought a *second-hand* car.

9. The lease was altered when the property *changed hands*.

10. Is it true that Mr Walker is *up to his eyes* in debt?

11. Would you mind *keeping an eye on* my bicycle while I go in here to buy something?

12. Pathma has never *seen eye to eye* with her husband about the carnival.

> **Meanings**
> a) used
> b) alert
> c) deeply
> d) ran away
> e) offend him
> f) readily available
> g) influence or persuade him to do what she says
> h) agreed completely
> i) passed from one person to another
> j) watching (and protecting)
> k) weak point or characteristic
> l) was hurt (financially in this case) by his own action

## Exercise 2

Explain what the expressions in *italics* mean.

1. Who is going to *foot the bill* for all the repairs?

2. Dozens of police surrounded the robbers' hideout and it soon became clear that the robbers *had no stomach* for a fight.

3. Business hasn't been good recently but I've decided to *keep my chin up* and hope for better times to come.

4. If you know what's good for you, you'd better *keep your mouth shut* and *your nose clean*.

5. The unexpected order from a German company will be a real *shot in the arm* for our company.

6. *Keep your fingers crossed*. Vimala is going to take her driving test this afternoon.

7. Some village shops enable the owner to *keep his head above water* but don't enable him to make a great profit.

8. *Keep your ear to the ground* and see what you can find out about vacancies in your department.

## 6.7 Study skills: using a thesaurus

In 1805, an English doctor, Peter Roget, wrote down a list of synonyms and antonyms to help him in his writing and speaking. Later on, he enlarged the list and divided thousands of words into six main groups. Each group contained many sub-groups. In 1852, Dr Roget published his *thesaurus* (as the book is called) containing 1000 categories such as:

    size  heat  motion  success  virtue  production  experiment
    time  music  water  respect  religion  violence  intelligence

The entries under 'Musical sounds', for example, contain lists of different kinds of music, musicians and over 120 musical instruments.

Each group contains the nouns, verbs, adjectives, adverbs and phrases showing some similarity of meaning. In another part of the same page, the book gives corresponding antonyms.

Below is a very simplified version of part of the thesaurus. Check that you know the meaning of the words in it. Then use the words to complete Exercise 3.

| Word | Synonyms | Antonyms |
| --- | --- | --- |
| serious | major, important, great, significant, considerable, huge, meaningful, massive, enormous, marked, immense | small, slight, superficial, trivial, paltry, shallow, unimportant, insignificant, trifling, flimsy, frivolous |
| hot | 1. heated, warm, burning, fiery, blazing, feverish, sweltering<br>2. spicy, pungent, stinging, sharp, strong, peppery, highly-seasoned | cold, cool, chilly, frigid, frosty, shivering, fresh<br>tasteless, insipid, flat, mild, wishy-washy |
| useful | helpful, serviceable, valuable, of use, good for, beneficial | useless, futile, pointless, worthless, unserviceable |
| broad | wide, thick, tubby, rather fat, plump, squat, ample, dumpy, well built | narrow, thin, slender, slim, skinny, meagre, emaciated, lean |
| love | fondness, liking, admiration, affection, devotion, passion, enthusiasm, rapture, adoration | hate, hatred, dislike, contempt, coldness, coolness, bitterness, loathing, aversion, animosity |

English Alive!

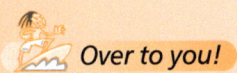 *Over to you!*

### Exercise 3

Make these sentences simpler and easier to understand by using synonyms in place of the underlined words.

1. One of the passengers received a <u>superficial</u> injury in the accident.
2. Some people prefer <u>pungent</u> food to <u>insipid</u> food.
3. Your suggestion will definitely be <u>beneficial</u> to the village.
4. The second robber was an <u>emaciated</u> man aged about 35.
5. The increase in the cost of petrol is really quite <u>trivial</u>.
6. The air-conditioning made us feel quite <u>chilly</u>.
7. It is <u>futile</u> to complain about delays caused by a hurricane.
8. The new tax will not have a <u>meaningful</u> effect on most people.
9. The increase in the number of accidents is not very <u>significant</u>.
10. There has been a <u>paltry</u> change in the rules of the competition but it will not affect our school.

## 6.8
## Grammar: agreement of subject and verb (revision)

### Exercise 4

These sentences are in pairs. Put in 'is' or 'are' each time.

1. a) The traffic ____ very heavy this morning.
   b) There ____ too many cars and lorries using this road.

2. a) All our luggage ____ over there.
   b) Our bags ____ just inside the door.

3. a) The reports in this newspaper ____ rather sensational.
   b) Most of the news ____ good today.

4. a) All the information from Guyana ____ very helpful.
   b) The facts in the first paragraph of the report on the proposed stadium ____ extremely interesting.

5. a) These machines ____ very economical to use and will cut production costs.
   b) The machinery in both of these factories ____ modern and efficient.

6. a) Some of the films on television ____ no good; they are boring.
   b) Drama ____ often broadcast on the radio in the evening.

7. a) All the pieces of equipment in the storeroom ____ getting rusty.
   b) Their equipment ____ old-fashioned and needs to be replaced.

8. a) Her behaviour ____ always very satisfactory.
   b) I assure you that her manners ____ exemplary.

9. a) All the family ____ waiting to welcome you when you return.
   b) Tony's family ____ certainly not a wealthy one.

10. a) Their team ____ full of veteran players and is very successful.
    b) Some of the players in our team ____ comparatively inexperienced.

11. a) Many rural scenes ____ very pretty and ____ admired by visitors.
    b) The scenery in many rural areas ____ very attractive.

12. a) Their clothing ____ not really suitable for tropical conditions.
    b) His clothes ____ simple but very practical.

## 6.9
## Grammar: relative pronouns (1)

Compare these two sentences:
   I know the girl. **She** won the 100 metres race.
   I know the girl **who** won the 100 metres race.

In the second sentence, 'who' is a **relative pronoun**. It replaces the pronoun 'She' and it links two statements about the girl: (a) I know her, (b) she won the 100 metres race. We can use 'that' instead of 'who', e.g.
   I know the girl **that** won the 100 metres race.

The expression 'who/that won the race' is an **adjectival clause**. We can put it after a noun near the beginning of a sentence or near the end, e.g.
   *near the beginning:* The girl **who/that** won the 100 metres race is Selva's sister.
   *near the end:* I know the girl **who/that** won the 100 metres race.

Notice that in sentences like those above, we use 'who' about people only. We can use 'that' to say something about a person, an animal or a lifeless thing.

 Over to you!

### Exercise 5

Join each pair of sentences by using 'who'. Leave out the words in *italics*.

1. Do you know that player? *He* is going to take the penalty.

2. What happened to the man? *He* was accused of being an illegal immigrant.

3. What's the name of the teacher? *She* teaches Maths in Form 5.

4. We must find somebody. *The person* can speak French well.

5. Where are the men? *They* were repairing that wall a few minutes ago.

6. Do you know the names of the two batsmen? *They* scored a century each.

7. You should speak to the girls. *They* are arranging the concert.

8. Mother is very friendly with the lady. *That lady* lives next door to us.

## Exercise 6

Join each pair of sentences by using 'who' or 'that'. This time put the expression with 'who' or 'that' early in the sentence after the noun it tells us about. Leave out the words in *italics*.

1. The police officer was praised for his bravery. *He* arrested two robbers.

2. The player is much better now. *He* was carried off the field.

3. Sandra says that the woman is her aunt. *The woman* made her new dress.

4. The Customs officers have to be very shrewd. *They* work at the airport.

5. The witness has made a statement to the police. *She* saw the accident.

6. Some of the passengers saw two huge whales. *They* were on the port side of the ship.

7. Most of the spectators managed to get one eventually. *They* arrived at the final without tickets.

8. The nurses work at our hospital. *They* are very experienced.

9. Both of the fishermen have been rescued. *They* were stranded on a tiny island near Tobago.

10. All the farmers have gone home already. *They* took part in a demonstration this morning.

## 6.10
## Grammar: relative pronouns (2)

Compare these two sentences:
> The Government is going to repair the road. **It** was damaged by the flood.
> The Government is going to repair the road **which/that** was damaged by the flood.

This sentence pattern is similar to those in 6.9. The only difference is that this time we are giving information about something which is *not* a human being. So we use 'which' or 'that' instead of 'who' or 'that'.

We put the **adjectival clause** after the word it tells us about. We can put it near the beginning or near the end of a sentence, e.g.

*near the beginning:* The road **which was damaged by the flood** is going to be repaired soon.

*near the end:* The Government is soon going to repair the road **which was damaged by the flood.**

In most cases, it does not matter whether we use 'which' or 'that' in this type of sentence. However, if we want to put a preposition before the relative pronoun, we must use 'which' and *not* 'that', e.g.

The Government is going to repair the road **on which** heavy lorries travel night and day.

That's the shop **at which** I bought these shoes.

That's the shop **in which** my cousin works.

## Exercise 7

Join each pair of sentences by using 'which' or 'that'. Leave out any words which are not necessary.

1. Miss Smith asked me about the book. The book was missing from the library.

2. My cousin pointed at the plane. It was just taking off.

3. We went to look at a boat. The boat had been blown right up on the shore.

4. We hope to catch the ferry. It leaves at seven thirty.

5. Jordan shut the door. It was banging to and fro.

6. You should tighten the nut. It keeps this bolt in place.

7. Who has the key? The key fits this lock.

8. What has happened to the donkey? It used to wander around at the back of Mr Patel's house.

9. Father is going to cut down two old trees. They block our view of the sea.

10. How can we get rid of the rats? They run around under our house.

11. The road is blocked by fallen trees as a result of the storm. The road leads to Castries.

12. Cruise ships are an important part of the local economy. They bring thousands of tourists here every month.

## 6.11

# Grammar: 'there is' and 'there are' (revision)

Compare these sentences:
- *dialect:* People say that *it have* more jobs in England than here.
- *standard English:* People say that **there are** more jobs in England than here.
- *dialect:* *It have* a kind of fish is no good to eat.
- *standard English:* **There is** a kind of fish which is no good to eat.

### Exercise 8

1. Put in 'there is' (with a singular subject) or 'there are' (with a plural subject). Notice that the subject comes *after* 'is' and 'are', so make sure that your verb agrees with it.
   a) ____ not many papaws on the trees this year.
   b) ____ more than one way of sending a parcel to London.
   c) ____ not much space in this room now.
   d) ____ a bus stop about fifty yards from our school.
   e) Sometimes ____ many passengers on our bus but sometimes ____ only a few.
   f) Is it true that ____ a storm on its way here?
   g) ____ not much to do in our village after dark.
   h) ____ usually a lot of excitement when ____ an election.
   i) Along the banks of the Essequibo River ____ many villages which rely on the river for transport.
   j) ____ a large supermarket not far from my home.
   k) In a quartet, ____ four musicians.
   l) Despite the ban on slavery, ____ still slaves in some countries.

2. Put in 'is there' or 'are there'.
   a) ____ any water in that well?
   b) ____ rice in that tin?
   c) ____ any oil under the sea near that island?
   d) ____ any bananas in the kitchen?
   e) ____ any mistakes in this letter?
   f) ____ many old houses in this part of the country?
   g) ____ any truth in the rumour about a change in the syllabus?
   h) ____ much space in the boot of the car?
   i) ____ two or three bedrooms in our new house?
   j) ____ a hyphen in 'eyebrow' or not?
   k) How many states ____ in the USA?
   l) How much petrol ____ in the tank?

## 6.12
## Grammar: 'there was' and 'there were' (revision)

Compare these sentences:

| | |
|---|---|
| *dialect:* | In another room *had* a billiards table. |
| *standard English:* | In another room, **there was** a billiards table. |
| *or:* | **There was** a billiards table in another room. |
| *dialect:* | *It had* two girls in St James used to write him. |
| *standard English:* | **There were** two girls in St James who used to write to him. |

### Exercise 9

Put in 'there was', 'there were', 'was there' or 'were there'.

1. ____ a big crowd at the stadium last Saturday.
2. ____ many people at the stadium yesterday?
3. Once upon a time, ____ a spider that wanted to be King of the Forest.
4. Last year ____ fewer cases of measles in the country.
5. ____ anybody in the factory when the fire started?
6. The watchman knew that ____ somebody hiding amongst the corn.
7. The hungry thief saw that ____ many ripe ears on the plants.
8. When we went round the bend in the road, we saw that ____ a car upside-down at the side of the road. ____ several people standing by it.
9. How many passengers ____ in the car when the accident happened?
10. Last week ____ a surplus of bananas available for export, so prices were low.

## 6.13
## Punctuation: using capital letters and full stops (revision)

We use capital letters:
- at the start of a sentence
- for days, months and festivals, e.g. 'Sunday', 'July', 'Christmas'
- for proper nouns and adjectives, e.g. 'Africa', 'African', 'India', 'Indian'
- in titles like 'Prime Minister', 'Dr Chin', 'Haji Ibrahim'
- for the main words in the titles of books, poems, films, etc.
- for the *first* word in the ending of a letter: 'Yours sincerely' (British), 'Sincerely yours' (American).

*English Alive!*

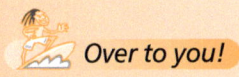 **Over to you!**

### Exercise 10

Put in capital letters and full stops when necessary.

1. this year christmas day is on a friday

2. uncle's plane leaves cheddi jagan airport in guyana on tuesday morning and should arrive at piarco airport in trinidad about an hour later we are going to meet his plane

3. when you see miss mattie, please give her this letter it is from mrs wilson make sure you don't lose it

4. we used to put 'yours faithfully' at the end of business letters but now most people prefer to use 'yours sincerely' it is more friendly and better for business

5. immigrants from the caribbean often find that life in canada, north america and britain can be unpleasant in the winter it can be very cold then most immigrants soon get used to the chilly weather

## 6.14 Enjoying poetry

Here are two different poems about dawn. The first is by Raymond Barrow of Belize.

Dawn is a fisherman, his harpoon of light
Poised for a throw – so swiftly morning comes:
The darkness squats upon the sleeping land
Like a flung cast-net, and the black shapes of boats
5   Lie hunched like nesting turtles
On the flat calm of the sea.

Among the trees the houses peep at the stars
Blinking farewell, and half-awakened birds
Hurtle across the vista, some in the distance
10  Giving their voice self-criticised auditions.

Warning comes from the cocks, their necks distended
Like city trumpeters: and suddenly
Between the straggling fences of grey cloud
The sun, a barefoot boy, strides briskly up
15  The curved beach of the sky, flinging his greetings
Warmly in all directions, laughingly saying
'Up, up, the day is here! Another day is here!'

*Raymond Barrow*

## Questions

1. In the first stanza, find at least one example of:
   a) personification
   b) a metaphor
   c) a simile.

2. Which of the word pictures in the first eight lines do you like most?

3. In line 8, we are told that the birds are 'half-awakened'. Since that is so, suggest a better word than 'hurtle' in line 9.

4. What is the attitude of the poet to dawn in this poem?

5. Taken as a whole, do you like the poem? Why or why not?

Now read this extract from a poem by Claude McKay of Jamaica:

### from When Dawn Comes to the City: New York

> The tired cars go grumbling by,
>     The moaning, groaning cars,
> And the old milk carts go rumbling by
>     Under the same dull stars.
> 5 Out of the **tenements**, cold as stone,         *large blocks of cheap flats*
>     Dark figures start for work;
> I watch them sadly shuffle on,
>     'Tis dawn, dawn in New York.
>
> The tired cars go grumbling by,
> 10     The crazy, lazy cars,
> And the same milk carts go rumbling by
>     Under the dying stars.
> A lonely newsboy hurries by,
>     Humming a recent ditty;
> 15 Red streaks through the gray of the sky,
>     The dawn comes to the city.
>
>                 *Claude McKay*

## Questions

1. In what way is the tone of this poem different from the tone of the first poem?

2. How does the poet create the tone he wants to convey to the reader?

3. How do the poets differ in their treatment of the stars?

4. Suggest a reason why the tone of McKay's poem is very different from the tone of Barrow's poem.

5. Do you think it is fair to say that one of these poems is better than the other? What is the reason for your answer?

### 6.15
### Writing

Write about *one* of the following:

1. Write another 250—350 words which continue the story of the corn thief in 6.2. Do *not* copy from the original story by Michael Anthony. You can decide how the story ends.

*or*

2. Write an original story about a teenager who tried to steal from a shop but was caught.

*or*

3. Write a poem about dawn, sunset or the night. You can decide the length. You may find it helpful to use personification, i.e. by writing about dawn, sunset or night as if it were a living creature.

# 7 Modelling

### 7.1
### Pre-reading

Would you like to be a model one day? What sort of a life does a model have?
Is modelling a suitable career? What problems do models have?
Read on and find the answers to these questions.

### 7.2
### Reading

## Modelling

When you see it on television, you look in wonder at this world. The men are tall and handsome, strong and rich. The girls are young, beautiful and ready for adventure. Together they dine in the finest hotels, buy the most expensive jewellery and travel first class across the world.

5   Or do they? What sort of life do models lead? Is it a worthwhile life for a young man or woman? Where do models come from – and where do they go?

A few models are well-known actors or actresses who make extra money by appearing in commercials. They include champion tennis stars, boxers and racing-drivers. But the majority are part-time aspirants, some of them still in Form 5 or 6
10  at local schools, who either hope to make a career out of modelling or who are curious to see what is involved in the work. There is no shortage of recruits for jobs as models. Many of the hopeful applicants are attracted by what they imagine is the glamorous image of the job. They know little of the difficulties, disappointments and hazards of the work.

15  Most people imagine that models earn a lot of money. This is true only of an elite few. Most models find it difficult to get work on a regular basis. Very few can earn enough to live on, and for all models the expenses are considerable. Their agents claim about 20 per cent of their earnings. They have to buy and maintain a good wardrobe of clothes so that they appear attractive to clients. Both men and women
20  have heavy hairdressing bills to pay. All models must maintain a 'book' – a collection of flattering photographs of themselves, to show prospective employers, and this adds to their expenditure. They have to pay to travel to interviews (or 'cattle-markets') and to reach locations where the work is to be done. A typical part-time model will get $200—$300 for a morning's work, of which 50% consists

25 of waiting for the scene to be set up for them. If we remember that many models may get only two jobs a week, the monthly total, less expenses and agent's fees, is hardly worth the effort.

Job interviews are known as 'cattle-markets' in the modelling world, and not without justification. An agent or employer inspects each hopeful model much as a
30 farmer inspects cattle at a market. Intelligence, qualifications and character count for little against good looks and the right figure. The girls may have to appear to be ideal mothers, outdoor sportswomen or disco regulars, depending on the nature of the job. For all except the few lucky ones, the life of a model is a continual search for work, trying to sell herself (or himself) in the face of cut-throat competition
35 and, sometimes, not particularly high moral standards on the part of some employers. Young people who set out on a career in modelling imagine that they will have a fairly easy, luxurious life, with high pay and no office hours. They are unaware of the insecurity of the job and that even if they succeed, the career of a model lasts no longer than her looks.
40 A girl who does succeed may achieve national or international fame. Her face may be in every magazine and on every television set – for a few short years. This exposure may result in a happy marriage. The girl may be sought after by the public and by famous figures. But she may become spoiled, arrogant or too expensive, and find that tomorrow she has been replaced by a younger, cheaper and more thrusting
45 aspirant to fame. Modelling is a fickle world with great financial rewards for a tiny minority who succeed and keep their heads, but with many dangers for the unwary. It is not for nothing that Immigration Officers look suspiciously at a girl whose passport claims that her occupation is 'Model' – and these officers are men and women of considerable experience of the world.

### 7.3
## Understanding

A Choose the best answer each time.
1. In line 1 of the passage, 'world' refers to ____.
   A. handsome men        C. both men and women
   B. beautiful women     D. the lifestyle of models

2. The writer asks: 'Is it a worthwhile life?' in line 5. He answers the question by ____.
   A. endorsing the lifestyle    C. advising considerable caution
   B. condemning the career     D. showing surprising jealousy

3. In line 9, 'aspirants' are people who ____.
   A. hope to become models    C. are still at school
   B. work part-time           D. know nothing about modelling

4. In line 14, 'hazards' is used with the meaning of ____.
   A. risks        B. hardships        C. dangers        D. obstacles

**B** Answer these questions about the passage.

1. What fact mentioned in the fourth paragraph explains why many models work part-time only?

2. Explain in your own words why the term 'cattle-markets' is used by models to describe interviews when they are seeking a job.

3. Give two possible reasons for the insecurity which a model may feel. Write two separate sentences.

4. What seems to be the main aim of the author of this passage?

5. Briefly explain the meaning of the following in the passage:
   a) heavy (line 20)   b) much as (line 29)   c) a fickle world (line 45)

## 7.4

# Vocabulary: meaning in context

**A** Choose the word(s) which best show(s) the meaning of the underlined words as they are used in the passage in 7.2.

1. who are <u>curious to see</u> what is involved (line 11)
   - A. worried about
   - B. strange as far as
   - C. wanting to find out about
   - D. afraid to know

2. no shortage of <u>recruits</u> for jobs (line 11)
   - A. opportunities
   - B. job-seekers
   - C. vacancies
   - D. enquiries

3. the glamorous <u>image</u> of the job (line 13)
   - A. general perception
   - B. lifestyle
   - C. reflection
   - D. custom

4. This is true only of an <u>elite</u> few. (line 15)
   - A. very fortunate
   - B. unusual and untypical
   - C. lucky minority
   - D. best and most successful

5. Their <u>agents</u> claim about 20 per cent of their earnings. (line 17)
   - A. representatives
   - B. employers
   - C. officials
   - D. assistants

6. All models must maintain a '<u>book</u>' (line 20)
   - A. novel
   - B. illustrated record
   - C. anthology
   - D. photographs of previous employers

86  *English Alive!*

**B** Match the underlined words with the meanings which they have in the passage.

| Words from the passage | Meanings |
|---|---|
| 1. a collection of <u>flattering</u> photographs (line 21)<br>2. to show <u>prospective</u> employers (line 21)<br>3. to reach <u>locations</u> (line 23)<br>4. <u>less</u> expenses and agent's fees (line 26)<br>5. not without <u>justification</u> (line 29)<br>6. to be <u>ideal</u> mothers (line 32)<br>7. in the face of <u>cut-throat</u> competition (line 34)<br>8. high <u>moral</u> standards (line 35)<br>9. <u>set out</u> on a career (line 36)<br>10. she may become spoiled, <u>arrogant</u> (line 43)<br>11. more <u>thrusting</u> aspirant (line 44)<br>12. dangers for the <u>unwary</u> (line 46) | a) places<br>b) adequate evidence<br>c) perfect<br>d) ruthlessly aggressive<br>e) embark<br>f) excessively proud and scornful<br>g) aggressively ambitious<br>h) not suspecting or aware of (trouble)<br>i) making them look better than they are<br>j) concerning good standards of behaviour<br>k) having deducted<br>l) possible future |

## 7.5
## Vocabulary: the emotive value of words

Many words create a good or bad impression in the mind of a person who hears or reads them. We call this the **emotive value of words**. Here are some examples:

| Good | Neutral | Bad |
|---|---|---|
| agreed<br>consented | said<br>spoke<br>discussed<br>mentioned<br>talked about | denied<br>alleged<br>demanded<br>retorted<br>objected<br>snapped<br>claimed<br>sneered |

 **Over to you!**

### Exercise 1

A young man aged 19 was caught breaking into a shop at night. When a policeman tried to arrest him, the man attacked him with a knife. The policeman had to use his revolver to defend himself. The young man was shot in his left leg and arrested. These headlines appeared in three different newspapers:

- PC guns down youth
- Thief shot in struggle with policeman
- Suspect injured in attack on PC.

1. Which of these headlines presents the policeman in an unfavourable light?
2. Which words help to create a bad impression?
3. Suggest a reason why the newspaper used this particular headline.
4. Do you consider that each headline is a fair report of the incident?

## Exercise 2

In each case say whether these words have a good, bad or neutral effect on *you*.

1. a man, a youth, a teenager, a boy, a male, masculine, a rascal, an old man
2. a woman, a lady, a girl, a hag, a female, feminine, an old woman, a young lady
3. to look, to peer, to stare, to gaze, to peep, to watch

## Exercise 3

Imagine a scale in which we give 'good' words a score of +1 to +10, neutral words a score of 0, and 'bad' words a score of -1 to -10. For example, you might give 'homework' a score of -6, and 'ice-cream' a score of +6.

Write down each of these words and the score that *you* would give it. If a word has two or more meanings, choose the meaning which first comes into your mind.

| | | | |
|---|---|---|---|
| 1. doctor | 6. husband | 11. hygienic | 16. models |
| 2. politics | 7. marriage | 12. money | 17. television |
| 3. mother | 8. prison | 13. dentist | 18. carnival |
| 4. river | 9. thirteen | 14. diet | 19. drugs |
| 5. roof | 10. fashionable | 15. holiday | 20. beach |

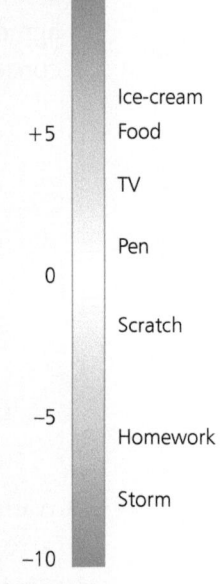

Compare your scores with those of other students in the class. You will probably find that a single word can have quite a different effect on different people.

## 7.6

## Grammar: using the Present Perfect tense (revision)

### Forms

|  |  | Examples |
|---|---|---|
| Active | has/have (not) + a past participle | Where **have** you **been**? What **have** you **done**? **Has** Pa **repaired** the TV yet? |
| Passive | has/have (not) been + a past participle | Pa **has been transferred** to the company's head office in Kingston, so we will all move there next week. **Has** the TV set **been repaired** yet? |
| Continuous | has/have (not) been + a present participle | It **has been raining** for the past three hours. How long **have** you **been learning** French? |

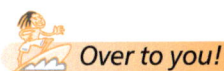

### Exercise 4

Put in the active (non-continuous) form of the Present Perfect tense of the verbs in brackets.

1. Doctor: How can I help you?
   Ranjit: I ____ (injure) my left arm. I think I ____ (break) a bone just here.

2. In recent years, there ____ (be) many changes in my country. Transport ____ (improve). The cost of living ____ (increase) and taxes ____ (go) up.

3. Mother: ____ you ____ (reply) to Uncle's letter yet?

   Francine: Yes, I ____ (write) a long letter to him. I ____ (tell) him about conditions here now. I think I ____ (answer) all his queries. I ____ (offer) to send him further information by email.

4. Krishna: What ____ (happen) to the storm? ____ it ____ (go) away?
   Jamie: Yes, I think so. It ____ (change) course and it ____ (weaken), so it's no longer a threat to the cricket match on Saturday.

5. Father: I can't find my keys. Somebody ____ (take) them. Who ____ (move) them?
   Mother: Nobody. They're still where you left them – on the table. Somebody ____ (put) the newspaper on them.

6. Several astronauts ____ (reach) the moon but nobody ____ (land) on Mars yet.

7. According to the radio, the police ____ (arrest) a tourist. They ____ (question) him and now they ____ (charge) him with attempting to smuggle drugs.

8. Look at this paragraph. You ____ (make) a mistake in the second line. You ____ (leave) out a word, and you ____ (spell) 'beginning' wrongly.

9. Mother: I hope you ____ (not forget) to water the plants.
   Susan: I ____ (just water) them and I ____ (sweep) the verandah too.
10. Shellyana: What's the matter with Mitzie?
    Kedeshia: She ____ (lose) her watch. She's been to the office but nobody ____ (find) it.

## Uses

The main uses of the Present Perfect tense are:

- (with non-continuous forms) for an action which has happened recently, especially with 'just', 'already', 'recently', 'now', 'never' and (in questions) 'ever'. However, if we say the time or date of a past action, we have to use the Simple Past tense, e.g.
   
   Mother: Don't waste your time watching television. Get on with your homework.
   Susan: I**'ve finished** all of it already.
   or: I **finished** all of it a few minutes ago. (time mentioned)

- to refer to completed future actions in sentences like these:
   
   This road will be much better when the workmen **have widened** it.
   You can go to your friend's house when you**'ve finished** your homework.

- for an action which started in the past and is still continuing, we use the continuous form, e.g.
   
   Hurry up! Uncle **has been waiting** for more than ten minutes. It's time for us to leave.
   People **have been complaining** about this road for many years. Now the Government has decided to do something about it.
   Mother: What **have** you **been doing** for the past hour?
   Jenny: I**'ve been helping** Alex with his Maths homework.

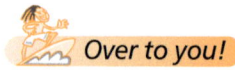 **Over to you!**

### Exercise 5

Put in the continuous form of the Present Perfect tense of the verbs in brackets.

1. Shall I wake Malina up? She ____ (sleep) for at least two hours and I know she wants to watch the film which starts in ten minutes' time.

2. I wonder what those two men want. They ____ (stand) out there for the past twenty minutes.

3. Ah, there you are! I ____ (look) everywhere for you. Where ____ you ____ (hide)?

4. Grandma ____ (live) in the same house for nearly seventy years.

5. I don't like the look of the river. It ____ (rain) for two days, and now the level of the river ____ (rise) steadily. I hope we're not going to have another flood.

6. Stella: Why are you going on a diet?
   Leela: I ____ (gain) weight for several months. Now I want to lose weight instead.

7. How long ____ you ____ (study) Chemistry? Who ____ (help) you?

8. Our neighbour ____ (grow) fruit and vegetables for as long as I can remember. She says it saves her a lot of money.

9. In recent years, more and more tourists ____ (visit) the Caribbean. That's good for business.

10. This tap ____ (leak) for weeks. Now Uncle says he'll repair it. He says he ____ (intend) to come for several weeks but was either too busy or forgot about it.

## 7.7

## Grammar: correcting mistakes

### Exercise 6

The mistakes in these sentences were all made by Form 3 (Grade 9) students. Find the mistakes and correct them. There is one mistake in each sentence.

1. A good leader will not accept nothing but the best from his assistants.

2. Now I will explain what I think the qualities of an hero should be.

3. A hero never set a bad example for others.

4. In many families a grandmother as a lot of responsibility for young children.

5. Mrs Wilson is undoubtedly a hard-working and dedicated fellow.

6. Sometimes tourists are surprised to find that customs in our country are different from their own country.

7. In my opinion, St Lucia is a very beautiful place, its mountains make it more interesting than a flat island.

8. Teachers spend more time thinking about the children their helping and less about themselves.

9. We should remember that everybody are equal, regardless of their colour or social position.

10. A good leader always have a definite goal to work towards.

11. Discipline in schools can be improve by setting certain standards and making sure that all students try their best to attain them.

12. A hero is a person noted or admired for strength of character, courage, outstanding achievements.

## 7.8

# Grammar: using 'It's time …'

The expression 'It's time …' refers to present time. These are common patterns:

- 'It's time for' + a noun, e.g.
  It's time for lunch/dinner/a rest/bed/a change.
  It's time for the start of the game/the final whistle.

- 'It's time for' + a noun/pronoun + an infinitive, e.g.
  It's time for us to go.
  It's time for the bell to ring.

- 'It's time' + subject + Simple *Past* tense, e.g.
  It's time we went home.
  It's time Uncle arrived. He's ten minutes late already.
  It's time you learnt to spell correctly.
  It's time we had a new car. This old one is nearly falling to pieces.

  Compare these sentences:
  *wrong:*   It's time we are going home.
  *right:*   It's time we **went** home.

  *wrong:*   It's time you are doing your homework.
  *right:*   It's time you **did** your homework.

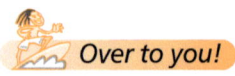

### Exercise 7

Make sentences which start with 'It's time …'. Use the Simple Past tense, as in the third pattern above. Add any other words which are necessary, e.g.
  you, go, see, dentist
  *It's time you **went** to see a dentist.*

  Uncle, return, Miami
  It's time Uncle **returned** from/to Miami.

1. you, go home
2. game, start
3. I, wash, hair
4. film, begin
5. you, go, bed
6. we, cook, food
7. you, iron, clothes
8. I, do, homework
9. rain, stop
10. Uncle arrive
11. somebody, repair, this road
12. you, finish, work
13. Lisa, write, to us
14. we, paint, kitchen
15. bus, into town, come

### 7.9
## Writing: making a summary

1. Read again the passage in 7.2 about modelling. Make a list of *three* benefits which a successful career as a model can bring. No item should be longer than *six* words.

2. Now make a list of *seven* unfavourable features of modelling as a career. No item should contain more than *six* words.

3. Use the information from (1) and (2) to write a summary of the advantages and problems or perils which can come to aspiring and/or successful models. Use 60–100 words. Start with these words:
    *The life of a model can bring both benefits and problems. …*

Include the above 11 words in your final summary. Before you hand in your work, show it to another student in your class. When he or she returns it, consider whether any improvements are necessary before your teacher sees your final summary.

### 7.10
## Enjoying poetry (1)

Read the following poem and try to decide who said what. You need to know that Purley is a suburb south of London. Victoria is one of the main railway stations near the centre of London.

### *On an afternoon train from Purley to Victoria*

Hello, she said and startled me.
Nice day. Nice day I agreed.
I am a <u>Quaker</u> she said and Sunday
I was moved in silence
5   to speak a poem loudly
for racial brotherhood.

I was thoughtful, then said
what poem came on like that?
One the moment inspired she said.
10  I was again thoughtful.

Inexplicably I saw
empty city streets lit dimly
in a day's first hours.
Alongside in darkness
15  was my father's big banana field.

A Quaker is a member of the Society of Friends. A Quaker is likely to be very sincere, honest and unprejudiced. Quakers have high moral standards and are practising Christians.

Where are you from? she said.
Jamaica I said.
What part of Africa is Jamaica? she said
Where <u>Ireland is near Lapland</u> I said.
20  Hard to see why you leave
such sunny country she said.
Snow falls everywhere I said.
So sincere she was beautiful
as people sat down around us.

James Berry

Ireland is nowhere near Lapland. As you know, Jamaica is not near Africa

## Discussion

Discuss what each person said in the poem and what you think the poet's replies mean. If you find that you do not understand the poem completely, don't worry. That is the poet's fault (or choice) – not yours.

### 7.11
### Writing: addressing an envelope

> Mrs M Williams
> 386 Elsenham Street
> LONDON
> SW18 5PZ
> ENGLAND

Check that you know how to address an envelope.
- Put the stamp(s) in the top right-hand corner.
- *If you like*, put the name and address of the **sender** in the top left-hand corner *or* on the back of the envelope – or don't give it at all.
- In modern times, people do not always put a full stop after an initial. Some people do not put a comma after any line. You can use full stops and commas if you want to. (See page 95.)
- Use one of these titles before the person's name (but this is not essential):
  – Mr for any male
  – Miss for an unmarried female (Some people use it before the name of *any* female.)
  – Ms before the name of any female: married or not
  – Mrs before the name of a married female.

- Give at least one initial of the person's name. There may be two or more people with the same name (e.g. grandfather, father, son) in one house. A letter addressed simply to Mr Williams will annoy the receiver and may cause confusion. Who should open it?
- Give the name of the house or the number and name of a street or road.
- Give the name of the city, town or village.
- Give the postal code (for the UK), e.g. SW18 5PZ. In the US it is called the 'zip code'. It is very important – it is the main guide for a post office sorter and for the person who delivers the mail.
- Give the name of the country. Notice that Northern Ireland, Wales and Scotland are in the UK (United Kingdom) but not in England. If you are writing to somebody in Scotland, the last two lines of the address will be 'Scotland, UK'.
- We can set out an address as in the example above or in this way:

    Mrs M Williams
    386 Elsenham Street
    LONDON    SW18 5PZ
    ENGLAND

- Here are some Caribbean addresses as they might appear on an envelope:

| Miss K Smith | Mr and Mrs S. Maniam, | Peter Martin |
|---|---|---|
| 16 Peaceful Drive | 478 Circular Avenue, | 123 Swan Street |
| Kingston 10 | St. James, | Bridgetown |
| JAMAICA | Port of Spain, | BARBADOS |
| WI | TRINIDAD, W.I. | WI |

 **Over to you!**

### Exercise 8

Write out these addresses as they would appear on an envelope:

1. Your own name and address.

2. The name and address of somebody living in a different Caribbean country.

3. The name and address of somebody living in a non-Caribbean country.

## 7.12

# Enjoying poetry (2): limericks

A limerick is a short, amusing poem. It has five lines with a rhyme scheme *a, a, b, b, a*. Here are some examples.

There was an old cook from <u>Bombay</u>
Who chopped off a finger one day.
He said, 'Let's not waste.
It has a good taste.
It can go in the soup of the day.'

'Bombay' is often chosen at the end of the first line because it is an easy word to find a rhyme for. It is difficult to find a rhyme for 'Barbados', 'Trinidad' or 'Antigua'.

There was a young man from Jamaica
Who hoped to become a good baker.
He lit a match in the dark
A gas leak to mark,
And now he's gone off to his Maker.

***

There was a young lady of Niger,
Who smiled as she rode on a tiger.
They returned from a ride
With the lady inside –
And a smile on the face of the tiger!
                *Cosmo Monkhouse*

***

A lady while dining at <u>Crewe</u>
Found a rather large rat in her stew.
Said the waiter, 'Don't shout
And wave it about,
Or the rest will be wanting one, too.'

an English town

***

There was an old man with a beard,
Who said, 'It is just as I feared.
Two owls and a hen,
Four larks and a wren,
Have all built their nests in my beard!'
                *Edward Lear*

***

There was a young girl from Antigua
Who said that it would not fatigue her
To cross the Atlantic,
Without getting frantic,
And turn up eventually in Riga.
                *Sandy Marshall*

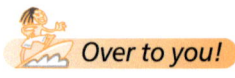 **Over to you!**

Make up some limericks and read them out in class.

## 7.13
## Writing

Write 250–350 words about *one* of the following:

1. Choose one of the people in the above photographs. Then give a brief account of what she perhaps did in the ten years *after* the photograph was taken, e.g. became a famous singer or a teacher of music, or became a doctor and carried out research into cancer or AIDS.

or

2. Choose one of the people in the photographs. Then write about a time when the person concerned had a very lucky day.

or

3. If you were offered a modelling contract (with a reputable agency) on your eighteenth birthday, what would you do – and why?

# 8 Medical Training?

### 8.1
## Pre-reading

In September 2001, terrorists crashed planes into buildings in New York, killing over 2000 innocent people. In the immediate aftermath of the slaughter, there were drastic reactions in many countries, since nobody knew where the next attack would occur. Many countries tightened their security systems. Planes were grounded without warning.

The passage in 8.2 shows what happened when one Caribbean student found that his medical training started sooner than expected. Read the passage and then decide for whom we should feel sorry: the student or his patient.

### 8.2
## Reading

## Medical Training?

In 2001 I was about to start my training to be a doctor when terrorists attacked the Twin Towers in New York. Our government decided to strengthen its medical facilities as a precaution. Volunteers were called for and I felt it was my duty to offer to help. I was put in charge of an old ambulance. I had two assistants of about
5  my own age: Francine was the driver, and Lloyd was to help carry the stretcher. After a week's instruction at the local hospital, I was supposed to be the first-aid expert. 'After all,' my supervisor said, 'you will probably be a doctor in a few years' time.'

We were sent out to practise our skills every evening. After a few days, we
10  decided to look for somebody to pretend to be a victim. We were driving on the outskirts of the town when we spotted an elderly gentleman walking his dog. We stopped and asked him if he would mind pretending to be injured for us, so that we could practise taking him to hospital.

'Well, all right,' the man agreed after a few explanations. 'Always pleased to help
15  in an emergency.'

We took out our stretcher and he lay down on it. We tucked a blanket round him and stood back, pleased with our work.

'Don't drop me,' he said with a laugh.

'Don't worry, sir,' I replied confidently. 'You're in good hands.' I bent down to
20  pick up one end of the stretcher. We were all wearing heavy metal helmets, since our supervisor had handed them out and had insisted that we wear them to simulate wartime conditions. As I bent down, my helmet fell off, hit our victim squarely on the head and knocked him unconscious.

98  *English Alive!*

'Oh, my goodness!' exclaimed Lloyd. 'What shall we do?'

'Take him to hospital, of course,' I said.

In something of a panic, we seized the stretcher and tried to push it into the rear of the ambulance but one of the man's hands swung down and became jammed under one of the stretcher wheels. The consequence was that the stretcher was stuck, half in and half out of the ambulance.

'Quick!' Francine said. 'Take the lead off the dog. Then we can tie the doors half-shut.' Lloyd passed me the dog's old leather lead and I tied it around the handles of the rear doors of the ambulance so that the stretcher could not slide out. Lloyd grabbed the perplexed dog and jumped in the front. Francine drove off at top speed.

I stayed behind to telephone the hospital. I remember having some difficulty explaining to the nurse at the hospital what had happened. I learnt the rest of the story from Francine later on.

She had driven off pretty fast, she admitted. Lloyd was sitting next to her, trying to pacify the dog, which by this time was missing its beloved master. Apparently the dog decided that it didn't like Lloyd, so it bit his arm. Lloyd leapt out of his seat, falling against Francine. She put her foot down hard on what she thought was the brake. Unfortunately it proved to be the accelerator. There was a corner ahead, and Francine pulled at the wheel, taking them round at a furious speed. This was too much for the dog's old leather lead, which surrendered under the strain. The rear doors flew open, and the stretcher and its unfortunate occupant shot out, rolled across the road and did their best to demolish a stone wall.

When the elderly gentleman was finally admitted to hospital, he was found to have concussion, two badly bruised fingers, a broken leg and three fractured bones in his left arm.

I went to see him the next day in hospital. The doctor surprised me by declaring that the old man had a strong constitution and should survive the ordeal. To my great relief, he was conscious and seemed to be recovering as well as could be expected. I was surprised to find that he was not angry at all, just a little sad.

'You see, this proves that my wife isn't always right,' he said, 'and she doesn't like that .'

'I'm sorry,' I said, 'but I don't quite understand.'

'Ah well,' he explained. 'Last night I was watching the TV peacefully at home. Then my wife told me not to be lazy. She told me to get up and take the dog for a walk. She said it would be beneficial for my health. Beneficial!'

## 8.3
## Understanding

**A** Choose the best answer each time.

1. In 8.1, tightening security systems was intended to be a ____.
   A. warning   B. threat   C. danger   D. precaution

2. The main reason for grounding planes (in 8.1) was apparently to ____.
   A. prevent further attacks   C. stop terrorists from escaping
   B. keep out immigrants   D. strengthen the economy

3. We can tell from the first paragraph of 8.2 that the writer was ____.
   A. patriotic   B. a doctor   C. apprehensive   D. a first-aid expert

4. It seems ____ that the writer was aged about 18–21 at this time.
   A. unlikely   B. certain   C. likely   D. definite

5. The Latin expression *non sequitur* means 'it does not follow logically'. In 8.2, which of these is an example of a *non sequitur*?
   A. Nobody knew where terrorists might strike next, so the government decided to take some precautions.
   B. You were going to become a doctor, so you must be a first-aid expert.
   C. Francine is a woman, so she can be the driver of the ambulance.
   D. We must improve our medical facilities so that we will be better prepared.

6. The explanations in line 14 probably included the words: ____.
   A. we want to be better prepared for a terrorist attack
   B. I'm going to become a doctor, so I need somebody to practise on
   C. it's better to practise on old people than young ones because it doesn't matter if something goes wrong
   D. this is the best way to get exercise for your dog

7. In line 18, the man's laugh probably showed his ____.
   A. fear   B. foolishness   C. frustration   D. confidence

8. In line 14, what words have been omitted before 'Always'?
   A. I have   B. I am   C. Are you   D. You are

9. The statement 'You're in good hands' proved to be somewhat ____ in the end.
   A. sarcastic   B. prophetic   C. ironic   D. accurate

10. In line 22, 'simulate' is somewhat similar in meaning to ____.
    A. re-create   B. escape from   C. prohibit   D. keep away from

**B.** Answer these questions about the passage.

1. What evidence can you find in the passage to suggest that the author's work for the medical services was (a) temporary and (b) not a full-time job?

2. What caused the panic in line 26?

3. What made Francine suggest that the men use the dog's lead?

4. How did the dog contribute to the injuries which its master received?

5. Why did the writer feel 'great relief' when he went to the hospital?

6. In line 54, to what does 'that' refer?

7. What did the old man imply by repeating the word 'beneficial' in the last line?

## 8.4 Vocabulary: meaning in context

**A** Choose the word(s) which best show(s) the meaning of the underlined words as they are used in 8.1 and 8.2.

1. In the immediate <u>aftermath</u> of the slaughter (8.1, line 2)
   A. subsequent events
   B. great confusion
   C. enquiry into
   D. causes

2. there were <u>drastic</u> reactions in many countries (line 2)
   A. quite unexpected   B. very severe   C. anticipated   D. caused by fear

3. strengthen its medical facilities as a <u>precaution</u> (8.2, line 3)
   A. something done to intimidate others
   B. act done to avoid future misfortune
   C. method of reducing costs
   D. way of encouraging people

4. I felt it was my <u>duty</u> to offer to help (line 3)
   A. right   B. privilege   C. opportunity   D. something I felt I should do

5. We were driving on the <u>outskirts</u> of the town (line 11)
   A. more peaceful parts   B. fringes   C. slums   D. busiest districts

6. 'Don't worry, sir,' I replied <u>confidently</u> (line 19)
   A. trying to give comfort
   B. certain that he would recover
   C. sure that nothing bad would happen
   D. trying to hide my real motives

7. my helmet fell off, hit our victim <u>squarely</u> on the head (line 23)
   A. full   B. heavily   C. painfully   D. fairly

8. The <u>consequence</u> was that the stretcher was stuck (line 28)
   A. cause   B. reason   C. result   D. trouble

**B** Match the underlined words with the meanings which they have in the passage.

| Words from the passage | Meanings |
|---|---|
| 1. the <u>perplexed</u> dog (line 33) | a) excessive |
| 2. She had driven off <u>pretty</u> fast (line 37) | b) knock down |
| 3. trying to <u>pacify</u> the dog (line 38) | c) natural health or spirit |
| 4. at a <u>furious</u> speed (line 42) | d) last through |
| 5. which <u>surrendered</u> under the strain (line 43) | e) unpleasant experience |
| 6. to <u>demolish</u> a stone wall (line 45) | f) good |
| 7. had a strong <u>constitution</u> (line 50) | g) puzzled and confused |
| 8. and should <u>survive</u> the ordeal (line 50) | h) calm down |
| 9. should survive the <u>ordeal</u> (line 50) | i) quite |
| 10. it would be <u>beneficial</u> for my health (line 58) | j) broke |

## 8.5 Vocabulary: homophones

Homophones are words which have the same sound but differ in their meaning, origin and (sometimes but not always) their spelling, e.g.

| | | | |
|---|---|---|---|
| *wait:* | Please **wait** for us. | *write:* | Don't forget to **write** to us. |
| *weight:* | What is your **weight**? | *right:* | Turn **right** at the end of the road. |
| | | *rite:* | This is a normal initiation **rite**. |

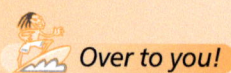

### Exercise 1

Give homophones for the following words and use them in your own sentences.

1. rain
2. heir
3. made
4. straight
5. veil
6. mail
7. rays
8. fair
9. torque
10. flower
11. meddle
12. grate
13. wood
14. quay
15. whole
16. cue
17. crews
18. flees
19. route
20. whether

## 8.6 Vocabulary: synonyms

The word **synonym** is often used to refer to a word which is similar in meaning to another word. However, synonyms are not necessarily used in exactly the same grammatical or situational way, e.g.

- slim, thin, skinny
    - When used to describe a girl, 'slim' may seem like a compliment.
    - If we call a girl 'thin', we imply that she should weigh more.
    - If we call a girl 'skinny', she may feel insulted.

- answer, reply
    - When these words are used as verbs, we put 'to' after 'reply' but not after 'answer', e.g.
        
        When are you going to **reply to** her letter?
        
        When are you going to **answer** her letter?
    - The two words can have different meanings. For example, in response to this question:
        
        What does 'craft' mean?
        
        *an answer would be:* A 'skill' of some kind.
        
        *a reply would be:* It depends on how you use the word.

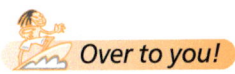 **Over to you!**

### Exercise 2

Choose the most suitable word in each case.

1. Vimala always takes great ____ to make sure that her calculations are accurate.
   A. aches          B. sores          C. pains          D. hurts

2. In ____ times, the ruler often had complete power over his subjects.
   A. ancient        B. old            C. elderly        D. old-fashioned

3. The outing will be popular with ____ member of our class.
   A. all            B. most           C. other          D. every

4. Mary is not very ____ on fishing, so I doubt whether she will come with us.
   A. enthusiastic   B. eager          C. fond           D. keen

5. Errol had not seen his cousin for several years, so when he met her at the airport, he did not ____ her at first.
   A. know           B. recognise      C. realise        D. acquaint

6. Two men broke into a shop and ____ a large quantity of cash.
   A. stole          B. robbed         C. shop-lifted    D. burgled

7. The notice in a supermarket said: 'People ____ stealing will be ____.'
   A. caught … persecuted              C. caught … prosecuted
   B. taken … prosecuted               D. taken … persecuted

8. Last night, the audience at the concert ____ mainly of teenagers.
   A. comprised      B. composed       C. contained      D. consisted

9. Is there ____ in the back of the car for another person?
   A. seat           B. place          C. size           D. room

10. We need to buy a new ____ of furniture for the lounge.
    A. suit          B. sweet          C. group          D. suite

### Exercise 3

In each case, give a word of similar meaning which we can use to replace the underlined word. Check that it has the right meaning, the right form and fits the structure of the sentence.

1. We thought the play was rather <u>tedious</u>, so we left before the end.

2. Are you <u>conversant</u> with the most modern methods of using moulds to make plastic articles?

3. Pathma's attitude to the proposal is rather <u>equivocal</u>, so we are not sure which side she will support.

4. The company has done well but we cannot afford to be <u>complacent</u> and sit still.

5. First, let us consider the <u>fundamental</u> principles on which the scheme is based.

6. Marlon's <u>associates</u> at his office think very highly of him.

7. Don't be so <u>disdainful</u> of his answer. He was trying his best and will learn in time.

8. The committee <u>resolved</u> to take no action on a complaint by a member.

9. One of the witnesses has <u>retracted</u> his statement, so the police may find it difficult to proceed with the case.

10. It is <u>unlawful</u> to act as a courier for drugs or to be concerned with the distribution of drugs in any way.

11. In some countries the <u>punishment</u> for drug trafficking is death.

12. The prisoner did not show any <u>remorse</u> for his crimes, so he received a heavier sentence.

## 8.7
# Grammar: questions with tags (1)

Questions with tags are often used in conversation. In these examples, the tags are in **bold**:
  The old man didn't die of his injuries, **did he**?
  The author was very inexperienced, **wasn't he**?

There are two main patterns for questions with tags. We can use + to show an affirmative expression and – for a negative expression:

- Pattern 1:  + – +   when the speaker expects the answer 'Yes'
- Pattern 2:  – + –   when the speaker expects the answer 'No'.

## Pattern 1

In this pattern, the speaker starts with a positive expression because he or she thinks that the answer will be 'Yes'. (However, sometimes the answer is 'No'.) E.g.

|  +                    –                  | + |
|---|---|
| Ken lives here, doesn't he? | Yes, he does. (*or* No, he doesn't.) |
| *Ken **does** live here, doesn't he? | |
| Ann found the money, didn't she? | Yes, she did. (*or* No, she didn't.) |
| *Ann **did** find the money, didn't she? | |

*The form is used for emphasis.

 *Over to you!*

### Exercise 4

Imagine that a tourist asked you these questions. Answer 'Yes', 'No' *or* 'I don't know'.

1. Your school is for both boys and girls, isn't it? (= Is your school for both boys and girls?)

2. You learn English at school, don't you? (= Do you learn English at school?)

3. Some of the children learn Latin, don't they? (= Do any of the children learn Latin?)
4. You do speak French at home, don't you? (= Do you speak French at home?)
5. Guyana is bigger than Jamaica, isn't it?
6. Some shops stay open until 7 p.m. or later, don't they?
7. When a hurricane comes, all the schools close, don't they?
8. Hurricanes do come here every year, don't they?
9. You have left school already, haven't you?
10. You go to church every week, don't you?
11. In Jamaica, the airport is near the harbour, isn't it?
12. Caribbean countries do export goods to the US and UK, don't they?
13. You slept at least ten hours last night, didn't you?
14. Trinidad invaded Barbados a few years ago, didn't it?
15. You've been to the UK, haven't you?

## 8.8
## Grammar: questions with tags (2)
### Pattern 2

In this type of question, the speaker starts with a negative expression because he or she thinks that the answer will be 'No'. (However, sometimes the answer is 'Yes'.) E.g.

      –              +              –

Coleen doesn't live here, does she?    No, she doesn't. (*or* Yes, she does.)
Dave didn't find the money, did he?    No, he didn't. (*or* Yes, he did.)

The auxiliary verb in the tag and answer depends on the tense of the verb in the question. Here are more examples:

Mia hasn't gone to St Lucia, has she?    No, she hasn't. (*or* Yes, she has.)
Tom wasn't waiting for you, was he?    No, he wasn't. (*or* Yes, he was.)
You can't lift that table, can you?    No, I can't. (*or* Yes, I can.)

**Important note:**
When you hear these questions, you can simplify them in your mind in this way:

Does Coleen live here?
Did Dave find the money?
Has Mia gone to St Lucia?    Yes. *or* No. *or* I don't know.
Was Tom waiting for you?
Can you lift that table?

You can ignore the tags at the end of questions when you are thinking about an answer.

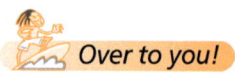 **Over to you!**

### Exercise 5

Imagine that a tourist asked you these questions. Answer 'Yes', 'No' or 'I don't know'.

1. You aren't still at school, are you?
2. You don't learn Spanish at school, do you?
3. You haven't been to the States, have you?
4. People don't still grow sugar cane here, do they?
5. Hurricanes don't come every month, do they?
6. Gold isn't as heavy as silver, is it?
7. I can't change Canadian money into local dollars here, can I?
8. There aren't any alligators or crocodiles in the Great Morass, are there?
9. You didn't watch the news on TV last night, did you?
10. Guyana didn't really used to be a British colony, did it?
11. Many people don't speak English at home, do they?
12. You wouldn't like to emigrate one day, would you?

 ## 8.9 Grammar: using the right pronoun (revision)

Remember that we use **personal pronouns** in these ways:

| As the subject of a verb | I | you | he | she | it | we | they |
|---|---|---|---|---|---|---|---|
| As the object and after a preposition | me | you | him | her | it | us | them |

*Examples:*

Between **you** and **me**, this is a present for Mother from Kimani and **me**.

These letters are for Kimberley. When **you** see **her**, please give **them** to **her**.

**We**'d better hurry. If **we**'re late home, Mother will be worried. **She** will be angry with **us**.

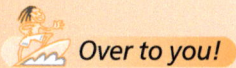 *Over to you!*

### Exercise 6

Choose the right words from the brackets.

1. Tanya is much younger than you, so look after (she, her) when you go shopping.
2. When our car broke down, a neighbour helped (we, us), so we were very grateful to (he, him) for (he, his) help.
3. Are these your keys? Father says (it, they) don't belong to (he, him, his).
4. Take this medicine. The doctor says (they, it) will soon make (it, you) better.
5. An old woman got off the bus, and after (she, her) came two tourists. (He, They) spoke to (we, us) and told (we, us) that (it, they) had come from New York.
6. Those old magazines are no good. You can give (it, them) to Kedeshia but if (her, she) doesn't want (it, them), ask (she, her) to throw (you, them) away.
7. All of (we, us) think that the team is the best (we, us) have, so don't change (it, them).
8. Hurry up! (now, It) is time for (we, us) to go to the airport. Uncle will be surprised to see (we, us) there when (he, she) arrives.
9. Michael stared at the dirty walls with graffiti scribbled all over (it, them) and wondered whether (he, him) should try to clean (they, them).
10. When I went into my grandmother's house, (her, she) stared at (I, me) as if (I, me) was a ghost. At first, (I, me) didn't know what to say to (she, her).

## 8.10
## Spelling: '-ce' and '-se' (revision)

Check that you can spell the following words correctly:

| | | | | | |
|---|---|---|---|---|---|
| *nouns use '-ce'*: | licence | practice | advice | device | prophecy |
| *verbs use '-se'*: | licensed | practises | advised | devised | prophesied |

### Exercise 7

Choose the correct words from the brackets.

1. I would (advice, advise) you to write more clearly and carefully.
2. Mark forgot his teacher's (advice, advise) and failed his examination.
3. It is an (offence, offense) to drive a car without a (licence, license).
4. According to Miss Menon, this (device, devise) will improve your breathing.

5. There are a number of (prophecies, prophesies) in the Bible.

6. In most countries, money-changers are (licenced, licensed) by the Government.

7. Donnaree can play the piano quite well but she needs more (practice, practise) if she hopes to play in the school concert next month.

8. We must (device, devise) some way of stopping the stream from flooding.

## 8.11
## Enjoying poetry

### Song of the Banana Man

Tourist, white man wiping his face,
Met me in Golden Grove market place.
He looked at my old clothes brown with stain
And soaked right through with the Portland rain.
5   He cast his eye, turned up his nose,
And said, 'You're a beggar man I suppose.'
He said, 'Boy, get some occupation,
Be of some value to your nation.'

I said, 'By God and this big right hand
10  You must recognise a banana man.'

Up in the hills, where the streams are cool,
Where mullet and janga swim in the pool,       small crayfish, shrimps
I have ten acres of mountain side,
And a dainty foot donkey that I ride,
15  Four Gros Michel, and four Lacatan,          types of bananas
Some coconut trees, and some hills of yam,
And I pasture on that very same land
Five she-goats and a big black ram.

That, by God and this big right hand,
20  Is the property of the banana man.

I leave my yard early morning time
And set my foot to the mountain climb.
I bend my back for the hot-sun toil
And my cutlass rings on the stony soil,
25  Clearing and weeding, digging and planting,
Till Massa sun drop back to John Crow mountain,
Then home again in cool evening time,
Perhaps whistling this little rhyme,
'Praise God and my big right hand
30  I will live and die a banana man.'

Banana day is my special day
I cut my stems and I'm on my way.
Load up the donkey, leave the land,
When the truck comes down I take a ride
35 All the way down to the harbour side.
That is the night when you, tourist man,
Would change your place with a banana man.

Yes, praise God and my big right hand
I will live and die a banana man.

40 The bay is calm and the moon is bright,
The hills look black though the sky is light,
Down at the dock is an English ship,
Resting after her ocean trip,
While on the pier is a monstrous hustle,

45 <u>Tally men</u>, carriers, all in a bustle,       workers who keep a
With stems on their heads in a long black snake     record of the bananas
Some singing the songs that banana men make.

Like 'Praise God and my big right hand
I will live and die a banana man.'

50 Then the payment comes, and we have some fun,
Me, Zekiel, Breda and Duppy Son.
Down at the bar near United wharf,
Knock back a white rum, bust a laugh,
Fill the empty bag for further toil
55 With saltfish, breadfruit, coconut oil.
Then head back home to my yard to sleep
A proper sleep that is long and deep.

Yes, praise God and my big right hand
I will live and die a banana man.

60 So when you see these old clothes brown with stain
And soaked clean through with Portland rain
Don't cast your eyes nor turn your nose,
Don't judge a man by his patchy clothes,
I'm a strong man, a proud man, and I'm free,
65 Part of these mountains, part of this sea,
I know myself, and I know my ways,
And will say with pride to the end of my days,

'Praise God and my big right hand
I will live and die a banana man.'

*Evan Jones*

### Questions

1. Do you think a modern tourist would behave and speak in a way similar to that in lines 6–8?

2. In line 1, the poet could have used 'fat', 'tall' or 'rude' instead of 'white'. Think of a possible reason why he chose to use 'white'.

3. What is the rhyme scheme in this poem?

4. What do you think the poet means by lines 36 and 37?

5. Imagine that you are the tourist to whom the banana man is speaking. What are you going to say when the banana man has finished his (excellent) account of his work and beliefs?

## 8.12
## Writing

Write about *one* of the following:

1. Write a story based on the picture below.

or

2. Write about a time (real or imaginary) in which you were involved in an accident (traffic or any kind) in which you were the victim, the guilty person or a witness.

or

3. Discuss realistic ways in which you think the number of casualties from traffic accidents could be reduced.

# 9 Emigration

### 9.1
## Enjoying poetry (1)

This poem was written at least 50 years ago when economic conditions in the Caribbean led large numbers of people to emigrate to (mainly) the USA and the UK in search of jobs and better living conditions.

## *Colonisation in Reverse*

    Wat a joyful news, Miss Mattie,
    I feel like me heart gwine burs'
    Jamaica people colonizin
    Englan in reverse.

5  By de hundred, by de t'ousan
    From country and from town,
    By de ship-load, by de plane-load
    Jamaica is Englan boun.

    Dem a-pour out o' Jamaica,
10 Everybody future plan
    Is fe get a big-time job
    An settle in de <u>mother lan</u>.    At this time, Jamaica was a colony.

    What a islan! What a people!
    Man an woman, old and young
15 Jusa pack dem bag an baggage
    An tun history upside dung!

    Some people don't like travel,
    But fe show dem loyalty
    Dem all a-open up cheap-fare-
20 To-Englan agency.

    An week by week dem shippin off
    Dem countryman like fire,
    Fe immigrate an populate
    De seat o' de Empire.

25 Oonoo see how life is funny,
Oonoo see de tunabout,
Jamaica live fe box bread
Outa English people mout'.

For wen dem catch a Englan,
30 An start play dem different role,
Some will settle down to work
An some will settle fe de <u>dole</u>.    **money paid to enable unemployed people to live**

Jane say de dole is not too bad
Bacause dey payin she
35 Two pounds a week fe seek a job
Dat suit her dignity.

Me say Jane will never find work
At the rate how she dah look,
For all day she stay pon Aunt Fan couch
40 And read love-story book.

Wat a devilment a Englan!
Dem face war an brave de worse,
But I'm wonderin how dem gwine stan
Colonizin in reverse.

*Louise Bennett*

Some of the 482 Jamaicans emigrating to the UK, 1948

### Questions

1. 'I feel like me heart gwine burs' ' (line 2). Why?

2. Suggest a reason why there is an apostrophe after 'burs' in line 2 but not after 'Englan' in line 4.

3. Change lines 9–12 into standard English.

4. In what way can the people 'tun history upside dung' (line 16)?

5. In lines 21–4, find (a) a simile and (b) a word used metaphorically.

6. How are Jamaicans able to 'box bread outa English people mout' '? (lines 27–8)

7. How would you describe the attitude of the poet to emigration? What evidence can you find to support your answer?

## 9.2
## Enjoying poetry (2)

Compare this poem with the previous one. In what ways are the two poems (a) similar and (b) different?

### *The Emigrants*

So you have seen them
with their cardboard grips       cases
felt hats, rain-
cloaks, the women
5   with their plain
or purple-tinted
coats hiding their fattened hips.

These are the Emigrants.
10  On sea-port quays
at air ports
anywhere where there is a ship
or train, swift
motor car, or jet
15  to travel faster than the breeze
you see them gathered:
passports stamped
their travel papers wrapped
in old disused news-
20  papers: lining their patient queues.
Where to?

They do not know.
Canada, the Panama
Canal, the Miss-
25 issippi painfields, Florida?
Or on to dock,
at hissing smoke-locked
Glasgow?

Why do they go?
30 They do not know.
Seeking a job
they settle for the very best
the agent has to offer:
jabbing a neighbour
35 out of work for four bob                    **shillings, a small sum of money**
less a week.

What do they hope for
what find there
these New World mariners
40 Columbus coursing kaffirs                  **black people**
What Cathay shores                            **(literally) Chinese, here 'Eastern'**
for them are gleaming golden
what magic keys they carry to unlock
what gold endragoned doors?                   **with dragons (carved or painted) on**
        *Edward Brathwaite*

## Questions

There are no right-or-wrong answers to some of these questions. Speak for yourself. Give your own honest opinion.

1. We could rewrite lines 1–8 in either of these ways:
   a) So you have seen them with their cardboard grips, felt hats, rain-cloaks; the women with their plain or purple-tinted coats hiding their fattened hips.

*or*

   b) So you have seen them
      With their cardboard grips,
      Felt hats, rain-cloaks;
      The women with their plain
      Or purple-tinted coats
      Hiding their fattened hips.

   From a poetical point of view, what difference is there between (a), (b) and the way in which the poet has set out the lines? Is the poet's method more effective?

114 *English Alive!*

2. What, if anything, is gained by splitting 'Mississippi' and putting it on two lines (lines 24 and 25)?

3. It is unlikely that the poet wrote the whole of the poem at one time in a few minutes. Poets often spend hours or days writing a poem and then rewriting it to improve it. Do you find that any parts of the poem are different from the rest?

4. How is the attitude of this poet to emigrants different from the attitude shown by the poet in 9.1?

5. Which of the two poems do you prefer? Why?

6. In your opinion, is 'The Emigrants' poetry or not? If possible, give your reason(s) for your opinion.

## 9.3
## Pre-reading

In 9.4, we can read part of a discussion about emigration. When you study the discussion, remember these points:

- Emigration affects at least two countries. For example, emigration from Jamaica to the UK affects both countries. The effect can be good or bad (or both good and bad). Thus the arrival of thousands of Jamaican immigrants in the UK can have both good and bad effects there. The departure of the same emigrants can have both good and bad effects in Jamaica.
- A report on emigration from Jamaica to the UK can be selective. Depending on the motives of the reporter, it can show favourable or unfavourable effects in either of the two countries. In other words, the report can be biased, unbalanced and unfair.

Read the discussion which is between Miss Jones, a tourist who is visiting Jamaica, and Errol Taylor and his wife, Avril Taylor, who live and work in Jamaica.

## 9.4
## Reading

### Emigration

**Avril:** How do people in the UK regard Jamaicans now? Is it true that Jamaicans have a negative image in the UK at present?

**Miss Jones:** Yes and no. In 2003, the British police arrested 20 people said to be involved in a drug-ring in Bristol. 17 of them were Jamaican 'Yardies' – or so the TV reported. At the same time, the Customs report that every plane from Jamaica is given special treatment because some of the passengers may be drug couriers. This type of publicity gives Jamaica a bad reputation but …

5

**Errol:** Surely 17 is nothing when compared to the hundreds of thousands of Jamaicans living peacefully in the UK?

**Miss Jones:** You took the words out of my mouth! I was just going to say that some of our best-known TV personalities are from the Caribbean. Sir Trevor McDonald has his own show. Then we often see Jamaican athletes and cricketers on TV. The Yardies are a tiny minority but they get a lot of publicity.

**Avril:** Is it true that the UK is recruiting teachers, nurses and even doctors from the Caribbean?

**Errol:** And recruits for the Armed Forces.

**Miss Jones:** Yes, I'm sure it is. There's a shortage of all those people in the UK, so recruiting teams have visited the Philippines, India, Australia and, of course, the Caribbean.

**Avril:** But that means taking away trained professionals! Surely it weakens the country they emigrate from?

**Miss Jones:** Maybe – or maybe not. That depends on whether a particular country has a surplus of people in one of those professions. And then there's the tricky question: Do we have the right to prohibit people from migrating if they see a chance to lead a better life?

**Avril:** I don't think so, not really. In any case, it would be difficult to enforce. Somebody could go off to the UK or the US for a holiday and never return.

**Errol:** I guess that's true. We can't introduce legislation to stop people from emigrating but it seems a shame to spend money training people and then see them go off to work in another country.

**Miss Jones:** Many of them remit money. That helps their families back home.

**Avril:** But isn't there a lot of opposition to immigrants in the UK now?

**Miss Jones:** Well, there's some opposition but I wouldn't call it 'a lot'. In any case, it's aimed mainly at economic migrants from East Europe, North Africa and Pakistan. People remember that many Jamaicans volunteered to serve in the British Armed Forces during both world wars, so that makes them more sympathetic towards Caribbean immigrants. In fact, if it weren't for drugs and the Yardies, there wouldn't be any criticism at all.

**Errol:** But how come that Britain needs more teachers and nurses?

**Miss Jones:** Some have emigrated to the US, Canada and Australia. Others have switched to different kinds of work. Both teaching and nursing can be stressful. Also the services have expanded, so more staff are needed.

**Avril:** But what about racial prejudice? I sometimes hear stories about it. Does it still exist in the UK?

**Miss Jones:** Officially, no. There are all sorts of laws to prevent racial discrimination, especially as far as job-seekers are concerned. Unofficially, yes, there is some racial prejudice, mainly amongst less educated people. They resent anybody who is not from the same race and class as themselves. It's like that in almost every country in the world. Isn't it true that racial prejudice exists here, in the Caribbean?

**Avril:** Well, if it does, we're not going to admit it!

|           |                                                                                                                                                                                                                                                 |
|-----------|-------------------------------------------------------------------------------------------------------------------------------------------------------------------------------------------------------------------------------------------------|
| Errol:    | I see your point. Tribal discrimination exists in Africa. Discrimination on account of religion exists in the Middle East and elsewhere.                                                                                                        |
| Miss Jones: | And Londoners are prejudiced against people from Liverpool or Manchester. Usually it's not much of a problem. It's becoming less with each new generation. A lot of the stars in our soccer and cricket teams are the children of Caribbean migrants and they're extremely popular. |
| Errol:    | Well, thanks very much for the chat. It's time for us to go home.                                                                                                                                                                               |
| Avril:    | Yes, thanks for the discussion. I have to go now. I want to phone my daughter. She's a nurse in London. Goodbye.                                                                                                                                |
| Miss Jones: | Goodbye. I really enjoyed our chat.                                                                                                                                                                                                           |

### 9.5
## Understanding

1. What is the meaning of a 'negative image' in line 2?

2. In line 3, Miss Jones said 'Yes and no.' In which subsequent line did she *start* to justify her use of 'no'?

3. Why did Miss Jones mention 'Yardies' in line 4?

4. What point is Miss Jones trying to make by mentioning Sir Trevor McDonald in line 13?

5. To whom does 'trained professionals' refer in line 22?

6. In line 43, what words can we use to replace 'how come' without changing the meaning of the question?

7. In line 56, Errol Taylor said, 'I see your point.'
   a) To whom does 'your' refer?
   b) Explain in your own words what the point was.

8. Do you think Avril Taylor is sympathetic towards people who emigrate or opposed to them? Give a reason for your answer.

### 9.6
## Vocabulary: meaning in context

**A** Choose the word(s) which best show(s) the meaning of the underlined words as they are used in 9.3 and 9.4.

1. A report … can be <u>selective</u> (9.3, line 8)
   A. prejudiced      C. particularly impressive
   B. covering a wide range      D. using certain points only

2. the report can be biased (line 10)
   A. deliberately favouring one side only   C. written too hurriedly
   B. completely truthful in all respects    D. uninformed

3. people said to be involved in a drug-ring (9.4, line 4)
   A. responsible for                C. taking part in
   B. innocent of any knowledge of   D. accused of

4. or so the TV reported (line 5)
   A. this is what   B. later on   C. then   D. it is said

5. every plane from Jamaica is given special treatment (line 6)
   A. refuelled and tested carefully         C. treated as a VIP
   B. regarded with considerable suspicion   D. given extra privileges

**B** Match the underlined words with the meanings which they have in the passage.

| Words from the passage | Meanings |
| --- | --- |
| 1. may be drug couriers (line 7) | a) seeking to obtain |
| 2. gives Jamaica a bad reputation (line 8) | b) refuse to allow |
| 3. our best-known TV personalities (line 12) | c) laws |
| 4. the UK is recruiting teachers (line 16) | d) unreasonable intolerance |
| 5. the tricky question (line 26) | e) do not like |
| 6. to prohibit people from migrating (line 26) | f) public image |
| 7. it would be difficult to enforce (line 28) | g) send back |
| 8. We can't introduce legislation (line 31) | h) similar to |
| 9. Many of them remit money. (line 34) | i) make sure that it is obeyed |
| 10. what about racial prejudice (line 47) | j) people who carry |
| 11. They resent anybody (line 52) | k) problematic |
| 12. It's like that in almost every country (line 53) | l) well-known people |

## 9.7
## Writing: making a summary

Make *one* of these summaries:

1. In 50–80 words summarise the information in 9.4 about why Jamaicans emigrate to the UK and why they are admitted.

or

2. In 50–80 words summarise what Miss Jones said about racial prejudice.

**Work in this way:**
1. Be absolutely sure that you know what information you are looking for.
2. Read the dialogue. Mark the places where you can find relevant information.
3. On some rough paper, make notes of the necessary information.
4. Join the notes up to make a fluent summary.
5. Check for length.
6. Ask a classmate to check your summary.
7. Make any changes which are necessary before you hand in your work.

## 9.8
## Spelling

1. Check that you can spell the words below and know how to use them. Then your teacher can test you or you can have a competition between two halves of the class.

   | | | | |
   |---|---|---|---|
   | appropriate | exhibition | invisible | separately |
   | batteries | explain | language | succeed |
   | beautiful | explanation | library | successful |
   | beginning | February | misbehave | surprise |
   | behaviour | friend | mysterious | survivors |
   | believed | government | professional | suitable |
   | ceiling | harbour | pronounce | thief |
   | conscience | ignorant | pronunciation | until |
   | conscious | illiterate | received | vehicles |
   | cultural | immigration | reliable | Wednesday |
   | disappointed | invincible | scenery | wonderful |

2. Complete these sentences by putting in words from the above list.
   a) An ____ person is somebody who cannot read or write.
   b) When a fishing-boat sinks, other boats try to rescue any ____.
   c) A ____ athlete is somebody who competes to get money.
   d) Your ____ will usually tell you whether what you are doing is right or wrong.
   e) Buses, trucks, taxis and lorries are different kinds of ____.
   f) The game won't start ____ the referee blows his whistle.
   g) For some students, the ____ of 'v' and 'th' is difficult.
   h) This torch won't work; it needs new ____.

## 9.9
## Grammar: making a complaint

There are two main ways of making a complaint:

- We can say what is wrong. Then we do *not* use 'complain' or 'complaint'. We often use this method in speech, e.g.

    There's something wrong with this radio.
    I've paid this bill already. Why have you sent it to me again?

It's 2 a.m. now. There's a party at a neighbour's home. They're making a lot of noise.

- We can use 'complain' or 'complaint':

| I want<br>I wish | to complain | to the manager. |
| I would like<br>I'd like | to make a complaint | about this radio. |

In both instances, we do two things: first we make a complaint; then we often say what we want somebody to do, e.g.

There's something wrong with this radio. I want a new one.
I would like to complain about this bill. Please check it and let me have a new one.
Miss Mattie complained to a police officer about two fierce dogs which her new neighbour had. She wanted the police to make her neighbour control the dogs.

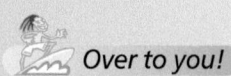 *Over to you!*

Exercise 1

Make up suitable complaints. Use at least two sentences each time, as in the examples above.

1. You bought a watch at a shop. Soon after you arrived home, the watch stopped and would not start again.

2. Mr Chan owns a shop near a school. Several times he has caught children from the school stealing things from his shop. He wants to complain to the principal of the school.

3. A tourist arrived at the airport. A taxi-driver charged her US $100 to drive her 6 miles to her hotel. She wants to complain to the Transport Department or whoever licenses taxis.

4. Miss Almeida's telephone is out of order. She has asked the telephone company to repair it but, two weeks later, nobody has come. Now she wants to write a letter of complaint to the telephone company.

5. Mrs Alicia Smith lives in a house near a large factory. She has a car-port and keeps her car under it at the front of her home. Several times she has found a big lorry from the factory parked outside her house so that she cannot get her car out in the morning to go to work. She wants to complain to the manager of the factory.

6. Mr Daljit Singh ordered some goods by email but the company sent the wrong things. He is going to return the goods but wants to send an email to the company, complaining about its carelessness. He intends to put a printed copy of his email in the parcel when he returns the unwanted goods.

## 9.10
## Writing

Write about *one* of the following topics:

1. Write a story in which one or both of the people in the pictures is involved.

or

2. If you have a chance to emigrate later in life, where would you prefer to go and why? What would you hope to do there?

or

3. Describe the types of poems you enjoy *and* those which you do not like. You can quote from some poems if you like but no quotation should be longer than four lines.

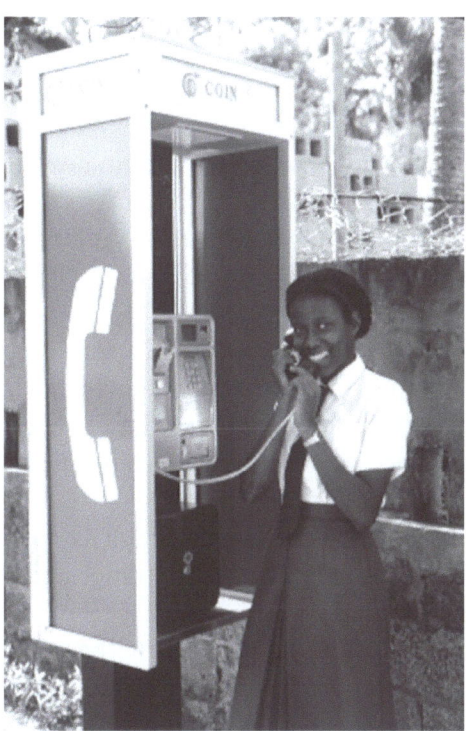

# 10 The Treeman

### 10.1
### Pre-reading

The passage in 10.2 is based on a report by Alexander Chancellor in *The Independent* newspaper. Notice the sympathetic tone of the report and the way in which a law-breaker is eventually persuaded to stop breaking the law. As the writer says, 'America is still the land of opportunity'.

### 10.2
### Reading

## The Treeman

Anybody visiting New York for the first time should take a room high up in one of the over-priced hotels at the southern end of Central Park, merely for the extraordinary view it provides. The park extends northwards until it is lost to sight: a sea of tree-tops flanked on each side by enormous impenetrable cliffs of stone and
5   cement.

During recent years, several legends have grown up among people who live near the park or often visit it. One story claims that the park contains whole tribes of mysterious tree-dwellers who play tomtoms at night. According to another story, there is a young and handsome man who has been spotted from time to time
10   lurking among the branches like a modern Tarzan.

It is not surprising that such rumours should exist. Central Park covers a huge area – some 850 acres – and accommodates a multitude of strange and sinister events. In this case, one of the rumours proved to be correct. There *was* a young and handsome man in the park, and he had been living among the tree-tops for
15   eight years before he was brought to book not long ago by the city authorities.

It is a touching tale. Bob Redman, now 22, had always been addicted to trees. He grew up in a tiny apartment and was always fascinated by the trees in nearby Central Park. When he was 14, he went into the park and quietly built himself a tree house. It was the first of 13 such houses he was eventually to build, each more
20   elaborate and lavish than the last. 'I like to be in trees,' he explained to a reporter from the *New York Times*. 'I like to be away from everything. I like the solitude. Most of all, I love to go up in the tree houses and look at the stars.'

Mr Redman built his tree houses with pieces of scrapwood that he managed to scrounge. He carried them little by little into the park and then hoisted them
25   secretly into the tree tops. A lean and muscular young man, he can scale tall and branchless tree trunks with remarkable agility. Entry to his houses was often 40 feet above the ground, with several levels above that.

His final house was the grandest of them all. Constructed at the top of a towering beech tree from 1000 lbs of timber, it was what an estate agent would describe as a five-room, split-level home commanding spectacular views of the city skyline and of all of Central Park. It included ladders and rope bridges – one leading to an adjacent tree – as well as wooden benches and tables he had made. Who can imagine what the rent would be?

Mr Redman would take great pains to conceal his tree houses, building them in neglected corners of the park and camouflaging them with branches and green paint. Friends would come to visit him in them, bringing sandwiches and radios, books and torches. They were given a set of rules which, among other things, prohibited branch-breaking, fires, litter and loud noise. His brother, Bill, sometimes brought a set of conga drums to the tree houses and played them late at night, giving rise to the rumours of a tree-dwelling tribe.

Although the park authorities quickly became aware of his activities, the houses would often go undetected for long periods of time. Some lasted as long as a year before the sleuths of the Parks Department would find them and tear them down, often with Mr Redman watching mournfully from a distance. His final and most magnificent structure went unnoticed for four months. Then they got him.
He was awoken one morning by the voice of Frank Serpe, Director of Horticulture for Central Park. 'Come down! The party's over!' he yelled from the foot of the tree. And Mr Redman climbed down to meet not only Mr Serpe but 10 officers of the Parks Enforcement Patrol. It was victory for Mr Serpe, who had been hunting Mr Redman for years. But, after his triumph, he paid Redman a generous tribute. 'We marvelled at the spectacular workmanship,' he said. 'The last house had floors strong enough to hold a truck, and not one nail was driven into the tree.'

You will be glad to know that the story had a happy ending. As the officers formed a huddle to decide his fate, Mr Redman offered to go up and help the workmen dismantle the tree house. 'I told him I supposed that was all right,' said one of the officers later. 'Well, he walked up the tree. It was amazing.' Mr Serpe concluded that, rather than lock Redman up, perhaps they should offer him a job. And now, having made a solemn promise to build no more tree houses, Mr Redman is a professional pruner and tree-climber for the Central Park

60 Conservancy. He says he still cannot believe that a job so perfect for him could possibly exist. His mother is happy too. He finally has work and is back living at home.

It all proves, I suppose, that America is still the land of opportunity in which dreams – even such seemingly impossible dreams – can become reality. And in the
65 tirelessly competitive atmosphere of the United States, it is comforting every now and then to remember that Mr Redman exists.

## 10.3
## Understanding

1. If the hotels in line 2 are over-priced, why should the writer recommend people to stay in one of them?

2. Why would a room on the first floor *not* prove satisfactory?

3. In line 4, which three words are redundant?

4. Two stories are mentioned in the second paragraph of the passage. Which of these stories proved to be partly or entirely true?

5. What figure of speech is used in each of the following?
   a) 'a sea of tree-tops flanked on each side by enormous impenetrable cliffs of stone and cement' (line 4)
   b) 'lurking among the branches like a modern Tarzan' (line 10)

6. What does the writer gain by using the figurative language mentioned in question 5?

7. Explain the meaning of 'brought to book' in line 15.

8. Find *three* reasons in the passage to show why Redman was able to build tree houses for eight years before he was finally caught.

9. Redman used 1000 lbs of timber to build his last tree house. Where did he get the timber from?

10. How would you describe the attitude of Mr Serpe to Redman?

## 10.4
## Speaking: making an oral summary

How good is your memory? Make an oral summary of the passage in 10.2 *without looking back at the passage*. You should include a few words (but not too many) about each of the following:

- Bob Redman and his tree houses
- 8 years
- caught by Mr Serpe. Offered a job.
- occupation now.

## 10.5
### Speaking: asking questions

Make up three questions about the passage in 10.2. Prepare the answers. Ask the questions in class and say whether the answers are correct or not.

## 10.6
### Vocabulary: meaning in context

**A** Choose the word(s) which best show(s) the meaning of the underlined words as they are used in 10.2.

1. a sea of tree-tops <u>flanked</u> on each side (line 4)
   - A. squeezed in
   - B. partly surrounded
   - C. having at the side
   - D. made to appear smaller

2. enormous <u>impenetrable</u> cliffs of stone and cement (line 4)
   - A. that nobody could get through
   - B. built to last for ever
   - C. impressive because of their height
   - D. being slowly washed away.

3. there is a young and handsome man who has been <u>spotted</u> from time to time (line 9)
   - A. seen
   - B. injured
   - C. heard
   - D. pursued

4. Central Park …<u>accommodates</u> a multitude of strange and sinister events (line 12)
   - A. provides space for
   - B. led to
   - C. witnessed
   - D. tries to exclude

5. he was brought to book not long ago by the city <u>authorities</u> (line 15)
   - A. MPs
   - B. officials
   - C. regulations
   - D. councillors

6. It is a <u>touching</u> tale. (line 16)
   - A. involving capture
   - B. long-winded
   - C. rather unexpected
   - D. making us feel sympathetic

7. Redman, now 22, had always been <u>addicted to</u> trees (line 16)
   - A. an admirer of
   - B. badly affected by
   - C. extremely fond of
   - D. harmed by

8. each more <u>elaborate</u> … than the last (line 20)
   - A. detailed and impressive
   - B. simple in design
   - C. difficult to locate
   - D. likely to last longer

9. each more …<u>lavish</u> than the last (line 20)
   - A. better equipped
   - B. secure
   - C. with a better view
   - D. attractive to friends

**B** Match the underlined words with the meanings which they have in the passage.

| Words from the passage | Meanings |
|---|---|
| 1. that he managed to <u>scrounge</u> (line 24)<br>2. then <u>hoisted</u> them secretly (line 24)<br>3. with remarkable <u>agility</u> (line 26)<br>4. <u>commanding</u> spectacular views (line 30)<br>5. leading to an <u>adjacent</u> tree (line 32)<br>6. in <u>neglected</u> corners of the park (line 35)<br>7. <u>camouflaging</u> them with branches (line 35)<br>8. <u>giving rise to</u> rumours (line 40)<br>9. <u>sleuths</u> of the Parks Department (line 43)<br>10. watching <u>mournfully</u> (line 44) | a) providing<br>b) next to<br>c) concealing<br>d) creating<br>e) men like detectives<br>f) get without paying<br>g) sadly<br>h) physical skill and liveliness<br>i) not cared for<br>j) pulled |
| 11. the officers formed a <u>huddle</u> (line 54)<br>12. to decide his <u>fate</u> (line 54)<br>13. <u>dismantle</u> the tree house (line 55)<br>14. Mr Serpe <u>concluded</u> (line 57)<br>15. made a <u>solemn</u> promise (line 58)<br>16. a professional <u>pruner</u> (line 59)<br>17. the Central Park <u>Conservancy</u> (line 60)<br>18. a job so <u>perfect</u> for him (line 60)<br>19. become <u>reality</u> (line 64)<br>20. the <u>tirelessly</u> competitive atmosphere (line 65) | k) finally decided<br>l) very serious<br>m) an organisation to protect<br>n) what was going to happen to him<br>o) completely suitable<br>p) happen<br>q) a closely gathered group<br>r) never slacking<br>s) somebody who trims trees<br>t) take to pieces |

### 10.7
# Grammar: compound adjectives

Many compound adjectives consist of two words joined by a hyphen, e.g.
    a **left-handed** girl
    a **split-level** house.

1. Make up compound adjectives to complete these sentences.
   a) A car park with many storeys is a ____ car park.
   b) A road down which vehicles can go in only one direction is a ____ road.
   c) Somebody who has a kind heart is said to be ____.
   d) A game in which one side is much better than the other is ____.
   e) A lion or tiger which eats people is called a ____.
   f) A shirt with short sleeves is a ____ shirt.
   g) A fence made of barbed wire is a ____ fence.
   h) A person aged 40-55 is ____.

*English Alive!*

2. What do we mean by these expressions?
   a) a mild-mannered reporter
   b) a cool-headed person
   c) an easy-going personality
   d) a tight-fisted person
   e) a far-sighted decision
   f) the long-awaited results

### 10.8
# Grammar: reflexive and emphatic pronouns (revision)

**Reflexive** and **emphatic** pronouns have the same form but are used in different ways.

| Singular | Plural |
| --- | --- |
| I enjoyed **myself** at the picnic.<br>Don't cut **yourself** with that knife, Sue.<br>Tom felt ashamed of **himself**.<br>Anna was pleased with **herself**.<br>One must defend **oneself**.<br>Our cat likes to wash **itself**. | We all enjoyed **ourselves**.<br>Behave **yourselves** at the party, boys.<br>The players were proud of **themselves**<br>when they won the inter-island cup. |

## Reflexive pronouns

Reflexive pronouns are used as the *object* of a verb or after a preposition. They are *not* used as the subject of a verb, e.g.

> *wrong:* Myself and my mother went shopping last Saturday.
> *right:* My mother and **I** went shopping last Saturday.
> *wrong:* Myself and brother like to play badminton.
> *right:* My brother and **I** like to play badminton.

**Remember:**
- The plural forms end in **ves**. None of the pronouns ends in 'fs'.
- Each pronoun is *one word*. Don't write one of these pronouns as two separate words.
- There is no such word in standard English as 'meself'.

### Exercise 1

Put in suitable reflexive pronouns.

1. Bob Redman made ____ several tree houses.

2. When friends visited him, he made sure that they behaved ____ and did not damage the trees or hurt ____ by falling to the ground.

3. May I help ____ to some ice-cream?

4. If you eat too much ice-cream, you may make ____ sick, Errol.

5. Don't try to lift that log by ____, Mark. I'll help you.

6. If a dog has fleas on it, it will scratch ____ frequently.

7. My sister is busy making ____ a costume for the carnival.

8. My friend and I went swimming but we dried ____ before we got on the bus to go home.

9. We blamed ____ for losing the game by not taking it seriously.

10. Why is it that birds never seem to lose ____ when they migrate?

## Emphatic pronouns

Emphatic (or emphasising) pronouns usually come immediately after a noun or pronoun. We use them to emphasise something, e.g.

I know the news is correct. Miss Smith **herself** told me.

We have moved to a new house. The house **itself** is very good but it is a long way from school.

### Over to you!

### Exercise 2

Put in suitable emphatic pronouns.

1. Don't interfere, Lisa. Let the boys ____ settle the argument.

2. Deena enjoyed the film but I didn't much like it ____.

3. The Park officers ____ admired Redman's skill in building tree houses.

4. There's nothing wrong with the computer ____. You haven't switched on the electricity.

5. There was nobody else at home, so I had to try to repair the leaking tap ____.

6. Thanks but I have your new address already. You ____ gave it to me last week.

7. Mrs Walker ____ is very nice but her husband is not so pleasant.

8. I doubt whether our team will win the tournament but the players ____ seem full of confidence, so perhaps they will win.

## 10.9
# Grammar: prepositions

### Exercise 3

Put in suitable prepositions.

1. Tourists should stay in a room high up ____ the extraordinary view it provides.

2. The park stretches towards the north until it is lost ____ sight.

3. According ____ one story, a young man has been seen ____ time ____ time lurking among the treetops ____ Central Park.

4. Bob Redman was addicted ____ trees and liked to be away ____ everything.

5. He was a young man ____ remarkable agility which had a great effect ____ Park officials when they saw him ____ work.

6. Redman camouflaged his tree houses ____ branches and green paint so that they would not be visible ____ searchers.

7. The park authorities were aware ____ his activities but Redman's tree houses went undetected ____ long periods of time.

8. The capture of Redman was a victory ____ Mr Serpe but he came ____ the conclusion that it would be wise ____ him to offer Redman a job.

9. Sometimes workers go ____ strike when they are dissatisfied ____ their pay or working conditions.

10. In a river, it is easier to swim ____ the current than to swim ____ it.

**Exercise 4**

Correct any mistakes with the use of prepositions. You may need to take out unnecessary words, change some or put some in.

1. It was nearly 10 p.m. when Durai reached to his home in Georgetown.

2. My sister has attended to Camperdown High School for four years.

3. Uncle spends most his time repairing people's cars, so he does not have much spare time.

4. Francine was born the 10th of January 1992, so she is too old to take part in the competition for students under 15.

5. It is the duty all citizens to obey to the laws of their country.

6. Can we rely to Tanya to vote in favour the proposal at the meeting?

7. In yesterday's football match, one of the players was sent out of the field for protesting the decision of the referee.

8. Another player was warned fighting with an opposing player.

9. Despite of the heavy rain, the game continued for another thirty minutes.

10. Hurricane Vera is approaching to our island, so heavy rain and strong winds are expected the next hour or two.

11. Miss Reynolds is busy at dealing to another customer at the moment, so please wait until she is free.

12. Some people dislike to watching films showing violence in television.

## 10.10

# Grammar: articles 'a', 'an', 'the' (revision)

### Exercise 5

Each of the following sentences contains one mistake in the use of articles. Correct the sentences. You may have to use a different article, omit one or put one in.

1. Sooner or later, each person has to learn how to fit into the society.
2. In a multi-racial community, it may be difficult for some people to communicate with the strangers unless there is a language known to everybody.
3. My sister often uses sewing-machine to repair or make clothes.
4. As the result, we spend less on new clothes than some families do.
5. A motorist was charged with driving under influence of alcohol and remanded on bail.
6. Susila has put forward an very useful suggestion which members of the executive committee should consider seriously.
7. Look at the map on next page and notice the changes in national boundaries since the start of the Second World War in 1939.
8. Darren speaks English as fluently as if he is an English, and this may be because he often speaks English at home.
9. You can travel to New York by sea if you prefer. On the one hand, it is cheaper but, on an other hand, it will take longer and may be more uncomfortable in rough weather.
10. As far as our wild life is concerned, we have to pay the high price for urban development.
11. At the wedding yesterday, the bride was wearing very beautiful white dress.
12. The Government has recently taken important steps to strengthen economy and boost employment.

### Exercise 6

Re-write these sentences, putting in 'a', 'an' or 'the' where necessary. If an article is not needed, do not leave a space.

1. The two young children chatted happily like ____ pair of parrots in spring.
2. Mr Serpe decided to take ____ photo of Redman's tree house before it was demolished.
3. Bob Redman climbed up the tree quickly, showing ____ remarkable agility. The Park Patrol admired ____ spectacular workmanship of ____ tree houses built by the young man.

4. When Redman was given ___ opportunity of joining ___ Horticultural Department as ___ professional pruner, he accepted with ___ gratitude. This was just ___ type of ___ work he had always hoped to get.

5. We all admired ___ tolerance and tact of ___ two police officers who had to deal with ___ drunk driver near ___ airport last night.

6. Their behaviour set ___ example for other police officers to follow. Although ___ driver was abusive and violent, ___ police officers showed ___ great restraint when they took ___ man into ___ custody.

7. If you want to become ___ member of ___ Police Force, ___ tolerance and ___ sense of ___ humour are very helpful qualities when dealing with ___ public.

8. When Redman's mother heard about her son's new job, she said to him, 'What ___ lucky fellow you are! What ___ marvellous opportunity for you to develop ___ career by working in ___ Central Park!'

## 10.11
## Punctuation practice

Here are two sentences without punctuation marks:
    Danielle has moved to a new house    She likes it very much

We must either use a full stop to separate these sentences or join them with a suitable connecting word. We cannot put a comma between them, e.g.
    *wrong:*    Danielle has moved to a new house, she likes it very much.
    *right:*    Danielle has moved to a new house. She likes it very much.
    *right:**    Danielle has moved to a new house, **and** she likes it very much.
    *right:*    Danielle has moved to a new house **which** she likes very much.

*When both sentences are short, the comma can be omitted.

Here are one and a half sentences without punctuation marks:
    Earl was late for school    because he missed the bus

The statement starting with 'because' is not a separate statement. It does not make complete sense by itself. The two statements must be punctuated as one sentence, e.g.
Earl was late for school **because** he missed the bus.

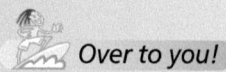 Over to you!

Exercise 7

Punctuate these sentences correctly. Correct any errors in them.

1. We went home by bus. When the show finished.
2. I phoned my friend's house there was no answer I assumed that she was out.
3. To save money. We decided not to buy an air-conditioner.
4. My cousin hopes to become an airline pilot one day. If he obtains the necessary qualifications and his family can pay for his training.
5. This is the same type of computer that Uncle Paul has, it is not very expensive, it is extremely useful.
6. Would you do me a favour post these letters when you go out please.
7. Our school team managed to win. Although we were one player short for most of the game.
8. The taxi stopped at the side of the road then a police officer came to speak to the driver.
9. Rabies is a fatal disease it is found amongst wild animals, sometimes dogs and even cats catch it, it can kill human beings.
10. The number of cars in our country is increasing too rapidly, therefore the Government is thinking of increasing the tax on them. Making it more expensive for the average person to buy a car.

Exercise 8

If you made some mistakes in Exercise 7, punctuate the following sentences correctly. If you made no mistake, omit this exercise.

1. Jamie heard somebody shout so he turned round and saw a friend waving to him from the other side of the road Jamie guessed that something was wrong his friend looked upset about something
2. If we work hard and are proud of our own country we can make it a better place for all people to live in
3. Mitzie has never had singing lessons, she has great natural ability, she could well make a very successful career out of singing she needs professional training

4. Don't eat that meat it is probably bad we must throw it away

5. Although Francine tried as hard as she could and spent nearly an hour on the question. She was unable to solve a Geometry problem, she had to ask her sister for help

6. On our way home from school we stopped to watch some men pulling down two old shops to make way for a new office block, the men were laughing and joking as they worked

7. Don't worry about your watch Uncle says he can repair it easily he'll be here on Saturday he can look at it then, if necessary he'll take it away to get spare parts for it

8. Grandma turned off the light and went to bed. Having completely forgotten that an electric iron was still on not surprisingly, about an hour later she woke up and smelt burning

## 10.12
## Enjoying poetry

### The Village

I know this village. I was born and bred here;
Grew up in that shanty there across the road;
Went to that little shop for groceries:
For things like flour, rice, salt-fish and pork;
5   And took my turn there at the village pipe.

This village is a part of me: I know no other.
Each little home, each jaunty little hut
Is just another part of me. These wooden homes
That look so bravely to the rising sun, are limbs –
10  My limbs. I watched them sprout through toil and agony.

For once this spot was all the world I knew:
It nourished me with wisdom from its breast.
As knowledge spiralled like an airy web,
This spot remained the hub and centre of my life,
15  And coloured all the texture of my dreams.

This village, too, has grown, but slow, so slow!
It seems to hang in space like yonder old mile-tree.
It has not learned to speak the language of the town,
Much to the sorrow of my friends. Ah no!
20  Its wisdom broods above the festooned cane.

Maybe, I'll roam to cities far and wide,
And learn to speak, some day, the language of the towns:
But here remains the one romantic spot
That has its roots deep, deep within my soul,
25 This and my mother, deep <u>primeval</u> ties.

William S. Arthur

going right back to the earliest times

## Questions

1. 'As knowledge spiralled like an airy web' (line 13)
   a) What figure of speech is used here?
   b) Where did the knowledge come from?
   c) Why does the poet say it was like an airy web?

2. The village has 'coloured all the texture of my dreams' (line 15)
   a) Line 15 can have two meanings. What are they?
   b) What else has the village done to the author?

3. 'Its wisdom broods above the festooned cane' (line 20)
   a) What figure of speech is shown by the first three words?
   b) What does the poet mean here?

4. What is the poet's attitude to his mother? What is your evidence for your answer?

## 10.13
## Writing and summarising

1. Read the passage in 10.2 again. Notice how it starts and then introduces Bob Redman when he was 14. This is not the only possible way of telling the story of Bob Redman.

2. Tell the story again. You can use your own words and/or take words from the passage. Choose one of the following ways to start:
   a) 'What! Another one! Number 13!' shouted Mr Serpe, Director of Horticulture for Central Park, N.Y. 'Are you sure!'
      'Absolutely, Boss,' the foreman said, 'and it's the biggest tree house we've ever seen.'
      'That does it!' Mr Serpe shouted. 'We've got to get this guy before we all go mad …'

   *or*

   b) Bob Redman was brought up in a tiny cramped apartment facing Central Park in New York. It is not surprising that he became dedicated to trees almost as soon as he could walk. When he was 14, …

   *or*

   c) As soon as her son came in, Mrs Redman knew that *something* had happened. In all his 22 years, he had never looked so happy. His eyes shone with joy. Mrs Redman wondered whether he had found a girl-friend at last.
      'Do you want to let me in on the secret?' she asked her son, Bob. …

Try to squeeze the rest of the story into another 150–250 words. You will probably find your work easier if you re-read the passage and then write from memory. The key facts are:

- Bob Redman loved trees.
- He built 13 tree houses in Central Park.
- He was caught by Mr Serpe, who offered him a job.
- Bob accepted the offer with great delight.

Those four sentences squeeze the key facts into 29 words, so you should have no problem squeezing them into 150–250 words.

## 10.14
## Asking questions

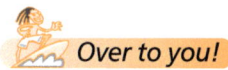 *Over to you!*

### Exercise 9

You are speaking to a friend. Make up questions to obtain the following information.

1. The place and time when an accident happened.
2. The number of people who were injured or killed.
3. The reason he/she was late for a meeting.
4. His/Her weight and height.
5. The cost of something he/she bought the day before.
6. The distance from his/her home to school.
7. What a film seen on television was about.
8. The reason a bridge collapsed.
9. What he/she has lost.
10. The place where he/she lost it.

# 11   Sherlock Holmes

### 11.1
### Pre-reading

Sir Arthur Conan Doyle (1859–1930) is regarded as the 'father' of detective stories. He created the famous detective, Sherlock Holmes, and his assistant, Dr Watson. In the 1880s, Doyle studied at Edinburgh University, in Scotland, and became a doctor. Between 1887 and 1925, he wrote 60 stories about his fictitious detective. He became so successful as an author that he gave up his medical practice. The character, Sherlock Holmes, is based on Dr Bell, one of Doyle's lecturers when he was at Edinburgh University. Dr Bell taught his students how to find out useful information from their patients by studying their hands, face and clothes.

The passage in 11.2 is based on one of Doyle's stories: 'The Adventure at Shoscombe Old Place'. In the passage, Holmes and Watson have gone to investigate the mysterious disappearance of Lady Beatrice Falder, a wealthy widow. They went to the village near Lady Falder's home. They borrowed Lady Falder's pet dog, which had been given to the owner of the local inn. They discovered that an old lady and her maid went for a drive in a horse-drawn carriage every morning. In this extract, Dr Watson is describing what happened.

### 11.2
### Reading

## Sherlock Holmes

When we reached two high iron gates, Holmes stopped. 'About midday, the old lady takes a drive, and her carriage must slow down while the gates are opened. When it comes through, and before it gathers speed, I want you, Watson, to stop the coachman with some question. Never mind me. I shall stand behind this holly-
5   bush and see what I can see.'

It was not a long vigil. Within a quarter of an hour, we saw a big yellow carriage coming from the main house, with two splendid high-stepping horses in the shafts. Holmes crouched behind his bush with the dog. A keeper ran out from the lodge and pulled the gates open.
10   The carriage had slowed to a walk, and I was able to get a good look at the occupants. A highly coloured young woman with flaxen hair and impudent eyes sat on the left. At her right was an elderly person with rounded back and a huddle of shawls about her face and shoulders which proclaimed the invalid. When the horses reached the gates, I held up my hand with an authoritative gesture, and as
15   the coachman pulled up I inquired if Sir Robert was at Shoscombe Old Place.

At the same moment, Holmes stepped out and released the dog. With a joyful cry it dashed forward to the carriage and sprang upon the step to greet its mistress. Then in a moment its eager greeting changed to furious rage, and it barked furiously at the black skirt above it.

20 'Drive on! Drive on!' shrieked a harsh voice. The coachman lashed the horses, and we were left standing in the road.

'Well, Watson, that's done it,' said Holmes, as he fastened the lead to the collar of the excited dog. 'He thought it was his mistress but he found it was a stranger. Dogs don't make mistakes.'

25 'But it was the voice of a man!' I cried.

'Exactly! We have added one card to our hand, Watson, but it needs careful playing, all the same.'

In due course, Sherlock Holmes solved the mystery. If you want to know exactly what happened, read 'The Adventure at Shoscombe Old Place'. It should be in any collection of the stories about Sherlock Holmes.

## 11.3
## Understanding

1. What is meant by saying in 11.1 that Sir Arthur Conan Doyle was the 'father' of detective stories?

2. How did Doyle's studies at Edinburgh University help him to become a famous writer?

3. Why did Holmes and Watson go to Shoscombe Old Place?

4. What made the dog angry?

5. What was the 'card' to which Holmes refers in line 26?

6. Why did the 'elderly person' order the coachman to drive on?

7. If you were Sherlock Holmes, what would you think as a result of this incident with the people in the carriage?

## 11.4
## Vocabulary: meaning in context

**A** Choose the word(s) which best show(s) the meaning of the underlined words as they are used in 11.1.

1. Doyle is <u>regarded</u> as the 'father' of detective stories (line 1)
   A. looked upon
   B. related to
   C. descended from
   D. much better than

2. He created the famous detective, Sherlock Holmes, (line 2)
   A. imitated            C. invented
   B. wrote about         D. admired

3. he wrote 60 stories about his fictitious detective (line 4)
   A. very clever         C. successful
   B. interesting         D. invented

4. he gave up his medical practice (line 5)
   A. sold        B. increased    C. left        D. boosted

5. he gave up his medical practice (line 5)
   A. learning    B. exercise     C. studying    D. business

**B** Match the underlined words with the meanings which they have in 11.2.

| Words from the passage | Meanings |
| --- | --- |
| 1. It was not a long vigil. (line 6) | a) blond, pale yellow |
| 2. Holmes crouched behind his bush (line 8) | b) revealed, indicated |
| 3. a … woman with flaxen hair (line 11) | c) sick or disabled person |
| 4. impudent eyes (line 11) | d) official-looking |
| 5. which proclaimed the invalid (line 13) | e) cried out shrilly |
| 6. proclaimed the invalid (line 13) | f) cheeky |
| 7. with an authoritative gesture (line 14) | g) hit with a whip |
| 8. an authoritative gesture (line 14) | h) wait and watch |
| 9. shrieked a harsh voice (line 20) | i) movement (of arm and hand) |
| 10. The coachman lashed the horses (line 20) | j) bent low |

## 11.5
## Grammar: making and using adjectives
### Common adjective endings

Here are some common adjective endings. Can you think of any more adjectives which have the same ending? Make sure that you know the meaning of these words:

-able  valuable, reliable    -ible  horrible, sensible    -less  hopeless, careless
-al    fatal, formal         -ic    acrobatic, civic      -ly    lovely, lonely
-ed    excited, damaged      -ing   exciting, amusing     -ous   ominous, humorous
-ent   different, silent     -ish   foolish, sheepish     -ual   gradual, perpetual
-ful   joyful, grateful      -ive   active, negative      -y     healthy, naughty

Note: There are at least another 20 common adjective endings.

## '-ed' and '-ing' endings

Check that you know the difference between adjectives ending in '-ed' and those ending in '-ing'. In pairs of words such as 'excited/exciting' and 'interested/interesting', we often follow these guidelines:

- **-ed** Adjectives ending in '-ed' show what has happened to a person or thing. They are often used *to describe a person*, e.g.

    annoyed    excited    worried      depressed
    amused     bored      interested   fascinated

- **-ing** Adjectives ending in '-ing' are often used *to describe a thing*. They show a quality of something or the effect which it can have on people, e.g.

    a **boring** film    an **interesting** book    an **amusing** tale    an **annoying** mistake

 Over to you!

### Exercise 1

Form adjectives from these words. Then use them in short sentences.
1. mud
2. ice
3. bone
4. triangle
5. threat
6. charity
7. fame
8. satisfy
9. clock
10. nature
11. legend
12. race
13. democracy
14. statue
15. cost

### Exercise 2

Choose the right words from the brackets.

1. When the dog approached the carriage, it was (surprising, surprised) to discover that its mistress was not in the carriage. It become very (annoyed, annoying) and (excited, exciting).

2. Sherlock Holmes found the actions of the dog (interested, interesting) because he could see that something was wrong.

3. We saw a very (amused, amusing) film on television last night. It was quite (interested, interesting).

4. When Miss Taylor opened the letter, she was (annoyed, annoying) to discover that it contained a bill which she had already paid.

5. When our team scored the winning goal, the noise in the stadium was almost (deafened, deafening), and most of the people near us were very (excited, exciting).

6. Cutting sugar cane can be a (tired, tiring) job, especially when you are not used to it.

7. When Natoya opened the parcel, she was (puzzled, puzzling) at first because the box inside it appeared to be empty. Then she was (surprised, surprising) to find an envelope stuck to one side of the box.

8. A robber was (embarrassed, embarrassing) when he tried to rob a man who turned out to be a detective and who promptly arrested him.

9. Mr Mohan was (disgusted, disgusting) when a friend borrowed $2000 from him and then disappeared from the country. He told everybody that his friend's behaviour was (disgusted, disgusting).

10. In recent years, the success of the West Indian cricket team has been really (surprised, surprising).

## 11.6

## Vocabulary: occupations

Check that you know these occupations. Say what each person does. You may like to have a competition between two halves of your class:

1. Somebody in team A names an occupation.

2. Somebody in team B must say what the person does.

Note that each of these jobs can be held by a man or a woman. When a word ends with 'man', it can be replaced by 'woman' or 'person'.

| List 1 | | | |
|---|---|---|---|
| accountant | beggar | caterer | doctor |
| actor | bus-driver | chauffeur | dressmaker |
| architect | butcher | chef | electrician |
| auctioneer | car dealer | chiropodist | farmer |
| baker | carpenter | chiropractor | fisherman |

a bank teller/clerk          an estate agent (a realtor)
a chemist/pharmacist      a (tourist) guide
a civil engineer               an IT (information technology) engineer

| List 2 | | | |
|---|---|---|---|
| clerk | judge | plumber | singer |
| glazier | librarian | policeman | surgeon |
| hairdresser | mechanic | salesman | tailor |
| jeweller | nurse | secretary | taxi-driver |
| jockey | optician | shelf-stacker | teacher |

an insurance agent                    a marine biologist
a lawyer (attorney, solicitor)      a postman (mailman, mail-carrier)
a machine operator                   a veterinary surgeon

## 11.7 Finding out somebody's occupation

1. Look at these pictures. What are the people doing? What are their jobs?

2. You can play this game in pairs or as a class.
   a) Somebody will write down the name of his/her occupation, choosing from Lists 1 and 2. The person will not show the class what he/she has written down.

b) The others must ask questions to find out the occupation. The person who has written down his/her occupation can answer 'Yes' or 'No' only.

You can ask questions like these. Your aim is to find out the person's occupation.
Do you wear a uniform?
Do you work in a building?
Do people give you money?
Do you sit down at work?
Do you work in a place where there are many people?
Is your work concerned with health?
Is your work usually done in the same place each day?
Are you very rich because of your job?
Are you a man?
Are you an electrician?
Do you make things?
Do you repair anything?

### 11.8

## Grammar: using the Past Perfect tense

### Forms

| | | |
|---|---|---|
| **Active** | 'had' + a past participle | had stopped |
| **Passive** | 'had been' + a past participle | had been stopped |
| **Continuous** | 'had been' + a present participle | had been stopping |

In this section, we will use the active form only.

### Uses

- The main use of this tense is to show that one past action happened before another, e.g.
    Natalie watched a film on television when she **had finished** her homework.
    Sherlock Holmes suspected that somebody **had murdered** Lady Falder.
    When the carriage **had stopped**, Holmes released the dog.
    After Samantha **had taken** the medicine, she began to feel better.

- We also use the Past Perfect tense in indirect (reported) speech when the verbs in the original (direct) speech were in the Present Perfect or Simple Past tense, e.g.
    *direct:* My father said, 'I lost my car keys yesterday.'
    *indirect:* My father said (that) he **had lost** his car keys the previous day.

    *direct:* Deena thought, 'I've sprained my left ankle.'
    *indirect:* Deena thought (that) she **had sprained** her left ankle.

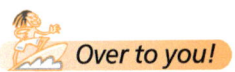
**Over to you!**

### Exercise 3

Put in the active form of the Past Perfect tense of the verbs in brackets.

1. I looked out of the window and saw that a lorry (collide) with a bus.
2. We heard on the radio that a factory (close) down and that many people (lose) their jobs.
3. Tanya saw a little girl crying in the supermarket. She asked her what was wrong. The girl said she (lose) her mother.
4. After Lisa (finish) her homework, she helped her mother with her work.
5. The dog was angry because somebody (take) the place of his mistress.
6. Sherlock Holmes was pleased because he (discover) that Lady Falder (disappear) and that somebody else (take) her place.
7. When Kimani came out of the shop, he was annoyed to find that somebody (steal) his bicycle. He (lock) it before going into the shop but somebody (cut) through the chain round one wheel.
8. After the hurricane (pass), we went out to inspect the damage. We discovered that the storm (knock) down several of our trees. It (damage) our wooden fence and (rip) the roof off a neighbour's home.
9. The storm knocked down two electricity poles, so we had no electricity until the workmen (put) the poles up again and (reconnect) the cables.
10. It took our team several minutes before they realised that they (win) the inter-schools championship. At half-time they were losing 2-0 and felt sure that they (lose) the game but they (play) much better in the second half and (beat) the favourites.

### 11.9

## Grammar: using the passive form of the Past Perfect tense

We saw in 11.8 that the passive form of the Past Perfect tense is made with 'had been' + a past participle, e.g.

A lot of people were pleased when the police reported that the escaped prisoners **had been recaptured**. The report mentioned that two of the prisoners **had been** slightly **injured** and that they were all now back in prison.
Sherlock Holmes was not sure whether Lady Falder **had been killed** or not. He suspected that she **had been kidnapped** and was being held to ransom.

## Uses

We use the passive form of this tense when the action is done *to* the subject and not *by* it. Compare these sentences:

*active:* Kimani told us that somebody **had stolen** his bicycle.

*passive:* Kimani told us that his bicycle **had been stolen**.

*active:* We saw that the wind **had blown** several trees down.

*passive:* We saw that several trees **had been blown** down.

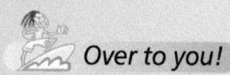 Over to you!

Exercise 4

Put in the passive form of the Past Perfect tense of the verbs in brackets.

1. When Leela reached her grandmother's home, she was surprised to see that it (repaint) and looked very smart. She noticed that the grass (cut) and a lot of new flowers (plant).

2. On her way back home, Leela stopped at the scene of an accident. Somebody told her that an elderly cyclist (knock) down by a car. The driver of the car (arrest) because he appeared to be drunk. He (take) away to the police station.

3. Last year the water at our village was contaminated, so we could not drink it until it (boil) for several minutes.

4. Miss Davis bought a new car but it had so many faults in it that she suspected that it (not check) properly before it was sold.

5. Somebody offered Errol some food at a barbecue but he did not like it because it (not cook) properly.

6. Last year a block of flats collapsed because they (not build) correctly. An investigation showed that too much sand (mix) with cement to make concrete. The work (not supervise) adequately.

7. Until last week, our team (not defeat) for over a year but last week we lost 1-0.

8. When Wayne returned to his village after an absence of 32 years, he hardly recognised it because many houses (demolish) to make way for a factory.

9. During a heavyweight boxing match, one boxer complained that he (bite) by the other boxer. He pointed to an ear and we saw that a piece (take) out of it.

10. Grandma complained that the veranda (not sweep) and the plants (not water) for two or three days.

## 11.10
## Grammar: prepositions

These sentences show common mistakes in the use of prepositions:
- *wrong:* We must emphasise on the advantages of the plan.
- *right:* We must put more emphasis **on** the advantages of the plan.
- *right:* We must emphasise the advantages of the plan.

In the incorrect sentence above, the writer is confusing the noun, 'emphasis' and the verb 'to emphasise'. The following incorrect sentence shows a similar mistake:
- *wrong:* You should stress on the first syllable of this word.
- *right:* You should put more stress **on** the first syllable of this word.
- *right:* You should stress the first syllable of this word.

Sometimes students confuse two expressions, e.g.
- *wrong:* A fire officer will investigate into the cause of the fire.
- *right:* A fire officer will look **into** the cause of the fire.
- *right:* A fire officer will investigate the cause of the fire.

Study the following *correct* expressions. Check that you can use them in your own work.

| | |
|---|---|
| We **accompanied** him. | to **go beyond** that level |
| **busy** talking to somebody | to **explain** your actions |
| She **continued** her story. | to **give an explanation of** your actions |
| They **made a demand for** money. | He **was afraid of** the man. |
| They **demanded** money. | He **feared** the man. |
| **despite** the heavy rain | She **lacks** experience. |
| **in spite of** the heavy rain | He **is lacking in** experience. |
| have a **discussion about** sport | to **request** an interview |
| to **discuss** sport | **Lower** your hand. |
| to **go into** a room | **Put** your hand **down**. |
| to **enter** a room | Don't **omit** anything. |
| to **exceed** that level | Don't **leave out** anything. |

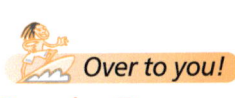 **Over to you!**

### Exercise 5

Re-write these sentences putting a suitable word in the space if necessary. If no word is needed, do not leave a space.

1. Two students raised ____ their hands to answer ____ my question.

2. He entered ____ the room and lay ____ the bed to rest ____ a while.

3. I expect we'll reach ____ our destination ____ about two hours' time.

4. She lacks ____ money but she is not lacking ____ intelligence and charm.

5. The place was quiet except ____ the noise of birds.

6. Mrs Wilson accompanied ____ her young daughter when she went for a medical examination.

7. The police sergeant recorded ____ Mr Moore's statement and promised to let him ____ know the results of the investigation ____ the incident.

8. I'm sorry ____ not meeting you yesterday. I was busy ____ helping my mother and that made me ____ forget all about the arrangement.

9. The workers requested ____ an interview ____ the manager ____ support ____ their demand … an increase ____ pay.

10. The company regretted ____ it was unable to raise ____ the basic rate of pay ____ that time but promised to consider ____ it ____ some future time.

11. This method has been used ____ hundreds of times ____ the past.

12. Please try to contact ____ Krishna and Daljit and get their opinions ____ the proposal.

13. ____ our opinion, Miss Aguilar is quite capable ____ dealing ____ the problem.

14. Krishna stated ____ his reasons ____ opposing ____ the scheme ____ its present form.

15. A vacancy ____ a sales assistant will occur in our company next month, so let your cousin ____ know ____ case she is interested ____ applying ____ the job.


## Exercise 6

Select the word or pair of words which best completes the sentence. If no word is needed, choose XXX.

1. If the price of the car exceeds ____ $12,000, don't buy it.
   A. XXX   B. beyond   C. over   D. by

2. I think I'll request ____ permission to take a day's leave on Friday.
   A. XXX   B. for   C. to   D. concerning

3. That side of the equation ____ the other side.
   A. equal   B. equals   C. is equal   D. has equal

4. Shops often raise ____ their prices when a hurricane approaches.
   A. up   B. XXX   C. above   D. higher

5. Please remove ____ that rubbish.
   A. out   B. off   C. away   D. XXX

6. We had a big surprise when we entered ____ the room.
   A. to          B. XXX          C. into          D. in

7. Uncle has just entered ____ negotiations to buy a new shop.
   A. into        B. XXX          C. in            D. to

8. I'm sure he regrets ____ what he wrote in the letter to you.
   A. XXX         B. for           C. to            D. about

9. Early ____ one morning, I heard people arguing outside our door.
   A. XXX         B. in            C. on            D. at

10. If you bargain ____ him, he'll probably lower ____ the price.
    A. with … down     C. XXX …. XXX
    B. to … off        D. with … XXX

## 11.11
## Listening practice

For each of the following, listen and then write down the letters A, B, C and D in the right order to show the order in which the four things happened.

1. A.        B.        C.        D.

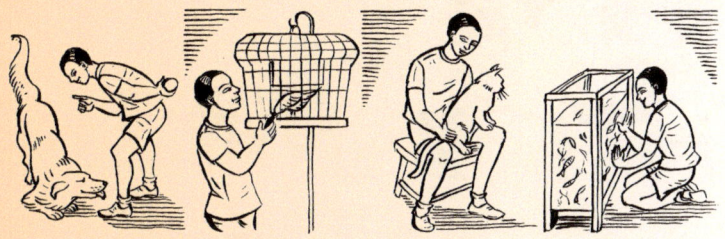

2. A.        B.        C.        D.

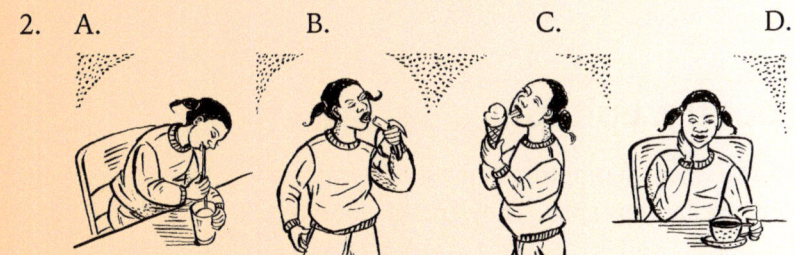

3. A.        B.        C.        D.

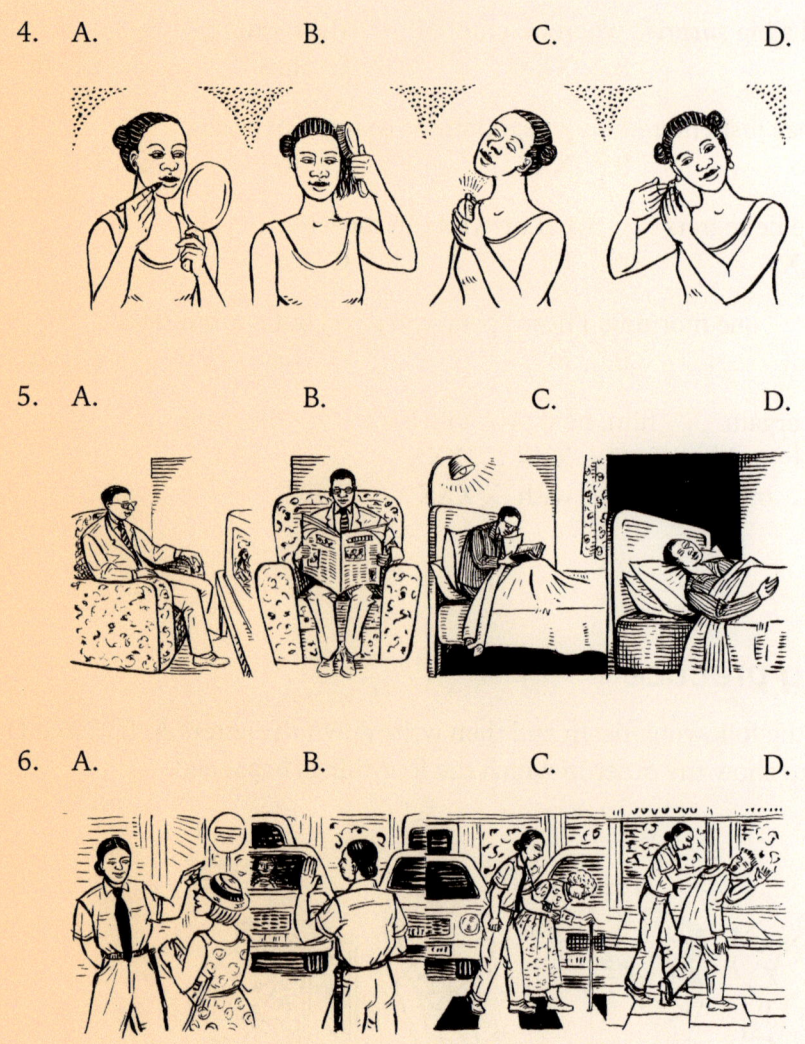

 **11.12**

# Enjoying poetry: epitaphs

An epitaph is a statement (sometimes in verse) which is written on a person's tombstone. Here are five epitaphs. They are all anonymous.

## Epitaph for a Poor Woman

Here lies a poor woman who always was tired.
She lived in a house where help was not hired.
Her last words on earth were: 'Dear friends, I am going
Where washing ain't done, nor sweeping, nor sewing;
5  But everything there is exact to my wishes;
For where they don't eat, there's no washing of dishes.

I'll be where loud anthems will always be ringing,
But having no voice, I'll be clear of the singing.
Don't mourn for me now; don't mourn for me never –
10   I'm going to do nothing for ever and ever.'

## Learning how to fly

There was an old man who <u>averred</u>           declared
He had learned how to fly like a bird.
Cheered by thousands of people
He leapt from the <u>steeple</u> –                 highest point on a church
5   This tomb states the date it occurred.

## An unlucky man

Here lies a man who was killed by lightning;
He died when his prospects seemed to be brightening.
He might have <u>cut a flash</u> in this world of trouble,   made a big impression
But the <u>flash</u> cut him, and he lies in the stubble.    flash of lightning

This is the epitaph which a husband put on his wife's grave:

Here lies my poor wife
Without bed or blankit,
But dead as a door-nail,
God be thankit.

And this is the epitaph which a wife put on her husband's grave:

To follow you I'm not content.
How do I know which way you went?

## 11.13
### Writing

Write 250–350 words about *one* of the following:

1. Write about the work of one of the people in 11.6, describing the work which the person does.

or

2. Write about a day in the life of one of the people in 11.6. You can describe a typical day or a rather unusual one.

or

3. Describe a time when a traffic police officer stopped somebody for speeding but then decided *not* to charge the motorist with speeding.

## 11.14
### Using a comma (revision)

Put in commas when necessary. Each sentence shows a different use of commas.

1. Don't forget to post my letter when you go out Kwesi.
2. Selva rode his bicycle carefully trying to avoid the worst pot-holes in the road.
3. My mother said 'Hurry up! It's time for you to leave.'
4. My best friend who lives opposite the hotel told us all about the fire and how it started.
5. The referee sent off Paul and the other player received first aid.
6. We rely heavily on such things as fruit vegetables fish and meat for our food.
7. Mr Jackson locked the door turned off the light in the living-room washed quickly and went to bed feeling very satisfied with his day's work.
8. 'Don't forget to thank Uncle for the present' my mother said 'and send him our best wishes.'
9. 'Fatima where did you put the keys to the car?' her mother said suddenly.
10. Most of the people in our village were not affected by the flood. A few houses however were flooded to a depth of about a metre.

# 12  Gun Hill

## 12.1
### Pre-reading

From the seventeenth century onwards, there were numerous uprisings of slaves in the Caribbean. The worst affected places were Haiti, Jamaica, Guyana and (later) Brazil and the southern states of the USA. Barbados was comparatively free from trouble until 1816 when a man known as Bussa led an uprising which resulted in the death of more than a thousand slaves. It also led to the building of a series of signalling stations. Gun Hill was one of these stations. Read about it in 12.2.

## 12.2
### Reading

## Gun Hill

About 10 km north-east of Bridgetown, the capital of Barbados, there is a spectacular watchtower known locally as Gun Hill Signal Station. Restored in a benevolent act by the Barbados National Trust, it is now part of the Bajan heritage and a popular tourist attraction. From it, a visitor can look out across rolling hills
5   to Bridgetown and beyond the city to the ocean.

Bridgetown is one of the oldest cities in the Caribbean. British settlers arrived on the uninhabited island in 1627, and Bridgetown was founded a year later. In subsequent years, indentured labourers arrived from England and Scotland, followed not long afterwards by slaves from West Africa. Sugar plantations brought
10  wealth to their owners but had no significant impact on the low standard of living of the workers.

In 1807, the British government abolished the slave trade but did not free existing slaves or make slavery illegal. Rumours spread throughout the island, falsely claiming that the colonial government had abolished slavery but that the plantation
15  owners were deliberately preventing abolition from being implemented on the island. Nine years later, there was a major uprising. An African slave named Bussa led other slaves in an attack on homes and crops. The uprising lasted only a few days. A small number of whites were killed or injured but more than a thousand slaves died in battle or were executed when the uprising collapsed.
20  Alarmed at the prospect of further uprisings or an attack by French or Spanish ships, the authorities on Barbados took urgent steps to improve their communications. Six sturdy watchtowers were built to provide a prompt warning for the various forts which had been built earlier. Soldiers in the watchtowers could view the whole of the island and its surrounding sea. By using semaphore, they

25 could warn each other and the garrison at Bridgetown. By day, trained signallers used flags to relay messages swiftly; at night, the flags were replaced by lanterns. Large numbers of soldiers remained on standby in the Bridgetown garrison, ready to set off at the first sign of trouble.

As the years passed by, the danger of an uprising or external attack diminished.
30 In 1838, all slaves were freed, and in 1878 compulsory education was introduced. Semaphore continued to be used for a time but only to report the safe arrival of cargo and passenger ships. When telephones were invented, the signal stations became superfluous, and after 1887 they were no longer manned. In the twentieth century, tourism brought additional wealth to the island, and most of the forts and
35 signal stations were allowed to deteriorate.

Now, however, visitors to Barbados can drive out to Gun Hill Signal Station and view the central and southern parts of the island. They can imagine how the soldiers must have felt, wondering when and where trouble was coming.

## 12.3
## Understanding

**A** Choose the best answer each time.

1. A word often used by British historians for an uprising (12.1, line 1) is a ____.
   A. riot          B. slaughter       C. rebellion       D. incident

2. In line 5 of 12.1, 'It' refers to ____.
   A. Barbados      B. Bussa           C. death           D. uprising

3. A signaller in the Gun Hill Signal Station who wanted to look towards Bridgetown would look towards the ____.
   A. north-east    B. south-east      C. north-west      D. south-west

4. In line 3 of the passage, the act of the Barbados National Trust in restoring the signal station is called 'benevolent' because ____.
   A. all the members of the Trust were volunteers
   B. they were kind to restore the tower
   C. members of the trust had to pay for the restoration out of their own pockets
   D. it was part of the Bajan heritage and should therefore have been destroyed

5. In line 10, the expression 'no significant impact' tells us that the ordinary workers on plantations ____.
   A. did not benefit from the success of the plantations
   B. were pleased because they did not lose their jobs
   C. made no contribution to the wealth of the plantation owners
   D. did not resent the wealth which sugar produced for plantation owners

**B** Answer these questions about the passage.

1. How did the British law of 1807 affect people in Barbados?

2. Which word first tells the reader that the rumours mentioned in line 13 were untrue?

3. What probably caused the uprising of 1816?

4. Name *two* of the 'urgent steps' which the British apparently took. (line 21)

5. What effect did the freeing of slaves in 1838 have on the signal stations?

## 12.4 Vocabulary: meaning in context

**A** Choose the word(s) which best show(s) the meaning of the underlined words as they are used in the passage in 12.2.

1. there is a <u>spectacular</u> watchtower (line 2)
   - A. solidly built
   - B. very impressive
   - C. used to keep an eye on events
   - D. of great historical value

2. <u>Restored</u> … by the Barbados National Trust (line 2)
   - A. written down in records
   - B. taken out of storage
   - C. put carefully into storage
   - D. brought back to its original condition

3. in a <u>benevolent</u> act (line 3)
   - A. good but wasteful
   - B. fine but pointless
   - C. showing goodwill or kindness
   - D. connected with past events

4. part of the Bajan <u>heritage</u> (line 3)
   - A. ancient history
   - B. ancestral lands
   - C. custom or tradition
   - D. things inherited from the past

5. Bridgetown was <u>founded</u> a year later (line 7)
   - A. discovered
   - B. found
   - C. established
   - D. named

6. In <u>subsequent</u> years (line 8)
   - A. other
   - B. some
   - C. difficult
   - D. later

**B** Match the underlined words with the meanings which they have in the passage.

| Words from the passage | Meanings |
|---|---|
| 1. no <u>significant</u> impact (line 10) | a) very serious |
| 2. <u>abolished</u> the slave trade (line 12) | b) chance that something might happen |
| 3. were <u>deliberately</u> preventing (line 15) | c) fearful |
| 4. a <u>major</u> uprising (line 16) | d) strong and well-built |
| 5. the uprising <u>collapsed</u> (line 19) | e) constantly available |
| 6. <u>Alarmed</u> at the prospect (line 20) | f) purposely |
| 7. Alarmed at the <u>prospect</u> (line 20) | g) no longer needed |
| 8. <u>took steps</u> to improve (line 21) | h) became less |
| 9. six <u>sturdy</u> watchtowers (line 22) | i) of any size or importance |
| 10. remained <u>on standby</u> (line 27) | j) started action |
| 11. the danger … <u>diminished</u> (line 29) | k) proved to be a failure |
| 12. became <u>superfluous</u> (line 33) | l) did away with |

## 12.5
## Semaphore

These pictures show one method of sending a message by semaphore. For the letters A to G, one flag is held straight down by the sender's legs. The other flag is rotated through seven positions. Different methods can be used as long as the sender and receiver have agreed in advance what letter (or word) each position shows. At night, lanterns were used instead of flags. Modern ships can use radio and/or the morse code sent by means of powerful lights.

A and 1
(LH down RH low)

B and 2
(LH down; RH out)

C and 3
(LH down; RH high)

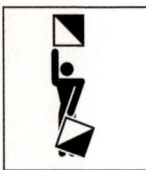
D and 4
(LH down; RH up –
or LH up; RH down)

E and 5
(LH high; RH down)

F and 6
(LH out; RH down)

G and 7
(LH low; RH down)

## 12.6
## Sending a cable or telegram

In modern times, most messages can be sent by telephone or email. However, it might be necessary to send a cable (or telegram) to somebody who does not have a telephone or computer. Then we can follow these guidelines:

- Say whether you want to send your cable at the ordinary rate, at the urgent rate (often double the ordinary rate) or at the letter rate (slower but cheaper).
- Give as much of the receiver's name and address as are necessary.
- Use as few words as possible (to keep the cost down) but **make sure that the meaning of your cable is clear**. Omit unnecessary articles, auxiliary verbs, etc.

Use the word STOP in place of a full stop. Omit all other punctuation marks.

- Give as much of your name as will identify you.

Look at these examples:

*Ordinary rate*:

```
SURESH KISSOON 34 ABARY STREET BETTER HOPE WEST COAST BERBICE
GUYANA
SINCERE CONGRATULATIONS ON YOUR MARRIAGE BEST WISHES TO YOU AND
BRIDE
JOHN NATHAN AND FAMILY
```

*Urgent rate*:

```
STACY MELVILLE 14 CHAPEL LANE GREEN HILLS KINGSTON JAMAICA
DONNAREE ARRIVING UA728 1430 MAY 18 STOP PLEASE ARRANGE
ACCOMMODATION AND MEET AT AIRPORT THANKS
NADIA
```

 **Over to you!**

Make up telegrams (cables) for these occasions. You will need to make up names, addresses, etc.

1. You want to congratulate a friend or relative on his/her success in passing an examination.

2. Donald Smith's brother is studying overseas. His grandfather has just died suddenly. You are Donald's brother or sister and you wish to tell him about the death. It is not necessary to ask him to come home.

## 12.7 Vocabulary: problem words

Check that you understand the meaning of these words and know how to use them.

| Words | Meaning |
| --- | --- |
| economic<br>economical | concerning the trade or finance of a community<br>not costing too much, a cheap method |
| lose<br>loose | be unable to find, fail to win<br>not tight, not held in place firmly |
| illegal<br>illegible<br>eligible | unlawful, against a law<br>difficult or impossible to read<br>able to be chosen or to do something |
| principal<br>principle | the most important (member of staff, point, idea, etc.)<br>a basic or guiding idea or belief |
| refrain<br>restrain | decide not to do something<br>stop somebody else from doing something |
| comprehension<br>comprehensive | understanding (usually of speech or written work)<br>covering everything (as in an insurance policy) |

Exercise 1

Choose the right word from the brackets each time.

1. Susila politely (restrained, refrained) from saying anything when she heard two women criticising her best friend.

2. A (comprehension, comprehensive) vehicle policy covers damage caused by the owner but a third-party policy does not cover that risk.

3. The Government has just published details of its (economic, economical) policy for next year.

4. First I will explain the (principal, principle) involved in this experiment.

5. Check that the chain on your bicycle is not too (lose, loose). If it is, it may come off.

6. Sorry, you're too old. To be (illegible, eligible) to enter this competition, you must be under 14.

7. To reduce costs, our company is trying to find a more (economic, economical) way of distributing its goods.

8. Please (assure, ensure) that all members of the team are on the field by 5 p.m.

9. You can probably solve the problem by drawing a graph. (Alternately, Alternatively,) you can use algebra to get the answer.

10. In the wild, all creatures have to learn to (adapt, adopt) to changed conditions if they want to stay alive.

Exercise 2

Choose the right word from the brackets each time.

1. What (affect, effect) will the change in the law have on us?

2. Thank you very much. We are most (thankful, grateful) to you for helping us to put out the fire.

3. When the results of the competition were announced, Pathma was so (exciting, excited) that she could not speak for a few moments.

4. At a special ceremony yesterday, the new Principal was (formerly, formally) introduced to the staff and students.

5. The (discovery, invention) of oil in and near Trinidad has brought a most welcome (source, sauce) of income to the country.

6. In the alphabet, the letter Q (proceeds, precedes) R and S.

7. If you need any (advice, advise) about growing vegetables, ask Grandpa.

8. That's a deep cut. (You, You'd) better keep it covered to make sure that it doesn't become (sceptic, septic). If it starts to look (worse, worst), go and see a doctor.

9. When a lorry hit our bus, two of the passengers were hurt but (there, their) (wounds, injuries) were not very serious and we (except, expect) them to (re-cover, recover) soon.

10. The police are looking for two youths (age, aged) 14–15 in connection with a series of (burglaries, thefts) from local shops.

## 12.8
## Vocabulary: affixes and roots

An understanding of affixes and roots is useful when you meet new words.

- An **affix** is a word or part of a word added to another word. **Prefixes** and **suffixes** are affixes. We put prefixes at the front of a word and suffixes at the end of a word.
- A **root** is the part of a word to which the affixes have been added. The root often comes from a word in another language, such as Greek or Latin.

For example, in 12.2, the writer said that eventually signal stations in Barbados became 'superfluous', meaning 'no longer needed'. The word 'superfluous' is an example of the way in which many English words have developed:

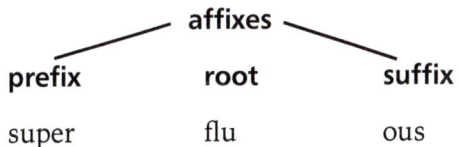

| | affixes | |
|---|---|---|
| **prefix** | **root** | **suffix** |
| super | flu | ous |

super    means 'above', 'over', 'beyond'
flu      means 'flowing' (like a river) – from Latin
ous      simply means 'with the quality of'
So 'superfluous' means 'flowing over' or 'too much' and thus 'unneeded'.

Other words which are made from the root 'flu' include:
    fluid
    fluent (speaking well
      like a flowing river)
    affluent (flowing with wealth)
    influence

    influenza (an illness which flows into the body
      from outside)
    effluent (something that flows out, e.g.
      sewage)

Sometimes a word has two prefixes, e.g. 'unconscious':

| | affixes | | |
|---|---|---|---|
| **prefixes** | | **root** | **suffix** |
| un | con | sci | ous |

un      means 'not'
con     means 'with'
sci     means 'knowing', 'being alive and aware of what is happening' – from Latin
ous     means 'with the quality of'

So, 'unconscious' means 'not having an awareness of what is happening' or 'not conscious'.

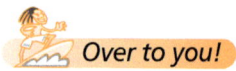 **Over to you!**

### Exercise 3

Here are some Latin roots. Think of English words derived from these roots. (The meaning of each root is given in brackets.)

1. mare (the sea)
2. nego (say no)
3. leges (laws)
4. ager (a field)
5. captum (taken)
6. servus (a slave)
7. femina (a woman)
8. migro (move to another place)
9. decem (ten)

 **12.9**

## Vocabulary: prefixes

Check that you know the meaning of these prefixes and the examples. Can you think of any more examples?

| Prefix | Meaning | Examples |
| --- | --- | --- |
| inter- | among, between | international, intersection |
| omni- | all | omnivorous, omnipotent |
| contra- | against | contradict, contraband |
| vice- | able to take the place of, next in position | vice-president |
| anti- | against | anti-aircraft, antiseptic |
| auto- | self | autobiography, autograph |
| bene- | well | benefit, benevolent |
| e-, ex- | out, away from | exit, exhaust, emigrate |
| il-, im-, in-, ir- | in, into, on, not | illiterate, irresponsible |
| mis- | badly, wrongly | misbehave, mistake |
| tele- | at a distance, far | television, telephone |
| per- | through, by means of | perspiration, perforated |

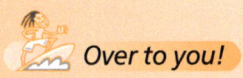 **Over to you!**

**Exercise 4**

Answer the questions.

1. 'Bio' means 'life'. 'Graph' means 'write'. What is the difference between a 'biography' and an 'autobiography'?
2. What is a perforated ear-drum?
3. Where can you see perforations on a stamp? What are they used for?
4. What is the purpose of an exhaust pipe on a car?
5. What is the purpose of an anti-personnel mine in wartime?
6. What is the difference between 'malevolent' and 'benevolent'? What does the prefix 'mal' mean?
7. What is the opposite of 'export'?
8. If the chairperson of a meeting is absent, who should take his or her place at a meeting?
9. What is the meaning of 'omniscient'?
10. What is telepathy? Is it possible?
11. What do you think 'scope' means in 'telescope'?
12. What is the meaning of the prefixes in these words?
    a) submarine   b) postpone   c) homicide   d) conscious   e) triangle

## 12.10
## Punctuation: using a question mark

We put a question mark after a **direct question** but *not* after an indirect question, e.g.

| With a question mark | Without a question mark |
| --- | --- |
| How old are you? | She asked me how old I am. |
| Where's Kevin? | I don't know where Kevin is. |
| Is Elaine at home now? | He wants to know if Elaine is at home now. |
| Do you need any help? | I wonder if she needs any help. |

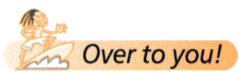 **Over to you!**

### Exercise 5

Put in a question mark or a full stop.

1. Quacy wanted to know where Wayne was going
2. Do you know how to get to Sam Lord's castle
3. If you're going to Bridgetown, shall we go together
4. What time does the supermarket close on Saturdays
5. It's not usually chilly at night, is it
6. Mary wondered where she had left her keys
7. Don't forget to phone us as soon as you get home, will you
8. Give me a call when the programme is about to start
9. Courtney says he's not sure when the last bus to Kingston goes
10. Ask her where she lives
11. What to do with rubbish can be a problem sometimes
12. Show us where you hurt your arm
13. How deep is the harbour at this point, Colin
14. Do you mind if we move the table nearer to the window

## 12.11
# Grammar: reporting orders

We saw in Book 2 that we can report orders in these ways:

| Direct | Indirect |
| --- | --- |
| She said, 'Hurry up!' | She told me to hurry up. |
| 'Lend me $20,' Paul begged me. | Paul begged me to lend him $20. |
| He said, 'Don't make a noise!' | He told me not to make a noise. |
| My mother said, 'Don't forget to take the right books to school.' | My mother reminded me not to forget to take the right books to school. |

160   *English Alive!*

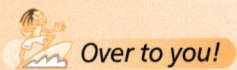 **Over to you!**

**Exercise 6**

Change these sentences into indirect speech. Pretend that you are telling somebody what another person said to you.

1. 'Bring a whistle to the game,' my friend said to me.

2. He told me, 'Make sure you are there by five p.m.' *(Use 'am' or 'was'.)*

3. 'Hold the bottom of the ladder,' my father told me.

4. 'Please water the plants on the veranda,' my grandmother said to me. *(Ignore 'Please'.)*

5. Miss Morris said to me, 'Please collect all the books. Put them on my table.' *(Put in 'and'. Use 'her'.)*

6. 'Finish your homework and put your books away,' my mother said to me. *(Use 'my' three times.)*

7. My grandmother said to me, 'Lock the door and turn off the light before you go to bed.' *(Use 'I went'.)*

8. She said, 'Don't forget to close the windows.'

9. 'Don't go too near the fire,' a police officer said. 'Keep away from it.' *(Use 'told' twice.)*

10. 'Don't tell anybody about the mistake,' my friend begged me.

11. Our Science teacher reminded us, 'Don't pour water into concentrated sulphuric acid.'

12. Miss Wilson said to us, 'Don't believe everything you see in newspapers or hear on the radio or TV.' *(Use 'we'.)*

## 12.12
# Grammar: reporting statements

When you report an order, a statement or a question, you may have to change some words in the original speech:

- You may have to change pronouns ('me', 'us', 'them') and possessive adjectives ('your', 'his', 'our') to make the meaning clear, as in some of the sentences in Exercise 6.

- You may have to change words showing time, e.g.

| In direct speech | In reported speech |
|---|---|
| now | then, at that moment, that day |
| today | that day, yesterday, two days ago |
| tomorrow | the next/following day |
| yesterday | the previous day |

- You may have to change words showing place, e.g.

| In direct speech | In reported speech |
|---|---|
| here | there (or name the place) |
| in my home | in his/her home |
| there | (perhaps name the place) |
| in our country | in his/her/their country (and/or name the country) |

- We do not use the original inverted commas or the comma after the speech verb.
- You may have to change the tense of verbs. We will study that later in this book.

The aim of all these changes is to make clear what somebody said and to whom he or she was speaking or referring. The changes are a matter of common sense.

We do *not* need to change the tense of verbs when:
- the reporting verb is in the Present tense ('he says')

or

- the original speech is about something which is always true (e.g. 'Ice melts in the sunshine.') or has not yet happened (e.g. 'Uncle is coming next week.').

Look at these examples:
*direct:* Uncle said, 'My car is two years old.'
*indirect:* Uncle says his car is two years old.
*direct:* Jolene said, 'My brother is coming from the UK to visit us next month.'
*indirect:* Jolene says her brother is coming from the UK to visit them next month.

If Jolene's speech were reported two months after she said it, we would use:
*indirect:* Jolene said that her brother was coming from the UK to visit them the following month.

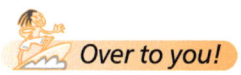 **Over to you!**

Exercise 7

Change these sentences into indirect speech. Do not change the tense of the original verbs.

1. Our Science teacher told us, 'Leaves absorb carbon dioxide and produce oxygen.'

2. My mother reminded us, 'Meat and fish soon go bad if you leave them out of a fridge.'

3. My aunt said, 'You ought to get your hair cut.'

4. Shaleen explained to the tourist, 'The price of fresh fish always goes up when a tropical storm comes. The fishermen can't go out to sea then.' (*Use one or two sentences.*)

5. I told the tourists, 'The temperature here never falls below about 20 degrees, even at night.'

6. David reminded me, 'My bicycle is older than yours.'

7. Lloyd said, 'Our parrot always says "Hello! Hello!" when it's hungry.'

8. Mr Porter often complains, 'The road outside my house is full of pot-holes.'

9. The girl at the travel agent's office said, 'The flight to the UK usually takes about eight hours but you should book well in advance if you want to travel on a particular day.'

10. My friend told me, 'My mother owns a small restaurant. She does most of the cooking herself. She is an expert cook.'

## 12.13

### Enjoying poetry

### Look Closer

What do you see, nurses, what do you see?
Are you thinking, when you are looking at me,
A <u>crabbit</u> old woman, not very wise,     **bad-tempered**
Uncertain of habit, with far away eyes,
5  Who dribbles her food, and makes no reply,
When you say in a loud voice, 'I do wish you'd try',
Who seems not to notice the things that you do,
And forever is losing a stocking or shoe,
Who, quite unrealistic, lets you do as you will

10　With bathing and feeding, the long day to fill?
　　Is that what you're thinking, is that what you see?
　　Then open your eyes, you're not looking at me.
　　I'll tell you who I am, as I sit here so still,
　　As I move at your bidding, as I eat at your will,
15　I'm a small child of ten, with a father and mother,
　　Brothers and sisters, who love one another,
　　A young girl of sixteen with wings on her feet,
　　Dreaming that soon a true lover she'll meet;
　　A bride now at twenty – my heart gives a leap,
20　Remembering the vows that I promised to keep;
　　At twenty-five now I have young of my own,
　　Who need me to build a secure, happy home;
　　A woman of thirty, my young now grow fast,
　　Bound to each other with ties that should last;
25　At forty my sons will soon all be gone,
　　But my man stays beside me to see I don't mourn;
　　At fifty once more babies play round my knee;
　　Again we know children, my loved one and me.
　　Dark days are upon me, my husband is dead.
30　I look at the future, I shudder with dread.
　　For my young are all busy, with young of their own,
　　And I think of the years and the love that I've known.
　　I'm an old woman now and nature is cruel,
　　'Tis her jest to make old age look like a fool.
35　The body it crumbles, grace and vigour depart,
　　There now is a stone where I once had a heart.
　　But inside this old <u>carcase</u> a young girl still dwells,　　(nearly) dead body
　　And now and again my battered heart swells.
　　I remember the joys, I remember the pain,
40　And I'm loving and living life over again.
　　I think of the years, all too few – gone too fast,
　　And accept the stark facts that nothing can last.
　　So open your eyes, nurses, open and see,
　　Not a crabbit old woman, look closer – see ME.

*Phyllis McCormack*

## Questions

1. In line 6, a nurse says: 'I do wish you'd try.' What does the nurse want her to do?

2. What does the writer mean when she says (in line 12): 'You're not looking at me'?

3. In line 17, what does 'with wings on her feet' mean?

4. What is the poet's attitude to the old woman?

5. Do you like or dislike this poem? Why?

Now read this poem on a similar subject but by a man.

## I Look Into My Glass

I look into my glass  
And view my wasting skin  
And say, 'Would God it came to pass  
My heart had shrunk as thin!'

For then, I, undistrest  
By hearts grown cold to me,  
Could lonely wait my endless rest  
With equanimity.

But Time, to make me grieve,  
Part steals, lets part abide;  
And shakes this fragile frame at eve  
With throbbings of noontide.

*Thomas Hardy*

Glass — mirror  
wasting — wasting away  
undistrest — not upset  
equanimity — a peaceful mind  
abide — stay with me  
at eve — in the evening of my life  
throbbings of noontide — the passions of a much younger person

### 12.14
## Writing

Write about 250–350 words on *one* of these topics:

1. Describe some of the things and/or places in your country which – like the Gun Hill Signal Station – are worth protecting and keeping for future generations to see.

*or*

2. Write about anything which you found interesting in a History or Geography lesson this year.

*or*

3. Do you think tourism is a good or a bad thing for your country?

*or*

4. Write an account of an incident involving an old woman or and old man.

# 13  The Best Sugar Boiler

### 13.1
### Pre-reading

In this extract from *Big Doc Bitteroot* by C. Everard Palmer, Nathan Berwick's workers have temporarily deserted him to support a newcomer to the village, Doc Bitteroot. The narrator in this extract is one of Nathan's sons. His father is angry because he believes that Doc Bitteroot is a fraud who is deceiving the villagers by falsely claiming to be able to cure all sorts of illnesses. The family are helping Nathan to extract sugar from sugar canes.

### 13.2
### Reading

## The Best Sugar Boiler

Boiling juice into sugar was a skill. Father was the best sugar boiler for miles around. You had to skim the muck off the boiling foamy juice and temper it with lime, using the right amount, and knowing just when it should cease boiling. It was hard work, but we managed. Mother and I finished carrying the canes, she
5   loading and unloading the donkey. I contributed by carrying on the head a bundle of canes on each trip. The fact that Doc Bitteroot was responsible for this hard work on my part really mobilised my feelings and set me against him. He was responsible for my working myself to death.

   The worst thing, however, was that we were left with this hideous amount of food:
10  two great pots of yams and a third with the tastiest curry goat that had perhaps ever been cooked on an outdoor fire. And we were too busy to eat heartily. We took small passes at the food, nibbling between jobs, but we did not sit down for a real meal. Jerry managed all right: by sundown he had ground three additional barrels of juice. Father boiled in silence, sour and thoughtful, knowing that Doc Bitteroot, the thorn
15  in his flesh, had won the minds of the men and succeeded in taking over the village. After this he would be able to extort money from them all. They were superstitious enough to pay him off for his supposed interception of evil to come.

   Night came and not one of the men returned. Lights flickered in the village and we heard the noise of cheering coming from the show. The people had always been
20  enthusiastic, but tonight seemed special. Word must have gone around of the powers of Doc, for the crowd seemed gigantic, to judge from the cheering, which was not only tumultuous but almost continuous. To say nothing of idolatrous.

   Father was talking to himself. 'I'll get that fraud.'

   'Nathan,' Mother said, 'you're talking to yourself.'

25      'I'll get that fraud,' Father repeated.
        'Can't you see, Nathan,' Mother asked, 'that you're no match for him? That man's as smart as a new coin and more crooked than a fox. He's got the village eating out of his hand.'
        'You must mean he's eatin' the village clean. No match for him, you say? He'll
30      make a mistake soon. Jus' one, Fran. That's all I'll ask for an' I'll be here to see he pays. I'll break him, you watch.'
        'You'll have the village down on you.'
        'They won't dare.'
        …

        In the days that followed, the people kept close to Doc as if for protection -
35      waiting, it seemed, to be warned of danger. Some came and left, then returned again; others hung around for the better part of the day. His lot was like a fair-ground. They did not come empty-handed, the wretches: there were gifts. They did not leave empty-handed, because there were purchases. In the following days, Doc nearly worked himself and his family to death, making and bottling
40      tonic. Father was worried. Money going down the drain, he said. Mother berated him.
        'It's out of your hands, Nathan. That's plain. There's nothing you can do.'
        Father ground his teeth so hard that the action was seen through his cheeks. He walked out of our store and behind, down to the field he kept there. For a
45      time, he walked among the corn plants. This was a way of killing his anger.

## 13.3
## Understanding

**A** Choose the best answer each time.

1.  It seems likely that Mrs Berwick was loading a donkey because ____.
    A. this was her normal work          C. she liked working with animals
    B. the normal workers were absent    D. she wanted to keep an eye on her husband

2.  In line 2 of the passage, 'it' (in 'temper it') apparently refers to ____.
    A. lime          B. juice          C. muck          D. cane

3.  In line 7, the word 'mobilised' is similar in meaning to ____.
    A. aroused.      B. represented.   C. showed.       D. quenched

4.  How was Doc Bitteroot responsible for the writer's predicament?
    A. He had forced the writer to work to earn money to pay him.
    B. His actions had led to Mr Berwick's workers leaving him, so the family had to deal with the sugar.
    C. He had extorted a lot of money from the writer's father.
    D. He had made the writer's father very bad-tempered.

5. The food mentioned in line 9 had probably been prepared for ____.
   A. a family celebration   C. the whole family
   B. the normal workers     D. Doc Bitteroot and his family

**B** Answer these questions about the passage.

1. In line 9, why does the narrator refer to the food as 'hideous'?

2. Who do you think Jerry was (line 12)? What is your evidence for your answer?

3. What *two* reasons are mentioned in the passage to explain why people flocked to Doc Bitteroot?

4. 'to pay him off for his supposed interception of evil to come' (line 17)
   a) What was Doc Bitteroot claiming that he could do?
   b) What does the narrator imply by using 'supposed'?

5. In lines 34–41, what evidence is there to justify the use of 'superstitious' in line 17?

## 13.4

# Vocabulary: meaning in context

**A** Choose the word(s) which best show(s) the meaning of the underlined words as they are used in the passage.

1. You had to skim the <u>muck</u> off the boiling foamy juice (line 2)
   A. surface     B. top        C. stones      D. impurities

2. and <u>temper</u> it with lime (line 2)
   A. modify      B. solidify   C. liquefy     D. sweeten

3. I <u>contributed</u> by carrying … canes (line 5)
   A. paid        B. kept busy  C. volunteered D. helped

4. this <u>hideous</u> amount of food (line 9)
   A. unpleasantly large        C. ugly and horrible-looking
   B. quite unexpected          D. repulsive and frightening

5. we were too busy to eat <u>heartily</u> (line 11)
   A. largely     B. enthusiastically   C. sincerely   D. for a long time

6. We took small passes at the food, <u>nibbling</u> between jobs (line 12)
   A. having a brief rest       C. chatting in a friendly way
   B. eating greedily           D. eating small amounts

7. Father boiled in silence, <u>sour</u> and thoughtful (line 14)
   A. in a bad mood             C. jealous and resentful
   B. remaining silent          D. feeling very angry with himself

8. he would be able to <u>extort</u> money from them all (line 16)
   A. get by fraudulent methods
   B. obtain by force, threats or other bad methods
   C. extract
   D. gradually draw out

**B** Match the underlined words with the meanings which they have in the passage.

| Words from the passage | Meanings |
| --- | --- |
| 1. They were <u>superstitious</u> enough (line 17) | a) very noisy and boisterous |
| 2. for his <u>supposed</u> interception (line 17) | b) somebody who uses trickery to get money |
| 3. for his supposed <u>interception</u> (line 17) | c) have the courage to do something |
| 4. which was not only <u>tumultuous</u> (line 22) | d) being wasted |
| 5. To say nothing of <u>idolatrous</u>. (line 22) | e) site |
| 6. I'll get that <u>fraud</u>. (line 23) | f) worshipping a person |
| 7. more <u>crooked</u> than a fox (line 27) | g) scolded |
| 8. They won't <u>dare</u>. (line 33) | h) ability to stop or turn aside |
| 9. His <u>lot</u> was like a fairground. (line 36) | i) quite obvious |
| 10. Money <u>going down the drain</u> (line 40) | j) dishonest and cunning |
| 11. Mother <u>berated</u> him. (line 40) | k) assumed but not proved to be true |
| 12. That's <u>plain</u>. (line 42) | l) believing without evidence that something can cause harm |

## 13.5
## Vocabulary: idioms

### Exercise 1

Complete the sentences by putting in the most suitable idiom from the list on page 170.

1. If you have a narrow escape from trouble, you can say it was ____.

2. If you want to warn a friend that somebody is dishonest and untrustworthy, you can say that the person is ____.

3. An achievement such as passing an examination can be called ____.

4. Money saved up for some future event is regarded as ____.

5. In an argument or a dispute, if you have ____, you have something which you can produce and give your opponent an unpleasant surprise.

6. If you buy a used bicycle or car without first having seen it, you are buying ____ and may wish you hadn't bought it.

7. If a problem is difficult to solve, people may call it ____.

8. ____ is a very special (usually good) day in somebody's life.

9. Something which is meant to deceive somebody, especially in an enquiry or an investigation, is often called ____.

10. If somebody has a fixed belief in his mind – even when the belief is not justified – people may say to him, 'You seem to have ____.'

| a card up your sleeve | a bee in the bonnet |
| a red letter day | a feather in your cap |
| a red herring | a pig in a poke |
| a nest-egg | a hard nut to crack |
| a close shave | a bad penny |

## 13.6
## Vocabulary: proverbs

Exercise 2

Match these proverbs with their meanings.

| Proverbs | Meanings |
| --- | --- |
| 1. Absence makes the heart grow fonder. | a) If you don't waste money and food, you won't be in need of things. |
| 2. Out of sight, out of mind. | b) A friend who helps you when you really need help is a true friend. |
| 3. Walls have ears. | c) When you are separated from somebody (whom you like or love), you will miss the person and like or love him or her even more. |
| 4. A friend in need is a friend indeed. | |

| Proverbs | Meanings |
|---|---|
| 5. You can't have your cake *and* eat it. | d) He complains and threatens but he doesn't take much action against people. |
| 6. A stitch in time saves nine. | e) You should make a greater physical effort. |
| 7. As you make your bed so you must lie in it. | f) If you repair something when the need first arises, you won't have to make much more extensive repairs later on. |
| 8. Practice makes perfect. | g) Don't try to get a double advantage. |
| 9. Waste not, want not. | h) If you are separated from somebody, you may soon forget about him or her. |
| 10. A fool and his money are soon parted. | i) Your future life depends upon what you make of your opportunities now. |
| 11. His bark is worse than his bite. | j) Be careful! Somebody may be listening. |
| 12. You ought to use more elbow-grease. | k) The more you try to do something, the better you will become. |
| | l) It is easy to get money away from a person who is stupid or who behaves in a silly way. |

### 13.7
## Grammar: using adjectives

In 13.2, Mrs Berwick said that Doc Bitteroot was 'as smart as a new coin' and 'more crooked than a fox'. We can use other adjectives to complete the similes, e.g.
  as ____ as a new coin (smart, bright, flashy, flamboyant, striking, colourful)
  more ____ than a fox (cunning, crafty, crooked, deceitful, treacherous, tricky, calculating, scheming, clever, stealthy)

1. Suggest adjectives which we could use to complete these comparisons.
   a) Doc Bitteroot was as ____ as a lion.
   b) Anne is very shy. At school she is as ____ as a mouse.
   c) After spending three days in the forest, the survivor of the wreck was as ____ as a starving wolf.

d) The Berwick family were as ____ as ants preparing sugar from the canes.
e) You will have to be as ____ as an ox to pull this load of cane.

2. What nouns can we use to complete these comparisons?
   a) My young brother is as lively as ____.
   b) What's for dinner? I'm as hungry as ____.
   c) He doesn't have a good singing voice. He sings like ____.
   d) Be careful! When he is angry, he is as dangerous as ____.
   e) Ugh! This meat is as tough as ____.

## 13.8
## Writing: the structure of a story

In Unit 5, we saw that a story needs these things:

|  | In *Big Doc Bitteroot* |
|---|---|
| A setting | The quiet village of Kendal in Jamaica |
| Conflict to form a plot | The clash between a stranger, Doc Bitteroot, and the existing leader of the village, Nathan Berwick |
| Development of the plot | Villagers leave Berwick and support Doc. A fight between Berwick and Doc. Doc fails to cure a dangerously ill child. Doc is accused of breaking the law by practising medicine without a licence. |
| Characters | Berwick and Doc and their families/supporters |
| A start | 8 lines to introduce the village; then the 'enemy' (Doc Bitteroot) arrives |
| An ending (a resolution) | Instead of forcing Doc to leave the village, Nathan Berwick forgives him and helps him to settle down and play a useful role in the village; everybody is happy. |
| Language | The author uses standard English so that the book can be read by people in any country where English is used. He could have written the book in dialect, but this would mean that far fewer people would be able to understand the story. |

## 13.9

## Writing: starting a story

When we start a written or spoken story, we have to consider two things: **where?** and **how?**

### Where shall we start the story of Big Doc Bitteroot?

We could start in one of these places:

- in a country, town, village or locality
- in the village – out on a road
- in the village store owned by Nathan Berwick
- in Nathan Berwick's home – he is speaking to his wife
- in one of Doc Bitteroot's wagons – he is speaking to his companion.

The author decided to start in the country and move quickly to a road in the village. This is how he started:

> Kendal lies at the head of a narrow valley. If you approach it from Green Island, a seaside market town four miles down west, you travel over a sinuous, winding road, sometimes of tar and sometimes of gravel. But you may also come from the east, over a backbone of hills called Cessnock. The road down from there is even more winding than the first, before it drops into our square, well done up in asphalt. **It was by this route that the strangers arrived.**
>
> 'Look't here!' chimed Ringo Pellman, pointing up the road. He was on the pavement in front of our store. 'What a sight!'

### How shall we start the story of Doc Bitteroot?

We could start by using one of these methods:

- a **statement**, e.g. describe the locality or a person
- describe an **action**, e.g. serving a customer in the store, pointing at wagons, flicking a whip over the back of a mule, running into or out of the store, etc.
- use **dialogue**
- use a proverb or quotation. (This method is not often used.)

If the story is for a play or film, we would have to consider the scenery and music as well. Which method did Mr Palmer decide to use?

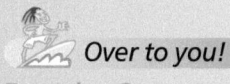

Exercise 3

Learn by heart these useful ways of starting a story – **SAD**:

S – **statement**
A – **action**
D – **dialogue**

Unit 13 · *The Best Sugar Boiler*

Then be ready to use one of these methods when you write your own stories.

### Exercise 4

Write up to 12 lines to start the story of Doc Bitteroot in a different way. For example, you could start in one of these ways:
- Nathan Berwick is working in his store when somebody rushes in to report the arrival of an impressive stranger.
- Berwick is talking to his wife at home. He is showing that he is worried because he is suspicious of a stranger (Doc Bitteroot) who arrived a day or two previously.

You can use one of these, or make up your own way of starting.

## 13.10

## Punctuation: using inverted commas (revision)

We can use inverted commas (speech marks or quotation marks) to show:
- direct speech, e.g.
    'Are you ready?' Peter asked.
- the title of a book or film, e.g.
    Have you read 'Shane'?
- foreign words in a sentence, e.g.
    Businessmen like a 'laissez-faire' policy.
- words used in a special way, e.g.
    Some tourists 'hunt' animals with a camera.
- words quoted from a passage, e.g.
    The 'Titanic' was said to be 'practically unsinkable'.

In most books and newspapers, *single* inverted commas are used. Then double inverted commas can be used for a quotation or speech within a speech. In handwritten work (including examinations), it may be wiser to use double inverted commas because they are more easily noticed, e.g.
    Paul asked me, 'Have you ever read "Big Doc Bitteroot"?'
*or*    Paul asked me, "Have you ever read 'Big Doc Bitteroot'?"

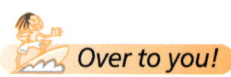 **Over to you!**

Compare each pair of sentences below. Explain any differences in the punctuation.

1. a) 'Wait until the bus stops,' the driver said. 'Then get off carefully.'
   b) 'Wait until the bus stops,' Miss Harris said, 'before you get off.'

2. a) 'We couldn't get on the bus,' Roy told his mother. 'It was full.'
   b) 'We couldn't get on the bus,' Anna told her mother, 'because it was full.'

Exercise 5

Punctuate these conversations correctly, putting in all necessary punctuation marks and capital letters. Remember that each new speaker starts a new paragraph.

1. are you going near the post office mrs reid asked her husband yes he said is there anything you want could you get me a small registered envelope please mrs reid said ive got to send some money to my sister in guyana ok mr reid said ill get a couple it may be useful to have a spare one available

2. when the telephone rang I ran to answer it thinking that it was probably a friend calling for a chat hello a lady said can I speak to the manager please Im sorry I started to say but she interrupted me mr reynolds I mean she said you've got the wrong number I replied the lady was surprised isn't that modern furniture she asked no I said Im very sorry she said that's all right I replied

## 13.11
## Listening practice

You work for a company which arranges the export of goods from Caribbean countries by sea. You want to know when ships are leaving various ports and what their destinations are. Listen to the information about ships. Then arrange the information in the form of a list, using these headings:

| Name of ship | Arrives | Leaves | Destination |
| --- | --- | --- | --- |
| | | | |

## 13.12
## Grammar: comparison of adjectives (revision)

| | Positive (one only) | Comparative (one of two only) | Superlative (one of three or more) |
| --- | --- | --- | --- |
| Group 1 | fat<br>big<br>clever<br>wealthy | fatter (than)<br>bigger (than)<br>cleverer (than)<br>wealthier (than) | (the) fattest<br>(the) biggest<br>(the) cleverest<br>(the) wealthiest |
| Group 2 | difficult<br>intelligent<br>beautiful<br>sensible | more difficult<br>more intelligent<br>more beautiful<br>more sensible | most difficult<br>most intelligent<br>most beautiful<br>most sensible |
| Group 3 | good<br>bad<br>little<br>much<br>many | better<br>worse<br>less<br>more<br>more | best<br>worst<br>least<br>most<br>most |

Unit 13 · The Best Sugar Boiler

- **Group 1** Nearly all adjectives of one syllable are compared in this way with '-er' and '-est'. We also compare adjectives of two syllables in a similar way if they have their stress on the second syllable, e.g. 'sincere', or end in '-er', '-le', '-ow' or '-y', e.g. 'clever', 'gentle', 'shallow', 'dirty'.
- **Group 2** Most long adjectives are compared in this way with 'more' and 'most'. When we put 'more' or 'most' before an adjective, we do *not* add '-er' or '-est' as well.
- **Group 3** There are a few adjectives with irregular comparisons. The important ones are given in the table.

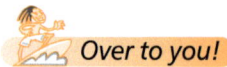
Over to you!

### Exercise 6

Four people decided to go on a diet because they weighed too much. This table shows what happened.

| Name | Age | Height in metres | Number of weeks on diet | Weight before (kg) | Weight after (kg) | Gain or loss |
|---|---|---|---|---|---|---|
| Nadia | 19 | 1.63 | 3 | 60 | 57 | –3 |
| Michelle | 18 | 1.68 | 6 | 64 | 59 | –5 |
| Kevin | 22 | 1.75 | 5 | 72 | 68 | –4 |
| David | 20 | 1.70 | 8 | 75 | 69 | –6 |

Answer these questions:

1. Who is the oldest person?
2. Who is the youngest person?
3. Who is the shortest?
4. Who is taller than David?
5. Who stayed on a diet for the longest period?
6. Who was the least heavy before a diet?
7. Who was heavier: Kevin or David?
8. Who lost most weight?
9. Who was on a diet for twice as long as Nadia?
10. Who lost the least weight?

### Exercise 7

How many of these questions can you answer?

1. Which is longer: a mile or a kilometre?
2. Which is shorter: 100 yards or 100 metres?
3. Quacy is 5' 10". Abiose is 1.9 m. Who is the taller?
4. Miss Johnson drove at 80 km/h (kilometres per hour). Miss Morris drove at 60 mph (miles per hour). Who was the faster driver?
5. Which island is the nearest to Guyana: Jamaica, Barbados or Tobago?

6. Which island is the nearest to St Lucia: Grenada, St Vincent or Barbados?
7. Which country has the most land: Guyana, Trinidad or Jamaica?
8. Which country has the biggest population: Trinidad, Guyana or Jamaica?
9. Which country produces the most oil: Antigua, Grenada or Trinidad and Tobago?
10. In triangle ABC, angle A is a right-angle and angle C is 45 degrees. Which of the three angles is the largest?
11. If X is the square root of C, and Y is the square root of X, which number is the biggest: C, X or Y?
12. It takes a plane 6 hours to fly from A to B. It takes a motorist 8 hours to drive from A to C. It takes a hiker 12 hours to walk from A to D. Which place is the nearest to A: B, C or D?

Make up some similar questions to ask in class.

## 13.13
## Enjoying poetry

The passage in 13.2 is taken from a book which describes events in a quiet Jamaican village. Now read this poem which describes the sort of village in which Nathan Berwick lived.

### In the Gentle Afternoon

Such commerce        activity
for a small village without a representative
on Central Government, without a village council,
without a working public toilet, with two
5    stand pipes, three rum shops and a cricket pitch;
such business
as citizens sit on benches and discuss
the latest test scores, last night's trouble
at the dance, Sunday's chance in the rounders match,
10    the price of cod fish, the problems of cross week;
such activity
late in the afternoon on Friday as mother
rushes over to seize her child; boys plot;
a girl shouts her directions, a jeep coughs
15    to a standstill by the shop, and erupts an eager crowd;
such peace
in the gentle afternoon, as the sun begins to die
and everybody drifts away to attend their affairs,
all part of the village family, all private people
20    with each a share of secrets, known by all.

*Royston Ellis*

Questions

1. In line 1, 'commerce' can refer to business activities, social relations or simply activities. What do you think 'business' means in line 6?

2. What do you think the poet's aim is in lines 2–5?

3. In line 15, 'erupts' could mean 'breaks up', 'attracts' or 'disgorges'. Which seems the most likely meaning here? Does it matter to the reader if he does not know the precise meaning of 'erupts' here?

4. What can we tell about the village people from the last line of the poem?

5. How would you describe the tone of this poem or the attitude of the poet to his subject matter?

6. This type of poem is said to be written in 'free verse'. What are the characteristics of free verse, as far as you can judge?

## 13.14
## Writing

Write about 250–350 words on *one* of the following topics:

1. Write (for a stranger) a description of the village or district in which you live or in which you once lived. You can do *one* of these things:
   a) Write mainly about the good or attractive features of the place. *or*
   b) Write mainly about the bad features of the place. *or*
   c) Combine (a) and (b). *or*
   d) Use your own method.

or

2. Read 13.1 and 13.2 again. Imagine that you are the son or daughter of Mr and Mrs Berwick. In a letter to a cousin overseas, describe the attitude of your father to the stranger, Doc Bitteroot, and explain why he has this attitude. Say what you think may happen in the near future.

or

3. Write a story in which the scene shown in *one* of the photographs on page 179 plays a part. (Do *not* just describe the scene.)

# 14 Bite-marks

### 14.1
### Pre-reading

The passage in 14.2 describes a legal precedent, i.e. the way in which a case was decided in a court of law for the first time. For example, the judge who first accepted fingerprints as legal evidence set a precedent. Judges in later cases would usually follow his decision. A precedent in one country is often followed by judges in other countries.

There are two words you need to understand before you read the passage in 14.2:

- 'forensic' – concerned in some way with a court of law (and often with crime)
- 'odontology' – teeth + study of; the scientific study of teeth.

So 'forensic odontology' (line 10) means the study of teeth in connection with crime or legal matters.

### 14.2
### Reading

## Bite-marks

A half-eaten Golden Delicious apple, abandoned at the scene of a fire, made legal history not long ago in the UK when Karl Johnson, a dustman, failed to have his conviction for arson quashed. The Court of Criminal Appeal decided that the tell-tale marks of teeth on an apple were evidence as valid as fingerprints. This was
5   the first time that bite-marks had been the sole evidence of identification in a criminal case, and it was enough for Johnson to be sentenced to three years in jail. Remarkably, the bite in the apple provided 46 points of similarity with Johnson's teeth, far more than in most fingerprint identifications.
    There was no other shred of evidence pointing to Johnson's involvement in the
10  crime. He had been caught by the science of forensic odontology – a little-known branch of dentistry that studies the often gruesome evidence of bite-marks at the scene of a crime. An office fire started around 2 a.m. on a Saturday. It destroyed most of the building, but in an unburnt room police subsequently found an apple with a single bite in it. They rushed it through traffic jams to the Liverpool home of
15  John Furness, the world's leading authority on bite-marks. He quickly bottled the apple in preserving fluid.
    Police picked up Johnson five days later. His home was only a few streets away from the damaged offices. His criminal record included an incident where fire had been used. Johnson's alibi was that he had been with friends until after midnight,

*English Alive!*

20  when he had returned home and watched a film on television. However, he agreed to have impressions taken of his teeth. The evidence provided by John Furness showed that Johnson was the man who had bitten the apple – which, it turned out, had come from the secretary's office drawer. The arsonist, feeling peckish, had taken the apple from the drawer while ransacking it.

25  When Johnson appealed against his conviction, the Court of Criminal Appeal looked at the status of forensic odontology and concluded that it was now a recognised science on a par with the evidence of fibres and fingerprints. Johnson's counsel argued in vain that odontology was new, untried and little more than a hobby. The forensic odontologists replied that, with 32 teeth in a full set, the odds
30  against two people having identical teeth are, as with fingerprints, two and a half billion to one.

Cases involving bite-marks have been known since 1906, when teeth marks in a piece of cheese were part of the evidence against a burglar. In 1960, however, a London magistrate warned that it would be 'utterly unsafe' to convict on the
35  evidence of bite-marks alone. Since then, John Furness has been one of a small group of dentists pioneering the increasingly sophisticated study of bite-marks. For over 20 years he supplied forensic evidence in more than 100 cases.

Furness explains, 'No two people's teeth wear in the same way. Just as each blacksmith will use his hammer in a slightly different way, so no two people chew
40  in the same way.

Their teeth take on unique characteristics. People can lie through their teeth but their teeth cannot lie.'

## 14.3
## Understanding

**A** Choose the best answer each time.

1. According to the evidence in the second paragraph, the statement about the apple in line 1 of the passage is ____.
   A. totally correct          C. not completely accurate
   B. totally false            D. an understatement

2. Apparently ____ was able to identify the apple as ____ originally.
   A. the police … a criminal's    C. Furness … his
   B. a secretary … hers           D. Johnson … Golden Delicious

3. After Johnson was arrested, he was charged with ____.
   A. stealing an apple from an office    C. illegally setting fire to a building
   B. burglary and theft                  D. assaulting a secretary in an office

4. As a result of his appeal at the Court of Criminal Appeal, Johnson's sentence was ____.
   A. changed.    B. reduced.    C. increased.    D. confirmed

5. We learn from the first paragraph that evidence provided by a bite-mark can be ____.
   A. unreliable at the trial of a criminal

        B. useless if a tooth is missing from a person's jaw
        C. even more convincing than evidence from fingerprints
        D. similar to the teeth of 46 other people

    6.  It seems likely that the police 'picked up' Johnson after the fire because of:
        I.   the bite in the apple
        II.  a report by John Furness
        III. a report on the fire at the office
        IV   his previous record
        A. I            B. II and III        C. I and II          D. III and IV

**B** Answer these questions about the passage.

1.  In what way was Johnson's case important to lawyers and the police?

2.  Why did Johnson appeal to the Court of Criminal Appeal? Did he succeed?

3.  What mistake did Johnson make when he entered an office?

4.  What did John Furness probably think of the decision of the Appeal Court? What is the reason for your answer?

## 14.4
## Vocabulary: meaning in context

**A** Choose the word(s) which best show(s) the meaning of the underlined words as they are used in the passage in 14.2.

1.  (he) failed to have his <u>conviction</u> for arson quashed (line 3)
    A. being suspected.          C. arrest by the police
    B. being found guilty        D. confession by a suspect

2.  (he) failed to have his conviction for <u>arson</u> quashed (line 3)
    A. carelessness with fire    C. breaking into an office at night
    B. attempted theft           D. deliberately setting fire to a place

3.  (he) failed to have his conviction for arson <u>quashed</u> (line 3)
    A. declared wrong            C. reduced in length
    B. postponed temporarily     D. lessened

4.  the <u>tell-tale</u> marks of teeth on an apple (line 4)
    A. deeply made    B. fresh    C. revealing    D. unexpected

5.  were evidence as <u>valid</u> as fingerprints (line 4)
    A. acceptable   B. common   C. widespread.   D. visible

6.  bite-marks had been the <u>sole</u> evidence (line 5)
    A. alone        B. lonely      C. definite      D. only

7.  <u>Remarkably</u>, the bite in the apple provided 46 points of similarity (line 7)

A. Worth noticing this time     C. Wonderfully
B. Rather surprisingly          D. Fortunately

**B** Match the underlined words with the meanings which they have in the passage.

| Words from the passage | Meanings |
|---|---|
| 1. no other <u>shred</u> of evidence (line 9) | a) horrible to see |
| 2. Johnson's <u>involvement</u> in the crime (line 9) | b) dense mass of vehicles |
| 3. the often <u>gruesome</u> evidence (line 11) | c) preventing deterioration |
| 4. police <u>subsequently</u> found an apple (line 13) | d) expert |
| 5. through traffic <u>jams</u> (line 14) | e) it was discovered later |
| 6. the world's leading <u>authority</u> (line 15) | f) proof of being somewhere |
| 7. bottled the apple in <u>preserving</u> fluid (line 16) | g) (small) piece |
| 8. Johnson's <u>alibi</u> was (line 19) | h) rather hungry |
| 9. which, <u>it turned out</u>, had come (line 22) | i) later on |
| 10. feeling <u>peckish</u> (line 23) | j) taking part |

**C** Match the underlined words with the meanings which they have in the passage.

| Words from the passage | Meanings |
|---|---|
| 1. while <u>ransacking</u> it (line 24) | a) considered equal to |
| 2. looked at the <u>status</u> of (line 26) | b) without success |
| 3. <u>on a par with</u> the evidence of fibres (line 27) | c) find a person guilty |
| 4. counsel argued <u>in vain</u> (line 28) | d) completely |
| 5. little more than a <u>hobby</u> (line 29) | e) doing work never done before |
| 6. it would be <u>utterly</u> unsafe (line 34) | f) advanced (and often complicated) |
| 7. to <u>convict</u> on the evidence (line 34) | g) searching through and taking from |
| 8. dentists <u>pioneering</u> the (line 36) | h) not found elsewhere |
| 9. <u>sophisticated</u> study of bite-marks (line 36) | i) accepted position and value |
| 10. <u>unique</u> characteristics (line 41) | j) something of interest but not studied very seriously |

## 14.5
### Writing: making a summary

You already know that when we make a summary we look for the main relevant points. Sometimes it is not easy to decide what these points are.
Read the passage in 14.2 again. We could make three different summaries based on the passage:

a) a summary of the information about Johnson

or

b) a summary of the status of bite-marks as evidence

or

c) a summary of the information about an apple.

So we need to choose a different set of main points for each summary:

| (a) Johnson | (b) bite-marks | (c) apple |
|---|---|---|
| criminal record. | 1906 – cheese | secretary |
| office | 1960 – unsafe | apple – desk |
| burglary | recently – OK | burglar – bite |
| apple | | preserved |
| bite | | studied – Furness |
| arrest | | evidence |
| trial | | legal precedent |
| sentenced | | |
| appeal failed | | |

Do you agree that these are the main points for each of the different summaries?
If you have to make a summary in real life or in an examination, make sure that you know *exactly* what you are supposed to look for.

 Over to you!

Exercise 1

Make a summary of the way in which an apple was responsible for sending Karl Johnson to prison. Use 80–120 words. Do *not* copy whole sentences from the passage.

## 14.6

### Vocabulary: idioms

At the end of the passage in 14.2, John Furness mentioned that people can 'lie through their teeth'. This is an idiom. What do the following idioms mean?

1. to lend an ear
2. to turn a deaf ear to
3. to turn a blind eye to
4. to turn the other cheek
5. to hold your tongue
6. to keep a stiff upper lip
7. to have your back to the wall
8. to see eye to eye with somebody
9. to take the words out of somebody's mouth
10. to have a swollen head

## 14.7

### Grammar: indirect (reported) speech

These are some of the common changes we make when we report a speech or pass on a message. If the original action has finished, we may need to change the tense of verbs.

|  | In direct speech | In indirect speech |
|---|---|---|
| **Time** | now<br>today<br><br>in five minutes' time<br>yesterday<br>tomorrow<br>an hour ago<br>in a week's time<br>next month | then, at that time<br>that day<br>on (+ the name of the day)<br>five minutes later<br>the previous day<br>the next/following day<br>an hour earlier/previously<br>a week later<br>in the following month |
| **Place** | here<br>in our house<br>in this room<br>in my car | there, in/at (+ name of a place)<br>in their house<br>in that room<br>in his/her car |
| **Pronouns and possession** | I<br>you<br>my key<br>your shoes<br>mine<br>our car<br>ours | he/she<br>I/me/you<br>his/her key<br>my/our shoes<br>his/hers<br>their car<br>theirs |
| **Tenses of verbs\*** | am, is, are<br>has, have<br>he wants<br>it finished<br>she has gone<br>it will start<br>can, may<br>it was found | was, were<br>had<br>he wanted<br>it had finished<br>she had gone<br>it would start<br>could, might<br>it had been found |

*We saw in Unit 12 that in many cases there is no need to change the tense of verbs when we report a speech. If an action mentioned in the original speech has not started or finished, we probably do not need to change the tense when we report the speech.

Look at these examples:

   *direct:*      The man said, 'My name is Paul Morris. I live in Antigua.'

   *indirect:*   The man said his name was Paul Morris and that he lived in Antigua.

   *or:*         … that he lives in Antigua *(if you think he still lives there)*

   *direct:*      Anna said, 'You can borrow my bicycle until yours has been repaired.'

   *indirect:*   Anna said (that) I could borrow her bicycle until mine had been repaired.

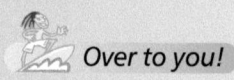 *Over to you!*

### Exercise 2

Somebody said these things to you several days ago. Tell another person what somebody said. Make any necessary changes.

1. Mrs Smith said, 'My daughter will give you the money tomorrow.'

2. Miss Jordan said, 'Your brother is waiting to see you, Mr Johnson.'

3. Mr Stuart said, 'The hotel is full. There are no vacant rooms. I'm sorry.'

4. The lady told us, 'I've sprained my ankle. I can't walk properly.'

5. A supervisor told us, 'The last bus has gone already. You'll have to walk or get a taxi.'

6. A lady at the desk said to me, 'You can go in the library if you leave your bag outside.'

7. One of the tourists said, 'We're staying at the Plaza Hotel until Thursday. We're going for a trip on a boat tomorrow.'

8. Peter said, 'My cat is older than yours, as far as I know.'

9. The woman said, 'I've lost my handbag, so I have no money.'

10. A man told us, 'The ferry is not working today. It will be all right tomorrow.'

11. My friend told me, 'My uncle is living in Canada now.'

12. The announcer on the radio said, 'The temperature is 28 degrees now and the humidity is 82%.'

### 14.8
## Punctuation: using a question mark (revision)

In section 12.10, we saw that we use a question mark after a **direct question** but not after an indirect one. Read 12.10 again if you have forgotten.

### Exercise 3

Say which sentences should finish with a question mark.

1. I wonder who that lady is
2. She asked me my name
3. When does the game start
4. How kind of her to help you
5. Did you enjoy the party
6. The police officer asked me why I wanted to enter the building
7. Do you happen to know when Sylvia's birthday is
8. Go and ask Nadia what Deena's telephone number is
9. Ask Francine if she liked the CD we lent her yesterday
10. I'm not sure whether this is the right answer or not
11. What's the date today
12. I wondered where the other boys were
13. How the men escaped is a mystery
14. Where to live is quite a problem
15. That's not your watch, is it

### 14.9
## Grammar: showing the purpose of an action

Check that you can use these ways of showing the purpose of an action:

| Way of showing purpose | Examples |
| --- | --- |
| a 'to' infinitive | Uncle stopped **to get** some petrol for the car. Farmers get up early **to take** their vegetables to the market. |
| in order to | Uncle stopped the car **in order to get** some petrol. We moved to higher ground **in order to escape** the flood. |
| so that (+ could/can) | Uncle stopped the car **so that he could get** some petrol. Sometimes I go to bed early **so that I can get up** early the next day. |
| so as to | Nnke climbed up a tree **so as to get** a better view of the game. Abiose tiptoed through the house **so as to avoid** waking anybody up. |
| in case | Take an umbrella with you **in case** it rains. When there is lightning in the sky, don't stand under a tree **in case** the lightning hits it. |

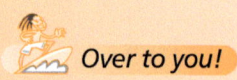 **Over to you!**

### Exercise 4

Combine the information in each pair of sentences to make one sentence. Use any of the sentence patterns shown on page 187. Make any necessary changes.

1. Sometimes police officers stop a bus. They want to look for a suspect.
2. Tourists often go to a money-changer. They want to get local money.
3. When a hurricane approaches, people stay at home. They want to protect their homes and keep out of danger.
4. Mr Walters set some traps. He wanted to catch mice in his home.
5. My grandmother bought herself a new pair of spectacles. She wanted to read the newspaper easily.
6. Sometimes a government has to raise taxes. It needs to obtain money to pay for schools, hospitals and other facilities.
7. Mrs Lall bought some flour. She intended to make some cakes.
8. Many people emigrate. They want to get a better job and save some money.
9. Miss Dixon bought a computer. She wanted to work at home.
10. Letitia turned off the television. She wanted to concentrate on her homework.
11. At most airports, Customs officers may search passengers and their luggage. They want to make sure that the passengers are not carrying any drugs.
12. You ought to send that letter by airmail. That will make sure that it gets to Nadia within a few days.

## 14.10

# Enjoying poetry

Read this poem in which a father is writing about his young daughter.

### *Ana*

While she was yet too young to crawl
my pride would picture her sunlit, outside
playing with flowers
like every poet's child;
5  the frills of her pink dress
waving in the gentlest whim
of her father observing

pen in hand, her little gestures
in her world of green.

10   It was a calm and quiet mental scene.

Instead, now,
she leaps at me
off kitchen counters
when my arms and mind are full
15   of other things:
I glimpse the little hands
lunging for my throat,
and in that stiffening split-second
I wish she would miss
20   (serve her damn right)
I pray she won't miss
(little monkey)
but infallibly I feel her hard fingers
her sharp nails
25   in the neutral father-flesh of my neck
and her barbaric howl of delight
stifles my angry shout.
I make to unhorse her with a wild shrug
she thinks it's a game,
30   'Do that again, Daddy',
and like a fool
Daddy does it again.

I've given up the prospect
of pink dresses and flowers;
35   I let her kick her somersaults
off my stomach, hardly noticing now
the muddy footprints on my shirts,
the scratches on my arms …
I think I must endure her thorny assaults
40   precisely because they seem
like self-inflicted wounds.

And yet when she is curled in sleep,
like a comma,
I can ponder still the possibility
45   of finishing all the stanzas
with images of her calm beauty
– lying so peaceful on the flower-patterned sheet,
all her brutal fangs of life
retracted behind the closed lids.

*Mark McWatt*

## Questions

1. What do lines 6 and 7 mean?

2. Did the vision described in lines 2--9 ever come true? What is the reason for your answer?

3. Change line 17 to make it less emotional and more as seen through the child's eyes.

4. Why do you think the poet calls the flesh of his neck 'neutral'? (Compare lines 19 and 21 to find an answer.)

5. In line 31 what does 'like a fool' tell us about the poet?

6. In what way are the scratches and thorny assaults 'self-inflicted wounds'?

7. What kind of person does the poet appear to be if we judge him by this poem?

## 14.11

# Writing: making up a story

In the CSEC examination, you may be given a picture and be asked to make up a story with instructions similar to these:

a) Write a story which includes the scene in the photograph.
b) Write a story based on the picture on the right.
c) Write a story suggested by the picture shown here.

## Guidelines

1. Study the instructions carefully. In (a) you have to include the scene. In (b) and (c), it is not essential to include the scene as long as your story is closely related to it.

2. Decide whether to write either a first person narrative or a third person one, e.g.

   | | |
   |---|---|
   | *first person (I):* | Last Saturday, I went to the beach with some friends … |
   | or: | A few days ago, I went swimming with some friends … |
   | *third person (he/she/they):* | Last Saturday, Leon and some friends went … |
   | or: | Not long ago, a group of friends decided to … |

3. When necessary, make up these things:
   - the names of one or more people involved
   - the name of the place
   - the date and (perhaps) the time of day: morning, afternoon, evening, night.

4. Use conflict to make up the outline of a plot. (See Unit 5 if you have forgotten what 'conflict' means.) This means that you have to think of a problem and find a way of solving it. Here are possible plots for the picture above:
   a) The young men are watching a girl in the sea. They think she may be drowning or in difficulty and are wondering whether to try to rescue her. They rescue her.

or

   b) As above but when they go to rescue her, they find that she is not in any difficulty but she appreciates their help and becomes friendly with one of them.

or

   c) As in (b) but the girl becomes annoyed and scolds her 'rescuers'.

or

   d) The young men have seen a stranger on the beach. Who is he? What is he doing in their territory. They set out to investigate: good or bad result.

or

   e) Similar to (a) but they are watching somebody in a boat and not in the sea. Is the person in difficulties? Then as in one of the scenarios above.

There are many more possibilities. Can you suggest a plot in class?

## 14.12
## Writing

Write about 250–350 words on one of these topics:

1. Write a story based on the picture on the previous page.

or

2. Write a story about a rescue at sea or on a river.

or

3. Is the sea (a) mainly helpful, (b) mainly harmful or (c) both helpful and harmful to your country?

# 15 Black Bart

### 15.1
### Pre-reading

'Black Bart' was never black. He was an unusual character who lived a double life more than a century ago in the USA. When he was alive, the only form of travel from town to town was by horse or stagecoach: a coach which took passengers from one stage (or place) to the next one. Two men (Wells and Fargo) formed a company which controlled most stagecoaches in the west of the USA. (The modern company is one of the leading banks in the USA.)

### 15.2
### Reading

## Black Bart

Black Bart was, without doubt, the most notorious of all stagecoach robbers in the USA. He was credited with 28 robberies between 1877 and 1883. Stage drivers throughout northern California lived in dread of the day when Bart would abruptly step out of the brush in some secluded ravine and call out politely, 'Will you please
5  throw down your treasure box, sir?' He encouraged drivers to comply by pointing a shotgun casually in their direction.

Bart's character and habits were just as interesting as his success rate. His working clothes were unique. He dressed in a long linen gown and wore a flour sack over his head with holes cut out for his eyes. He was always on foot and
10  carried only a shotgun and a blanket roll in which was tucked an old axe that he used to break open the strongboxes. Bart chose his locations shrewdly and always waited for the stagecoaches at sharp bends or on hills, where the horses would be moving at a walk.

Bart was considerate towards his victims and never harmed drivers or
15  passengers. It was revealed later that he never owned a single cartridge for his shotgun and could not have fired it even in self-defence. Bart earned an initial reputation as a minor poet by leaving short verses at the scene of two early robberies. He signed the poetry as 'Black Bart, the PO8' [po-ate].

This colourful career came to an end when Bart was wounded while escaping
20  from a hold-up near Copperopolis. He accidentally dropped a handkerchief with the laundry mark 'FX07'. The mark was traced to a customer of a San Francisco laundry, and police made one of the most surprising arrests in the city's history. Black Bart, the feared highwayman, turned out to be Charles E. Bolton, one of San Francisco's more prominent citizens and a man with close connections with the
25  police department.

After his arrest, Bolton confessed to the crimes of Black Bart and told a strange tale of his life as a type of Jekyll and Hyde. He was born in Illinois as Charles E. Boles and grew up as an intelligent, well-educated citizen. After serving in the Civil War, he emigrated to California in search of gold. Unable to find any legally, Boles decided to try his luck as a highwayman.

He worked for a time as a clerk in a stage office and studied shipments and schedules. He was soon able to familiarise himself with the normal workings of the Wells Fargo transport system. Then in August 1877, he transformed himself into Black Bart and made his first hold-up. His prior knowledge of stage routes and drivers made the job relatively simple. He tried again, this time in a different area. Again everything went smoothly. Success brought him prosperity. Boles moved to San Francisco, assumed the name of Charles Bolton, and quickly built a reputation as a non-smoking, non-drinking, God-fearing and eminently reliable man with big business interests in the mines. He was seen frequently in prominent social circles, always very neatly dressed and wearing fine rings.

Whenever more cash was needed to support this high life, Boles-Bolton-Bart would put aside his hat and cane, and pack up his linen gown and shotgun. Off he would go to the foothills, rob a convenient stagecoach, and return to more champagne and fine rings.

Black Bart's fascinating life did not end with his arrest. During his trial, newspapers made him a legend by distorting his exploits, ballooning the size of his ill-gotten gains and grossly exaggerating his talent as a poet. Amid much publicity, this new folk-hero was convicted and sentenced to six years in San Quentin prison. He served his sentence, with time off for good behaviour, and was released.

For a while, Bart stayed around San Francisco. Then early in 1888 he left for the San Joaquin Valley where he quietly disappeared into the dusty heat. There was a rumour that Wells Fargo had pensioned off the ageing robber and sent him away after he agreed not to rob any more coaches.

## 15.3
## Understanding

**A** Choose the best answer each time.
1. On average, Black Bart carried out ____ robberies a year before he was caught.
   A. 28    B. 2    C. nearly 3    D. nearly 5

2. We are told that Bart spoke to the drivers of stagecoaches 'politely' (line 4). Which word later in the passage echoes the idea of politeness?
   A. unique    B. considerate    C. colourful    D. reputation

3. 'His working clothes were unique.' (line 8) This tells us that his clothes were ____.
   A. intended to frighten people   C. intended to conceal his identity
   B. cheap and easy to carry       D. unlike those of other people

4. Bart carried a shotgun mainly ____.
   A. as a bluff                C. to shoot the horses
   B. to defend himself with    D. to help him open the strongboxes

5. Bart was eventually caught as a result of ____.
   A. a tip from an eye-witness    C. not paying a laundry bill
   B. information from Wells Fargo    D. his own carelessness

6. In line 27, the reference to Jekyll and Hyde echoes the words '____' in 15.1.
   A. a double life    C. When he was alive
   B. more than a century ago    D. to the next one

**B** Answer these questions.

1. What apparently led Boles to become a highwayman?

2. Suggest a reason why Boles never took any cartridges with him when he went out to rob a stagecoach.

3. What probably caused Bart to drop a handkerchief?

4. What do we mean if we call somebody a Jekyll and Hyde character?

5. Why do you think newspapers distorted Bart's exploits?

6. What benefit could Wells Fargo obtain by giving Bart a pension?

## 15.4
## Vocabulary: meaning in context

**A** Choose the word(s) which best show(s) the meaning of the underlined words as they are used in the passage in 15.2.

1. the most <u>notorious</u> of all stagecoach robbers (line 1)
   A. active for several years    C. well known and with a bad reputation
   B. successful at first    D. bold and daring

2. He was <u>credited with</u> 28 robberies (line 2)
   A. praised for his    C. managed to evade capture during
   B. wanted by the police for    D. believed to have been involved in

3. Bart would <u>abruptly</u> step out of the brush (line 3)
   A. in a threatening way    C. suddenly and unexpectedly
   B. dangerously    D. in a frightening manner

4. in some <u>secluded</u> ravine (line 4)
   A. very narrow    C. unpopulated
   B. not easily seen    D. with steep sides

5. in some secluded <u>ravine</u> (line 4)
   A. a narrow steep-sided valley    C. lonely forest area
   B. quiet time of the day    D. area of brush and semi-desert

6. He encouraged drivers to comply (line 5)
   A. act swiftly
   B. defend themselves
   C. do as they were told
   D. stop their horses

7. Bart chose his locations shrewdly (line 11)
   A. operations   B. tactics   C. methods   D. sites

8. Bart chose his locations shrewdly (line 11)
   A. swiftly   B. cleverly   C. by chance   D. bitterly

**B** Match the underlined words with the meanings which they have in the passage.

| Words from the passage | Meanings |
| --- | --- |
| 1. Bart was considerate towards his victims (line 14) | a) of less importance |
| 2. It was revealed later (line 15) | b) at first |
| 3. an initial reputation (line 16) | c) leading |
| 4. as a minor poet (line 17) | d) followed back |
| 5. This colourful career (line 19) | e) links |
| 6. traced to a customer (line 21) | f) disclosed |
| 7. more prominent citizens (line 24) | g) lists of departures and movements |
| 8. with close connections (line 24) | h) know all about |
| 9. shipments and schedules (line 32) | i) kind and thoughtful |
| 10. to familiarise himself with (line 32) | j) with interesting and lively events |

**C** Match the underlined words with the meanings which they have in the passage.

| Words from the passage | Meanings |
| --- | --- |
| 1. he transformed himself (line 33) | a) wealth |
| 2. His prior knowledge (line 34) | b) extremely |
| 3. made the job relatively simple (line 35) | c) reporting falsely |
| 4. brought him prosperity (line 36) | d) greatly but in a bad way |
| 5. assumed the name (line 37) | e) changed |
| 6. eminently reliable man (line 38) | f) achievements |
| 7. by distorting his exploits (line 46) | g) comparatively |
| 8. by distorting his exploits (line 46) | h) making much greater |
| 9. ballooning the size (line 46) | i) took on |
| 10. grossly exaggerating (line 47) | j) obtained earlier |

## 15.5
### Vocabulary: a cloze passage

Choose the best words from the lists below to put in the blank spaces in this passage.

Charles Boles went to California in the 1870s to search for (1) ____. When he was unsuccessful, he got a job (2) ____ a clerk in the (3) ____ of a company (4) ____ operated stage-coaches (5) ____ towns in Northern California. He was not satisfied (6) ____ his salary as a (7) ____, so in 1877 he decided to (8) ____ a highwayman.

During the six years (9) ____ 1877 (10) ____ 1883, Boles carried out (11) ____ least 28 robberies. One of his favourite (12) ____ was to (13) ____ at a sharp bend in the road, where a stage-coach (14) ____ have to go (15) ____ and then (16) ____ appear and demand all the valuables (17) ____ carried on the coach.

Boles used the name 'Black (18) ____' and was successful (19) ____ he carelessly left (20) ____ a handkerchief (21) ____ his laundry mark on it. The police (22) ____ to trace the laundry mark to (23) ____ (which was his assumed name) and (24) ____ him with highway robbery. His (25) ____ received a great deal of (26) ____ in the newspapers, and Bolton was eventually (27) ____ to six years in prison. He was (28) ____ before the end of his sentence (29) ____ of good (30) ____ and eventually disappeared.

1. A. wife
   B. friends
   C. silver
   D. gold

2. A. was
   B. like
   C. as
   D. became

3. A. desk
   B. office
   C. headquarters
   D. worker

4. A. that
   B. it
   C. who
   D. whose

5. A. between
   B. going
   C. calling
   D. of

6. A. to
   B. about
   C. with
   D. on

7. A. time
   B. clerk
   C. reason
   D. driver

8. A. became
   B. becomes
   C. becoming
   D. become

9. A. from
   B. between
   C. of
   D. with

10. A. end
    B. and
    C. with
    D. but

11. A. it
    B. not
    C. at
    D. no

12. A. method
    B. trick
    C. technique
    D. methods

13. A. conceal
    B. waits
    C. hide
    D. appear

14. A. would
    B. does
    C. is
    D. must

15. A. passed
    B. walk
    C. slowly
    D. quick

| 16. | A. to<br>B. he<br>C. do<br>D. is | 21. | A. had<br>B. has<br>C. was<br>D. with | 26. | A. public<br>B. publishing<br>C. publicity<br>D. publisher |
|---|---|---|---|---|---|
| 17. | A. which<br>B. that<br>C. been<br>D. being | 22. | A. failed<br>B. succeeded<br>C. managed<br>D. wanting | 27. | A. appointed<br>B. sentenced<br>C. punished<br>D. given |
| 18. | A. Tart<br>B. Brat<br>C. Boles<br>D. Bart | 23. | A. Bolton<br>B. Boles<br>C. Jekyll<br>D. Hyde | 28. | A. relieved<br>B. redeemed<br>C. pardoned<br>D. released |
| 19. | A. until<br>B. when<br>C. because<br>D. after | 24. | A. charged<br>B. arrested<br>C. accused<br>D. sentenced | 29. | A. account<br>B. basis<br>C. because<br>D. despite |
| 20. | A. down<br>B. behind<br>C. out<br>D. off | 25. | A innocence<br>B. sentence<br>C. box<br>D. case | 30. | A. behaved<br>B. conduct<br>C. luck<br>D. fortune |

### 15.6

## Grammar: using 'as'

'As' can have several different meanings. Be careful when you see 'As' at the start of a sentence. Find out what it means.

| Uses | Examples |
|---|---|
| as = while, when | **As** I was walking to school one day, I happened to find some money. |
| as = because | **As** it was raining, I took an umbrella with me. |
| work as (showing a person's occupation) | Boles **worked as** a clerk in a Wells Fargo office. |
| use as (showing similarity) | If you want to draw a straight line, you can **use** the edge of a book **as** a ruler. |
| the same ... as | Boles used **the same method** in his robberies **as** he had used in his first two hold-ups. |

| Uses | Examples |
|---|---|
| as if | It looks **as if** it is going to rain. |
| as + adjective or adverb + as | My friend is (not) **as tall as** I am. |
| as usual | Mick is late, **as usual**. |
| as well | Natoya went to the concert, and Deena went **as well**. |
| as a rule = normally | **As a rule**, Father comes home by six o'clock. |

 *Over to you!*

### Exercise 1

Look at the example for 'as' + adjective or adverb + 'as' above.
Make sentences based on the information below. Use 'not as' + an adjective + 'as'.

1. silver, gold (*heavy*)
2. St Lucia, Trinidad (*big*)
3. Guyana, Jamaica (*crowded*)
4. men, women (*honest*)
5. rivers, the sea (*deep*)
6. the moon, Earth (*suitable for life*)
7. most fish, sharks (*dangerous*)
8. a tropical storm, a hurricane (*powerful*)
9. Sean is 16. Anna is 14. (*young*)
10. lemons, oranges (*sour*)

## 15.7 Grammar: indirect questions (1)

There are two reasons why a knowledge of indirect questions is useful:
- Sometimes we want to report a question, e.g.
  *direct:* A woman asked me, 'Has the last bus gone?'
  *indirect:* The woman asked me if the last bus had gone.
- Many sentence patterns contain an indirect question, e.g.
  I wonder if the last bus has gone.
  We must find out what time the last bus goes.

### Guidelines

- Do not put a question mark after an indirect question unless it is part of a direct question, e.g.
  *no question mark:* The woman asked me **if the last bus has gone**.
  *with a question mark:* Do you know **if the last bus has gone?**
- Do not use inverted commas.
- Do not put a comma after the speech verb.

- Put the subject *before* the verb (and not in the middle of it or after it as in a direct question). Notice the word order:
  direct: Leela asked me, 'What's the time?'
  indirect: Leela asked me what the time was.
- Make any necessary changes in pronouns, possessive adjectives and words showing time or place, as in 14.7 on page 185.
- Move the tense of the verb back in time *if this is necessary*.

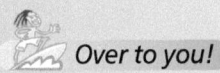 Over to you!

### Exercise 2

A few minutes ago, a girl asked you the questions below. Now somebody else wants to know what the girl asked you. Make indirect questions. Start with 'She asked me …'. It is not necessary to change the tenses but be careful with the order of the words, e.g.
  direct: 'What's the name of the girl with long hair?'
  indirect: She asked me what the name of the girl with long hair is.
  direct: 'What did the driver of the car say to you?'
  indirect: She asked me what the driver of the car said to me.

1. 'What's your name?'
2. 'Where do you live?'
3. 'When does the film start?'
4. 'Which CD do you want?'
5. 'What does Leela want?'
6. 'Who was sitting next to the driver?'
7. 'What's the score?'
8. 'What kind of bike did your brother buy?'
9. 'What did the referee say to you?'
10. 'How long does it take to get to Kingston?'

### Exercise 3

The situation is the same as in Exercise 2 but notice how we change these questions into indirect ones, e.g.
  direct: 'Are you still at school?'
  indirect: She asked me **if/whether** I am still at school.

  direct: 'Have you ever been to the States?'
  indirect: She asked me **if/whether** I have ever been to the USA.

Now change these questions into indirect ones. Start with 'She asked me …'.

1. Is your brother older than you?
2. Can you swim well?
3. Do you have an email address?
4. Is it going to rain tomorrow?
5. Have you spent all your money?
6. Do you know the answer to question 4?
7. Did you see the fire start?
8. Should I tell Kevin about the concert?
9. Are you related to Mrs Palmer?
10. Can I borrow your bike this weekend?

## 15.8

## Pronunciation: syllable stress

Many words can be used as a noun or verb:

- **nouns:** stress the *first* syllable, e.g. a ´rebel, an ´insult, e.g.
  It is an insult to call somebody a liar and a cheat.
- **verbs:** stress the *second* syllable, e.g. to re´bel, to in´sult, e.g.
  You may be arrested if you insult a police officer.

 *Over to you!*

1. Say these words:

   | Nouns | Verbs | Nouns | Verbs |
   |---|---|---|---|
   | a ´rebel | to re´bel | a ´decrease | to de´crease |
   | an ´insult | to in´sult | ´transport | to trans´port |
   | ´exports | to ex´port | a ´convert | to con´vert |
   | his ´conduct | to con´duct | ´imports | to im´port |
   | an ´increase | to in´crease | a ´contract | to con´tract |
   | a ´convict | to con´vict | a ´suspect | to sus´pect |

2. Say these sentences. Notice that the stress mark comes *before* the stressed syllable. (In some dictionaries, it comes after a stressed syllable.)
   a) Every week goods are ex´ported from the Caribbean in large con´tainers.
   b) One aim of missionaries is to con´vert people to their religion.
   c) The Government has just signed a ´contract to in´crease the size of the airport.
   d) After a long trial, three men were con´victed of smuggling drugs into the country. They will be de´ported after they have served their sentence.
   e) A ´convict is somebody who is im´prisoned for breaking the law.
   f) Changes in the price of oil often lead to an ´increase or a ´decrease in the cost of electricity. Companies are usually quicker to in´crease the cost than to de´crease it when the cost of oil changes.
   g) A ´suspect is somebody who the police think may be responsible for a crime. In some cases, they sus´pect a relative or acquaintance of a dead person.
   h) In some countries, people who re´bel against a government are called ´rebels by their enemies but ´patriots by their supporters.

## 15.9

## Pronunciation: the letter 'h'

- If the '**h**' at the start of a word is silent when we say the word, we use 'an' instead of 'a' before it, e.g.

  an hour    an honest man    an honour    an heiress    an heirloom
  a harbour    a very honest man    a house    a hurdle    a highway

- In the great majority of words, 'h' is pronounced at the beginning of a word. However, some words cause problems, so we can hear these words on television and in conversation:

  | a hotel | a history book | a herb |
  | an 'otel | a/an historical novel | an 'erb* |

- The letter 'h' is silent when we say these words:

  | vehicles | rhyme | rheumatism | honorary | silhouette |
  | verandah | rhythm | rhinoceros | exhume | exhibition |

*British people say 'a herb'. American people say 'an 'erb'.

## 15.10

## Grammar: indirect questions (2)

*Question:* Do we change tenses when we report questions?
*Answer:* It depends on the situation. Look at this example:

**On Friday morning,** Santok said to Daljit, 'Are you going to the game tomorrow?'
**On Friday evening,** somebody asked Daljit what Santok had said. He replied: 'She asked me if **I am** going to the game **tomorrow.**'
**On Saturday,** another person asked Daljit what Santok had said. He replied: 'She asked me if **I am** going to the game **today.**'
**On Monday.** a different person asked Daljit what Santok had said. He replied: 'She asked me if **I was** going to the game **last Saturday.**'

In most tests and examinations, we do not know the situation, so it is wise to change the tense of reported verbs (unless this changes the meaning).

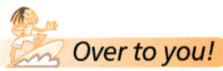

### Exercise 4

Change the following into reported (indirect) speech.

1. 'My watch has stopped,' Michelle said to Rick. 'What's the right time?'

2. 'I'm just going shopping,' Mrs Blake said to her husband. 'Is there anything I can get for you?'

3. 'How shall we get home if the car breaks down again and won't start?' Brian asked his father. 'There's a storm due tonight.'

4. 'My computer won't start,' Delroy said. 'Has anybody been playing games on it?'

5. 'What's Latoya's email address?' Natalie asked her brother. 'I wrote it down on a piece of paper but now I can't find the paper.'

6. 'Do you know anybody who wants to sell a computer?' Festus asked his sister. 'I'd like to buy one but I can't afford to buy a new one.'

7. 'Have you finished your homework yet?' Errol asked his sister. 'I'm waiting to watch a boxing show on TV.'

8. 'Did you see the car hit the cyclist?' Sgt Bennett asked me. 'Where were you standing when the accident happened?'

## 15.11
# Grammar: using 'used to'

We can use 'used to' to refer to a past action which was a habit but has now stopped. Then we pronounce 'used' in this way: /yoost/. Make sure that you do not leave off the 'd' at the end of 'used' in sentences like these:

Grandma **used to** live in Jamaica but now she lives in Florida.
Guyana and Trinidad **used to** be colonies but now they are independent countries.
I **used to** go to a primary school but now I go to a secondary school.

 Over to you!

### Exercise 5

Use the information in these sentences. Make up a new sentence containing 'used to' each time, e.g.

Suresh lived in Guyana for six years. Now he lives in Trinidad
*Suresh used to live in Guyana but now he lives in Trinidad.*

1. My father played football for several years. Now he plays badminton instead.

2. My family grew sugar cane here for many years. Now the land is needed for new homes.

3. Mrs Collins taught History for several years. Now she teaches English.

4. This district was very peaceful for many years. Now it is crowded and noisy.

5. Grandpa often played football when he was younger. He never plays now because he is too old.

6. Mr Dosman was a police officer for twenty years. Now he owns a shop.

7. Grandma drank coffee for many years. She never drinks it now because it keeps her awake at night.

8. There was a shop on this corner of the road for many years. There isn't one here now.

## 15.12
### Enjoying poetry

*For My Mother*
*(May I Inherit Half Her Strength)*

My mother loved my father.
I write this as an <u>absolute</u>      indisputable fact
in this my thirtieth year –
the year to <u>discard absolutes</u>.    stop being
                                        absolutely certain
5   He appeared, her fate disguised,   about things
    as a Sunday player in a cricket match.
    He had ridden from a country
    one hundred miles south of hers.

    She tells me he dressed the part:
10  visiting dandy, maroon blazer
    cream serge pants, seam like razor,
    and the beret and the two-tone shoes.

    My father stopped to speak to her sister,
    till he looked and saw her by the oleander,
15  sure in the kingdom of my blue-eyed grandmother.
    He never played the cricket match that day.

    He wooed her with words and he won her.
    He had nothing but words to woo her.
    On a visit to distant Kingston he wrote,
20  'I stood on the corner of King Street and looked,
    and not one woman in that town was lovely as you.'

…

    When he died, she sewed dark dresses for the women among us,
    and she summoned that walk, straight-backed, that she gave to us
    and buried him dry-eyed.

25   Just that morning, weeks after
      she stood delivering bananas from their skin
      singing in that flat hill country voice,
      she fell down a note to the realization that she did
      not have to be brave, just this once
30   and she cried.

      For her hands grown coarse with raising nine children
      for her body for twenty years permanently fat
      for the time she pawned her <u>machine</u> for my sister's   **sewing-machine**
      Senior Cambridge fees
35   and for the pain she bore with the eyes of a queen
      and she cried also because she loved him.

*Lorna Goodison*

This is only about half of the original poem. The missing lines describe the wedding of the poet's parents and then describe both parents.

## Questions

1. In line 5, what was 'her fate'?

2. Look at lines 7 and 8. Then look at line 19, where Kingston is described as being 'distant'. Then look at line 15 – 'in the kingdom of my blue-eyed grandmother'. Where, perhaps, did the Sunday cricket match take place?

3. What evidence is there in the poem to support the expression 'visiting dandy'? (Justify the use of *each* word.)

4. What is the meaning of 'seam like razor'? What figure of speech is this?

5. In line 23, suggest a reason why the poet chose to write 'summoned that walk' instead of saying 'walked'.

6. Is the poem meant to be a tribute to the poet's father or to her mother, as far as we can tell from this extract?

## 15.13
## Writing

Write about 250–350 words about *one* of the following topics:

1. Look at the last paragraph of the passage about Black Bart in 15.2. Then finish the story in a different way. Make up information about what happened to Bart after he was released from prison. Your account can have a happy, unhappy or boring ending. You can use a first-person narrative (pretending to be Bart) or a third-person narrative.

*English Alive!*

*or*

2. You are a lawyer taking part in the trial of Black Bart. He has confessed to the robberies and has pleaded 'Guilty' in court. Choose *one* of these roles:
   a) As the prosecution lawyer, write a speech to the court, saying why Bart should be dealt with severely. *or*
   b) As the lawyer defending Bart, write a speech urging the court to be lenient and giving reasons for leniency.

*or*

3. What effect, if any, does crime in your own country have on you and/or your family?

## 15.14

## Uncountable nouns (revision)

We call these words *uncountable* (or *mass*) nouns. They have **no plural form** and we use a **singular** verb with them.

| blood | gold  | traffic   | luggage   | thunder   | punctuation |
| bread | rice  | scenery   | baggage   | firewood  | information |
| dirt  | mud   | fiction   | evidence  | rainfall  | homework    |
| dust  | music | dictation | furniture | lightning | housework   |
| fun   | smoke | equipment | knowledge | rubbish   | stationery  |

Use 'a little' and '(not) much' before an uncountable noun.
Use '(a) few)' and '(not) many' before a countable noun.

### Exercise 6

Choose the right words from the brackets.

1. We're lucky. We don't have (many, much) homework today.
2. We just have a (few, little) Maths problems to solve.
3. There (are, is) not (many, much) traffic on the road at night.
4. There (are, is) only a (few, little) cars after midnight.
5. We don't need (many, much) new furniture in this room.
6. There (is, are) not (many, much) old chairs in our house.
7. Uncle did not bring (many, much) cases with him.
8. There (is, are) not (many, much) luggage to put in the car.
9. Last night there (was, were) not (many, much) lightning (or, nor) thunder.
10. The rain did not cause (many, much) flooding in our district.

# 16 Tantie's Tooth

### 16.1
## Pre-reading

The passage in 16.2 is an extract from *Crick Crack, Monkey* by Merle Hodge. It describes a time when a young girl went shopping with her aunt at a village shop. The shop is owned by Ling, who has a young son, Henry.

The passage starts when Tantie arrives at Ling's shop on a weekly shopping trip.

### 16.2
## Reading

### Tantie's Tooth

Almost every Friday night there was a friendly exchange between Tantie and Ling on the subject of honesty: 'Ling, yu too thief, man, oh Gord, it never had a Chinee man thief like you!' Ling's reply was always good-natured: 'Me no thief, Miss Lrosa, all we got to live, no?' and the beam that creased his eyes and his whole
5   face would almost conquer Tantie.

Ling still spoke what was to us a rather quaint pidgin. His wife spoke nothing at all (only Chinese) – she mostly held the fat baby, smiled amiably and helped Ling pack groceries. It was Henry, who was a miniature Ling and who was known as The Doc, who stepped into the breach when customer complaints took on a more
10   involved nature. Even in the rum-shop he would face ominous rum-soaked companies of men, separated from them by only a flimsy plank of a counter, and coldly argue the morality of a three-cents rise on the price of a flask.

There was one time when Tantie felt herself more than bearably hard done by in the matter of groceries. The salt-fish was mostly bone, there were *three* nails in the
15   chicken-feed, and the last straw came when, biting into a crisp warm slice of bake, she heard a horrible crunch and spat out a lily-white pebble, accompanied by a lily-white front tooth.

That Friday night when we walked into the shop customers moved aside so that Tantie could march straight up to the counter, and silence fell. This was due as
20   much to the fact that they were familiar with the indiscriminate nature of Tantie's wrath as to the fact that a lil noise was always welcome on a Friday-night-in-the-shop, and a lil noise involving Tantie was sure to be one of the highest order.

206   *English Alive!*

Tantie had in her hand a paper bag containing three nails, the stone-hard remnants of a bake, a pebble and a tooth. Ling seemed to duck a few inches when he saw her coming. He started to beam in advance. Tantie grimly untwisted the paper bag and turned it upside down on the counter. The contents rolled out, the tooth lurching away from the other objects. There was a burst of laughter, quickly repressed as Tantie turned and glared at the assembled company. She turned again to the business in hand.

'What yu t'ink o' all that, Ling?' she inquired.

'How yu mean, Miss Lrosa?' asked Ling, his eyes darting nervously from the display on the counter to Tantie's face and realising with dismay that it was not a situation to be beamed out of.

'Come Ling, do' play stupid here for me now, because you an' I know yu blasted smart! What all this was doin' in the goods? Watch that big-stone dey an' watch mih mout'!' and Tantie leaned over the counter and bared her front teeth at him, causing him to start violently; there was another burst of hilarity and while Tantie turned to glare Ling took the opportunity of hurrying out into the back of the shop in search of Henry. Henry emerged, a few paces in front of his father, bespectacled and with a pencil stuck behind his ear, looking like a preoccupied scholar annoyed at the interruption.

'Well yu could jus' send he back. I ain' come to argue wid a lil chile; go back an' do yu home-lesson, dou-dou.'

But only Tantie would conceive of calling Henry dou-dou, for you might just as well walk up and pat the Judge on the head. Ling was talking to him in Chinese, pointing at the little pile on the counter. Henry continued to look unimpressed.

'Ah say sen 'im back – yu wouldn' like me say a bad-word in front o' yu chile?'

Ling did not catch this and Henry translated rapidly for him – their eyes exchanged an amused twinkle.

'Ah, Miss Lrosa,' beamed Ling, glad of the diversion, 'my son Henry he know all bad-word already!'

'Awright, awright, wha 'bout mih teet' way fall-out?'

'Yu sure it ain' goods yu buy up the road, Miss Rosa?' Henry put the question mildly.

'Goods I buy up the road yu father head! Is now I going an buy goods up the road!'

And though we stormed out and marched up to Ramsaran, for the whole time that we traded up there Tantie always reminded me to pass in the back street, or we sneaked past Ling's door like thieves. When we went back to Ling it was the Friday night after Uncle Herman had sent Tantie to get her gold tooth put in. Tantie was in the best of humour, flashing smiles all around.

'Ah! Miss Lrosa! So yu come-back from the country!' beamed Ling, with his eyes creased in joy.

'Yes, man,' said Tantie: then leaning across the counter she confided to him in a thunderous whisper, 'You pigtail sweeter!'

Ling beamed on and nodded steadily throughout the bewildering burst of hilarity.

## 16.3
### Understanding

Answer these questions about the passage.

1. According to the first paragraph, how did Tantie often attack Ling? How did he defend himself?

2. What was Henry's role in his father's shop?

3. In line 20, we are told that customers at the shop were 'familiar with the indiscriminate nature of Tantie's wrath'.
   a) What does this tell us about Tantie?
   b) What did the customers do as a result?

4. What probably made Ling realise that Tantie's visit to the shop was 'not a situation to be beamed out of' (lines 32–33)? How did he try to get out of it?

5. What did Tantie do to try to prevent Ling from knowing that she had gone to a different shop? Why did she do it?

6. What did Tantie *really* think of Ling?

7. In the passage find at least two examples of the humorous style of the author.

## 16.4
### Vocabulary: meaning in context

**A** Choose the word(s) which best show(s) the meaning of the underlined words as they are used in the passage in 16.2.

1. Ling still spoke what was to us a rather quaint pidgin. (line 6)
   A. uneducated.
   B. quite attractive
   C. very difficult to understand
   D. unusual or old-fashioned but amusing

2. His wife … smiled amiably (line 7)
   A. mechanically
   B. in a friendly way
   C. without understanding the reason
   D. trying to impress other people

3. when customer complaints took on a more involved nature (line 10)
   A. complicated    B. hostile    C. prejudiced    D. distasteful

4. he would face ominous rum-soaked companies of men (line 10)
   A. potentially troublesome
   B. likely to bring bad luck
   C. angry because of drink
   D. hostile and dangerous

5. a flimsy plank of a counter (line 11)
   A. narrow    B. thin and weak    C. short and unbalanced    D. broken

208  *English Alive!*

6. coldly argue the morality of a three-cents rise (line 12)
   A. priorities    B. correctness    C. factors    D. consequences

7. Tantie felt herself more than bearably hard done by (line 13)
   A. dealt with wrongly        C. cheated out of money
   B. almost overlooked         D. not given sufficient attention

**B** Match the underlined words with the meanings which they have in the passage.

| Words from the passage | Meanings |
|---|---|
| 1. the indiscriminate nature (line 20) | a) got out of by smiling alone |
| 2. nature of Tantie's wrath (line 21) | b) distraction |
| 3. quickly repressed as Tantie turned (line 28) | c) noisy laughing and joking |
| 4. a situation to be beamed out of (line 33) | d) look angrily at somebody |
| 5. another burst of hilarity (line 37) | e) considerable anger |
| 6. Tantie turned to glare (line 38) | f) came out |
| 7. Henry emerged (line 39) | g) think |
| 8. a preoccupied scholar (line 40) | h) not aimed at a particular person only |
| 9. Tantie would conceive of calling (line 44) | i) stifled |
| 10. glad of the diversion (line 50) | j) busy thinking about something and not well aware of other matters |

### 16.5
# Punctuation: using an exclamation mark

We can use an **exclamation mark** (or 'point') to show strong emotion, e.g.

| | |
|---|---|
| pain: | Ow! That hurts! |
| joy: | Welcome, Tantie! Come in! |
| a need for help: | Help! Help! |
| getting attention: | Hey! |
| revulsion: | Ugh! What a horrible sight! |
| affection: | I love you! |
| admiration: | What a beautiful ring! |
| anger: | How dare you deny that! |

 **Over to you!**

Exercise 1

Find as many exclamation marks as possible in the passage in 16.2. In each case, say what emotion is shown.

## 16.6
## Writing: developing character in a story

These are some of the ways in which a writer can develop the character of people in a story:

- by describing the person's **clothes**
- by describing the person's **face and body**
- by describing the person's **movements**, especially the way he/she walks
- by letting the person's **speech** reveal his/her character
- by making the person's **actions** reveal something about his/her character
- by revealing what **other people** say about, or do to a person, or how they react to him or her.

To use these methods, a writer has to choose the right adjectives, adverbs and verbs.

 Over to you!

### Exercise 2

1. Make a list of every piece of information (in 16.2) which helps the reader to form a picture of Ling in his/her mind.

2. Similarly, make a list of all the information about Henry.

### Exercise 3

1. What do we learn about Tantie from these words and expressions?
   a) the shop customers **moved aside** (line 18)
   b) Tantie could **march** straight up to the counter (line 19)
   c) the **indiscriminate nature** of Tantie's **wrath** (line 20)
   d) a lil noise involving Tantie was sure to be **of the highest order** (line 22)
   e) Tantie **grimly** untwisted the paper bag (line 25)
   f) Tantie **glared** at the assembled company (line 28)

2. Find more words or expressions which help to reveal Tantie's character.

## 16.7
## Discussion: would you like to be an author?

Perhaps one day you will be a famous author. What qualities does an author need? How can you get those qualities?

## 16.8
## Vocabulary: changing dialect to standard English

When you change dialect into standard English, a word-for-word translation will often be inadequate. You may have to change the original sentence structure, add words and omit words, e.g.

*dialect:* Ling, yu too thief, man, oh Gord, it never had a Chinee man thief like you!

*standard English:* Ling, you really are too dishonest, man. God! There never was a Chinese man as dishonest as you!

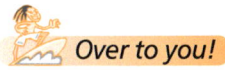 **Over to you!**

### Exercise 4

Change the following into standard English. Use correct punctuation.

1. Me no thief, Miss Lrosa, all we got to live, no? (lines 3–4)

2. What yu t'ink o' all that, Ling? (line 30)

3. Come Ling, do' play stupid here for me now, because you an' I know yu blasted smart! What all this was doin' in the goods? Watch tha big-stone dey an' watch mih mout'! (lines 34–6)

4. Well yu could jus' send he back. I ain' come to argue wid a lil chile; go back an' do yu home-lesson, dou-dou. (lines 42–3)

5. Yu sure it ain' goods yu buy up the road, Miss Rosa? (line 53)

## 16.9

## Grammar: correcting common errors

### Exercise 5

There is one mistake in each of the following. Find the mistakes and correct them. Notice that they may be mistakes of punctuation, use of capital letters or grammar.

1. When we were walking across the park, we saw a old man fast asleep under a tree.

2. A good dictionary can provide us with information on the meaning and derivation of a word, as well as its correct spelling and pronunciation.

3. After the shock of the bad news, Grandpa was trembling so bad that he could hardly tell us what had happened.

4. Do you remember them days when we used to fish in the river with your uncle?

5. The policeman asked the witness if he could identify the driver but the man shook he head and said, 'No, I can't.'

6. We followed the path for nearly a mile, it led us to a stream with an old wooden bridge across it.

7. What will you do if the landlord don't agree to let you build an extension at the rear of the house?

8. My friend and I was very excited when we saw the results of the examinations.

9. Every christmas, we have a big dinner and most of our relatives come to it.

10. When I was younger, my grandmother use to tell me stories about her life many years ago.

11. In some rural areas, you can see a number of abandon houses not far from the road.

12. The woman wanted to know how often do the buses go to the airport.

Exercise 6

There is one mistake in each of the following. Find the mistakes and correct them.

1. Many years ago, it had a shop over there but now it has disappeared.

2. Small boats cannot go very far from land when bad whether comes, so the local fishermen suffer and do not earn much money.

3. Last week our refridgerator broke down, so we had to get somebody to find out what was wrong with it.

4. The children swam and played in the sea for nearly an hour. When they came out, they were annoyed to discover that there shoes had disappeared. Somebody had stolen them.

5. Last night it had a very exciting film on television. It was about aliens who landed on Earth and started to control people's minds.

6. My best friends name is Claudia Smith. She lives about a hundred yards from our house, so we always go to school together.

7. A national hero is a person who does not accept nothing but the best, and who always has high principles.

8. If you want to succeed in cricket, tennis or any other sport, you must be determine and learn all the skills needed for success.

9. We stared at the ruins of the building. The walls were dirty and had graffiti scribbled all over it. There were holes in the roof and even in two of the walls.

10. Although the rain became heavier and heavier, the referee didn't stopped the game, so we played on until the end of the normal 90 minutes.

11. When Mr Edwards did not return at his usual time, his wife wondered what might of happened to delay him. As time passed, she grew steadily more worried.

12. We went to the airport to meet Uncle but we had to wait three hours because his plain had been delayed and was not due to arrive until nearly 6 p.m.

# 16.10
## Understanding: comparing pie charts

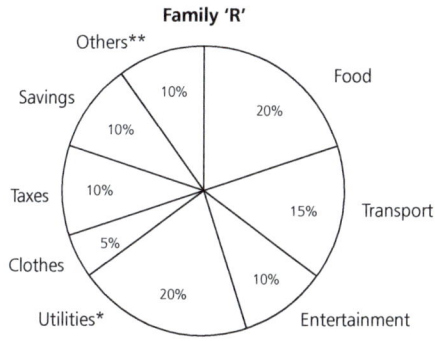
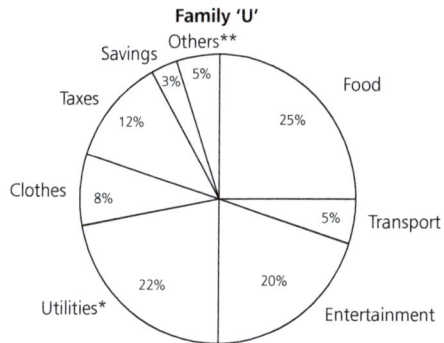

Study the pie charts. They show what percentage of annual income two families – Family R, a rural family, and Family U, an urban family – spend on various things such as food and transport. Each family contains the same number of people. Their ages are similar.

Now answer these questions:

1. Suggest two reasons why Family U spends more on food than Family R does.

2. If you compare the amounts spent on transport, what do you notice? Explain why there is a difference.

3. If Family U earns twice as much in a year as Family R, will Family U save more money or less money than Family R?

4. Suggest a reason why Family U spends more money on clothes than Family R.

5. 'Family U ____ spends more on electricity than Family R does.' Which of these words can we truthfully put in the blank space: 'definitely', 'always', 'never', 'perhaps', 'reluctantly', 'gladly', 'possibly'?

6. Make an accurate sentence comparing the amount which each family spends on entertainment each year. Then make another sentence trying to explain the difference in the amounts spent.

7. What do both families get in return for paying their taxes?

8. Imagine that you are the person who has to make important decisions in *one* of the two families. For various reasons, the income of the family is about to fall sharply, so you need to make some economies. In which areas should the family spend less money in future?

## 16.11

# Grammar: adjective or adverb? (revision)

| Adjectives | Adverbs |
| --- | --- |
| Nadia is a **good** singer. | Nadia can sing **well**. |
| Miss Dixon looked **angry**. | She spoke **angrily**. |
| Neville is a **careful** worker. | He always works **carefully**. |
| This job is **temporary**. | He is working here **temporarily**. |

Exercise 7

Choose the right words from the brackets.

1. Sandra waited (nervous, nervously) for her turn to see the dentist.
2. Mr Moktar looks (sad, sadly) but his wife looks quite (happy, happily).
3. We all waited (patient, patiently) for a bus to come.
4. (Lucky, Luckily) for us, the bus was not full.
5. Brush your hair before you go out! It looks very (untidy, untidily).
6. That man is a (careless, carelessly) driver and has been fined in the past for driving (reckless, recklessly).
7. The police investigated the complaint (thorough, thoroughly) and came to the conclusion that it had been made (malicious, maliciously).
8. Michelle became (suspicious, suspiciously) when she saw two men taking furniture from a neighbour's home. The men looked (suspicious, suspiciously) to her, so she phoned the police (quick, quickly).
9. Pathma was delighted when her application for a job was (successful, successfully).
10. The two men on the raft stared (hopeful, hopefully) at the horizon.
11. Tantie glared at Ling (angry, angrily) and demanded to know how three nails had got into the food. Ling beamed at Tantie (cheerful, cheerfully) and pretended that he did not understand her.
12. Henry greeted Tantie (polite, politely) and listened to her complaint in a (respectful, respectfully) manner before replying.

## 16.12

## Grammar: using the right preposition

### Exercise 8

Correct any mistakes in the use of prepositions and other words in these sentences.

1. There has been no improvement of his work this year.
2. He has been absent at school in many occasions this year.
3. Hitting another player deliberately is contrary the rules of the game.
4. Grandpa was annoyed at himself for losing his watch again.
5. Uncle will return from Florida in October the tenth.
6. Most of the men in the crowd were supporters to the Government.
7. Now let us consider the influence of Africa and Asia to the West.
8. This morning the bus was crowded of people going to work.
9. Can you give me the answers of these queries?
10. As a result of the new industries, the demand of labour has increased.

### Exercise 9

Put in suitable words.

1. My friend lives … the outskirts of the town and comes to school … bus.
2. Mohan felt ashamed … himself when his mother found … that he was telling lies.
3. There is a vacancy … a waiter at the Rex Hotel, so my cousin is going to apply … the job.
4. One of the guests complained … the manager … the food.
5. He said he was not satisfied … the way the food was cooked and disliked the way … which it was served.
6. The heavy rain prevented us … going out and forced Obi to find some way … keeping himself busy at home.
7. The car came round the corner … high speed and collided … a stationary lorry.
8. Do you take me … a fool? I know what tricks you are … to.
9. John has been ill … five days but is … the road to recovery now.
10. It is difficult to repair a television set … the help … an IT expert.

## 16.13

### Enjoying poetry

Read this poem written in the dialect of Barbados. What impression do you get of 'yuh ole muddah'?

## Letter to England

Girl chile darling yuh ole muddah hay
Praisin' de Lord fuh 'E blessing an' 'E mercies
You is many many blessin's an' all o' me mercies
Glory to God!
5   Uh get de 5 pound an' de Christmas card
God bless yuh!
But de carpenter ain' come to put on de shed-roof
So uh spen' it an uh sen' Rosy pretty to de
Exhibition gal, yuh should see she!
10   Next month when yuh sen me allowance again,
We will see wuh kin happen in de name o' de Lord.
De Cashmere sweater dat yuh sen' muh so soft
An so warm, uh kin nevah fuget muh
Poor li'l' chile. Sister Reed can'
15   Brag pun me like before, tink she one got
Daughter in England? Uh wear um down to
Service t'ree Sunday mornin' straight an'
Den all bout de place fuh to show dem
I en common, but Lord I haffa tell yuh
20   Dat it ketch 'pon a nial in de kitchen, so,
Bless you love don' f'get to sen' aneddah one.
Uh paint up de place an' varnish de furnitures
An' Lord mek peace dat t'ief charge muh so
High dat I ain't got a cent lef' to brighten
25   Muh face, so de Lord will bless yuh
Don' fo'get you ole muddah, lonely
An' t'ankful, wukkin' she finger to de
Bone, she soul case droppin' out. Wuh law!
I does pray day an' night fuh yuh
30   Come back child, I does, I does grieve but
De Lord unde'stand, I closes now
Wid love an' gratitude, care yuhself
Doan le' da man dat yuh married
To upset yuh, le' de Lord
35   An' yuh poor ole muddah keep a
Place in yuh heart. Amen. Amen.

*Bruce St John*

### Questions

1. How would you describe the attitude of the poet to his topic?

2. Why does the mother mention the shed-roof, the Cashmere sweater and painting her home?

3. Why did the mother say: 'Don' fo'get you ole muddah'?

4. Suggest a reason why the poet spells 'forget' in different ways (in lines 13, 21 and 26).

5. Pretend that you are the daughter mentioned in the poem. Make up 5–10 lines of poetry in any dialect in reply to 'yuh ole muddah'. Thank her for her letter and enclose 5 pounds.

### 16.14
# Writing

Write about 250–350 words on *one* of the following topics:

1. Describe a visit you have made to a dentist *or* one which somebody else made.

or

2. Does Tantie, Ling or Henry remind you of somebody you know? If so, describe the person and your contacts with her or him. (Your answer can be based on truth or it can be a product of your imagination.)

or

3. Imagine that you are Henry Ling. You have recently discovered that although Uncle Herman sent Tantie to get a gold tooth put in her mouth, it was your father who paid the bill. In your private diary (or journal) at home, write an account of the incident with Tantie and her tooth. Write in the first person because you are Henry.

# Appendix 1: Learning About Verbs

## Verb forms

### Infinitive

| | | |
|---|---|---|
| **Present active:** | (to) help | Mary likes **to help** people. |
| **Present passive:** | (to) be helped | Mrs Harris needs **to be helped**. |
| **Perfect active:** | (to) have helped | We ought **to have helped** that old man. |
| **Perfect passive:** | (to) have been helped | He might **have been helped** by Susan. |

### Present participle

**Active form:** helping
**Passive form:** being helped

*Examples:* Stella watched some men **helping** to find a leak in a water-pipe.
After the crash, we saw a passenger **being helped** from the damaged car.

### Past participle

helped

*Example:* **Helped** by a strong wind, the yacht soon finished the race.

### Perfect participle

**Active form:** having helped
**Passive form:** having been helped

*Examples:* **Having helped** his team by scoring two goals, Peter was very happy when the final whistle blew.
**Having been helped** a lot by two teachers at his school, Bob went on to become one of the finest batsmen in the Caribbean.

### Gerund

| | | |
|---|---|---|
| **Active form:** | helping | breaking |
| **Passive form:** | being helped | being broken |

A **gerund** is a noun made from a verb. It is often called a 'verbal noun', so it is not really a verb form. Unlike other nouns, a gerund can have an object, e.g.

**Helping** other people is an excellent thing to do.
Caribbean athletes like **breaking** world records.
Sometimes young children dislike **being helped** because they want to do something on their own..
When a hurricane approaches, many people put boards or shutters over their windows to stop them from **being broken.**

## Tenses

There are a number of tenses in English. Some tenses can be:
*active*: Mrs Harris often **helps** other people.
*passive*: Many people **are helped** by friends or relatives.
*continuous (progressive)*: Today Mrs Harris **is helping** a neighbour to make a wedding cake.

Grammarians sometimes use different names for the same tense, so you may find alternatives to some of the names used below. For example, some grammarians use 'progressive' instead of 'continuous'.

| Tense | Examples using 'to kick' | |
|---|---|---|
| | **Active form** | **Passive form** |
| Simple Present | I kick | I am kicked |
| Present Continuous | I am kicking | I am being kicked |
| Past Continuous | I was kicking | I was being kicked |
| Simple Past | I kicked | I was kicked |
| Present Perfect | I have kicked | I have been kicked |
| Present Perfect Continuous | I have been kicking | – |
| Past Perfect | I had kicked | I had been kicked |
| Past Perfect Continuous | I had been kicking | – |
| Simple Future | I shall/will kick | I shall/will be kicked |
| Future Continuous | I shall be kicking | – |
| Future Perfect | I shall have kicked | I shall have been kicked |
| Future Perfect Continuous | I shall have been kicking | – |
| Present Conditional | I should kick | I should be kicked |
| Present Conditional Continuous | I should be kicking | – |
| Perfect Conditional | I should have kicked | I should have been kicked |
| Perfect Conditional Continuous | I should have been kicking | – |

See Appendix 2 for the main uses of the more common tenses. For more about 'active' and 'passive', see 'Voice' on page 220.

## Transitive and intransitive verbs

A **transitive verb** is one which has an object. An **intransitive verb** does *not* have an object. Many verbs can be used transitively or intransitively. In many dictionaries, the letters *v.i.* (verb intransitive) or *v.t.* (verb transitive) show whether a verb is transitive or not.

*transitive:*    Sometimes Sharma sings old Hindi songs. *(with an object)*
*intransitive:*  Sharma can sing beautifully. *(no object)*

Common intransitive verbs include 'be', 'go', 'lie', 'seem' and 'appear'.

## Finite and non-finite (infinite) verbs

We can say that a **finite verb** is a working verb. It has a subject and is used in a tense, e.g.

   It **started** to rain when we **were walking** home.
   Peter **will help** you repair the puncture in that tyre.

A **non-finite verb** is not used with a subject. It may be an infinitive or a participle. In the above examples, 'to rain' and 'repair' are infinitives. In the second example, we can use 'repair' or 'to repair' after the verb 'help'.

> **Punctuation note**: A sentence must contain at least one finite verb with a subject. We *cannot punctuate* the following expressions as sentences. They do not contain a finite verb with a subject.
>    . . . walking down the road yesterday evening at about half past five
>    . . . damaged during the storm two days ago and left at the side of the road

## Voice

We can use most verbs in the **active voice** or in the **passive voice**.
When a verb is used in the **active voice**, the subject does the action, e.g.

   A careless motorist **injured** an elderly cyclist.
   Somebody **stole** John's bicycle during the night.

When a verb is used in the **passive voice**, the action is done *to* the subject and not *by* it. We often use a passive verb when we do not know (or do not care) who did the action, e.g.

   An elderly cyclist **was injured** by a careless motorist.
   John's bicycle **was stolen** during the night.
   A lot of sugar **is exported** to other countries.
   The two men who escaped from prison **have been recaptured.**

## Mood

### Indicative mood

We say that a verb is in the indicative mood if it is used to make a statement or a question, e.g.

   Many tourists **visit** the Caribbean every year.
   Sometimes lightning **hits** a tree and **starts** a fire.

## Imperative mood

The imperative mood is used for orders, commands or prayers, e.g.
> **Stop** making a noise! **Get on** with your work!

## Subjunctive mood

We say that a verb is in the subjunctive mood if it expresses doubt or (sometimes) a wish, e.g.
> If I **were** you, I wouldn't buy that old bicycle.
> If Uncle **were** here now, he would know what to do.
> I wish we **lived** nearer to my school.

## Auxiliary verbs

Verbs such as 'be', 'do', 'have', 'may', 'shall' and 'will' help to form the tenses of other verbs, e.g. 'it is raining', 'he has gone', 'they do not live here'. We can call these verbs **auxiliary** (or helping) **verbs** when they are used in this way.

# Appendix 2: The Main Uses of Tenses

## The Simple Present tense

**Active forms:**  I like, he likes
I do like, he does like

**Negatives:**

| I, They | do not | grow vegetables. | She | does not | live here. |
| You, We | don't | live near Mohan. | He, It | doesn't | like meat. |

**Questions:**
Do I/we/you/they know him?        Does he/she/it drink milk?

The form with 'do' and 'does' is also used when we want to emphasise a statement, e.g.
Oh! I **do** like your new shoes! Where **did** you get them?

Paul: Are you sure that Ajmir lives in this road? I thought he'd gone to the UK.
Jane: That's not true. He **does** still live here. His sister told me that yesterday.

**Passive form:** 'am', 'is' or 'are' + a past participle. It is used when the action is done to the subject and not by the subject, e.g.
More than 100 people **are employed** in this factory. They **are paid** every week.

## Uses

The main use of the Simple Present tense is for actions which are habits, routine or are always true. This tense is sometimes used for actions happening at the time of speaking and for some past and future actions, as shown below:

*continuous* (in a sports commentary):    Smith runs up and bowls. It's a bouncer. Lara steps forward and hits it hard.
*past actions* (in a history time chart): 1939:    Germany invades Poland. WW2 starts.
1945:    Germany surrenders. WW2 ends.
*past actions* (in a news headline): HELICOPTER SAVES FOUR.
*future actions:*  Uncle leaves for Miami tomorrow and returns on Saturday.
If it rains tomorrow, our game will be postponed.
When Auntie arrives, show her that letter.

## The Present Continuous tense

**Active form:** 'am', 'is' or 'are' + a present participle.

| Statements | | | | Questions | | |
|---|---|---|---|---|---|---|
| I | am | (not) | waiting for Errol. | Am | I | doing this correctly? |
| He/She/It | is | (not) | eating now. | Is | he/she/it | waiting for Ann? |
| We/You | are | (not) | listening to him. | Are | you/we | doing this correctly? |
| They | are | (not) | waiting for you. | Are | they | waiting for Ann? |

## Uses

The main uses of this tense are:
- for a temporary action which is happening at the time of speaking, e.g.
    Now I **am reading** this book. Deena **is looking** out of the window.
- for planned future actions, especially connected with movement or travel, e.g.
    Auntie **is coming** to visit us tomorrow. She **is bringing** Vimala with her.

**Passive form:** 'am/is/are' + 'being' + a past participle, e.g.
    We can't use Room 6 this week. It **is being redecorated**.
    Grandpa **is being discharged** from hospital this afternoon.

## The Past Continuous tense

**Active form:** 'was/were' + a present participle, e.g.
    It started to rain when we **were playing** football.
    What **were** you **doing** when the lights went out?
    **Was** Francine **waiting** for you when you got off the bus?

**Passive form:** 'was/were being' + a past participle, e.g.
    The house caught fire while it **was being redecorated**.
    Two of the men tried to escape when their car **was being searched**.
    **Was** the road still **being repaired** when you went into town this morning?

## Uses

The main use of this tense is to show what was happening at some past time. It is also used when we report a speech containing a verb in the Present Continuous tense, e.g.
    *direct:*    'Pa is leaving for Miami tomorrow,' Mrs Swaby told her children.
    *indirect:*  Mrs Swaby told her children that their father **was leaving** for Miami the next day.

## The Simple Past tense

**Active form:**   he helped, he did help      we went, we did go
**Negatives:**     he did not help             we did not go
**Questions:**     did he help                 did we go

## Uses

The main use of this tense is to show a completed past action. Notice that this tense has *two* forms: 'helped' and 'did help'.

We can use the form with 'did' to show emphasis. It is also used for negatives and questions, e.g.

You have a poor memory, Lloyd. I'm sure Paul **did go** fishing last Saturday. **I saw** him coming home with his fishing-rod. You **spoke** to him.

Paul: Who **repaired** your shirt for you?
John: Sylvia **did**.

> **Reminders:**
> - Don't use the Simple *Present* tense for a completed past action. In most cases, use the Simple *Past* tense.
> - After 'not', use the infinitive form of a verb and *not* the Simple Past form:
>   *wrong:* We did not went swimming yesterday.
>   *right:* We did not **go** swimming yesterday.

**Passive form:** 'was/were (not)' + a past participle, e.g.
Several trees **were blown** down during the storm but, luckily for us, our house **was not damaged**.
**Was** anybody **injured** in the accident? **Were** both cars completely **wrecked**?

## The Present Perfect tense

**Active form:** 'has/have' + a past participle, e.g.
Mitzie: What**'s happened**? (= What **has happened**?)
Sonia: There**'s been** an accident. (= There **has been** an accident.)
**Have** you **finished** your homework yet?
Uncle **hasn't written** to us for nearly a month.

## Uses

This tense is often used for an action which happened recently. Then we do *not* say the exact time or date of the past action. If we want to say the time or date, we have to use the Simple Past tense and *not* the Present Perfect tense. Compare these sentences:

*wrong:* Thank you for your letter which I have received yesterday.
*right:* Thank you for your letter which I received yesterday.
*right:* Thank you for the parcel which has just arrived.
*right:* Thank you for the parcel which arrived a few minutes ago.

**Passive form:** 'has/have been' + a past participle, e.g.
The road outside our school **has** just **been repaired**.
**Have** all your answers **been checked**?
Uncle's car **has** not **been cleaned** for several days.

## The Past Perfect tense

**Active form:** 'had (not)' + a past participle
**Passive form:** 'had (not) been' + a past participle

## Uses

The main use of this tense is to make quite clear which of two past actions happened first, e.g.
>When we reached Rosa's house, we found that she **had gone** out already.
>Brian told us that he **had lost** some money, so we helped him to look for it.
>The man on the phone told us that Father's car was not ready. He said that the mechanic **had** not yet **finished** the repairs.
>**Had** the goalkeeper **been sent** off before you reached the stadium?

The Past Perfect tense is often used when we report a speech containing a verb in the Simple Past or Present Perfect tense, e.g.
>*direct:* 'I've just arrived from Florida,' the woman told us.
>*indirect:* The woman told us that she **had** just **arrived** from Florida.

## The Simple Future tense

**Active form:** 'shall/will' + an infinitive without 'to'
**Passive form:** 'shall/will be' + a past participle

## Uses

We can use the Simple Future tense for both planned and unplanned future actions. Some people prefer to use 'shall' when the subject is 'I' or 'we', but we can use 'will' with any subject except in questions. Then we often use 'Shall' before 'I' and 'we', e.g.
>**Shall** I **turn** the light on?
>**Shall** we **go** swimming this evening?
>Who **will win** the 200 metres race?
>Grandad wants to know when he **will be told** the results of the X-ray?

**Note:** If there is some doubt about a future action, we can use 'may' (or 'might') instead of 'will' or 'shall', e.g.
>It **may rain** during the night.
>If you break the law, you **may be caught**. Then you **may be sent** to prison.
>One day I **may be** a doctor or a nurse.

## The Future Perfect tense

**Active:** 'shall/will have' + a past participle
**Passive:** 'shall/will have been' + a past participle

## Uses

We use this tense to refer to something which will be done or finished by the time of speaking or by some future time, e.g.

Uncle left on the six o'clock plane, so he **will have reached** Miami by now.
Those two men who escaped from prison **will** probably **have been arrested** by the time it gets dark.

## Pronouncing verbs which end in '-ed'

Some students do not pronounce the consonant sound at the end of a verb in the Simple Past tense, e.g. the /d/ at the end of 'turned' or the /t/ at the end of 'laughed'. Make sure that you pronounce the final sound at the end of a verb. Do not write the Simple Present form of a verb when you write about past actions.

Check that you know how to pronounce the final '-ed'.

| Final sound | Examples |
|---|---|
| /d/ | In most verbs, the final '-ed' is spoken with the /d/ sound in 'good': turned, moved, played, borrowed, enjoyed, answered, rescued |
| /t/ | Final '-ed' is spoken with the /t/ sound in 'ten' and 'hat' when it comes after verbs which end with these sounds:<br>/ch/ marched, watched, fetched, patched, pitched, bewitched<br>/f/ laughed, coughed, stuffed, puffed, staffed, handcuffed, knifed<br>/k/ kicked, picked, packed, smacked, baked, looked, cooked<br>/p/ hoped, helped, wiped, stopped, typed, whipped, hopped<br>/s/ faced, raced, placed, chased, ceased, promised, reduced<br>/sh/ washed, pushed, crashed, rushed, finished, wished, dashed<br>/th/ (as in 'path') berthed, bathed (in a bath) |
| /id/ | After the sounds /d/ and /t/, final '-ed' is spoken with the sound of /id/ in 'hid'.<br>The same sound is used for '-ied' at the end of 'ry' verbs which have at least two syllables.<br>/t/ waited, fated, suited, hated, voted, fitted, dated, contemplated<br>/d/ waded, folded, mended, faded, aided, blinded, befriended<br>-ied carried, married, hurried, worried, buried, queried, varied |

# Appendix 3: Irregular Verbs – Principal Parts

The following list shows the infinitive, Simple Past and past participle of some irregular verbs. Some verbs have the same form for all three, e.g. 'set', 'hurt', 'hit', 'cut', 'cost', etc. Some verbs have the same form for the Simple Past and the past participle, e.g. 'bring', 'buy', 'catch', 'fight', 'have', etc.

| Infinitive | Simple Past | Past participle |
|---|---|---|
| arise | arose | arisen |
| awake | awoke | awoken |
| be | was/were | been |
| bear | bore | born(e) |
| beat | beat | beaten |
| become | became | become |
| begin | began | begun |
| bend | bent | bent |
| bet | bet | bet |
| bind | bound | bound |
| bite | bit | bitten, bit |
| bleed | bled | bled |
| blow | blew | blown |
| break | broke | broken |
| breed | bred | bred |
| bring | brought | brought |
| broadcast | broadcast | broadcast |
| build | built | built |
| burn | burnt or burned | |
| burst | burst | burst |
| buy | bought | bought |
| cast | cast | cast |
| catch | caught | caught |
| choose | chose | chosen |
| come | came | come |
| cost | cost | cost |
| creep | crept | crept |

| Infinitive | Simple Past | Past participle |
|---|---|---|
| cut | cut | cut |
| deal | dealt | dealt |
| dig | dug | dug |
| do | did | done |
| draw | drew | drawn |
| dream | dreamt or dreamed | |
| drink | drank | drunk |
| drive | drove | driven |
| dwell | dwelt | dwelt |
| eat | ate | eaten |
| fall | fell | fallen |
| feed | fed | fed |
| feel | felt | felt |
| fight | fought | fought |
| find | found | found |
| fling | flung | flung |
| fly | flew | flown |
| forbid | forbade | forbidden |
| forecast | forecast | forecast |
| forget | forgot | forgotten |
| forgive | forgave | forgiven |
| freeze | froze | frozen |
| get | got | got |
| give | gave | given |
| go | went | gone |
| grind | ground | ground |
| grow | grew | grown |
| hang | hung, hanged | hung, hanged |
| have | had | had |
| hear | heard | heard |
| hide | hid | hidden |
| hit | hit | hit |
| hold | held | held |
| hurt | hurt | hurt |
| keep | kept | kept |
| kneel | knelt | knelt |

| Infinitive | Simple Past | Past participle |
|---|---|---|
| know | knew | known |
| lay | laid | laid |
| lead | led | led |
| lean | leant or leaned | |
| leap | leapt or leaped | |
| learn | learnt or learned | |
| leave | left | left |
| lend | lent | lent |
| let | let | let |
| lie | lay | lain |
| light | lit or lighted | |
| lose | lost | lost |
| make | made | made |
| mean | meant | meant |
| meet | met | met |
| pay | paid | paid |
| put | put | put |
| read | read | read |
| ride | rode | ridden |
| ring | rang | rung |
| rise | rose | risen |
| run | ran | run |
| saw | sawed | sawn |
| say | said | said |
| see | saw | seen |
| sell | sold | sold |
| send | sent | sent |
| set | set | set |
| sew | sewed | sewn |
| shake | shook | shaken |
| shed | shed | shed |
| shine | shone | shone |
| shoot | shot | shot |
| show | showed | shown |
| shrink | shrank | shrunk |
| shut | shut | shut |

*Appendix 3 · Irregular Verbs – Principal Parts*

| Infinitive | Simple Past | Past participle |
|---|---|---|
| sing | sang | sung |
| sink | sank | sunk |
| sit | sat | sat |
| sleep | slept | slept |
| slide | slid | slid |
| smell | smelt | smelt |
| sow | sowed | sown |
| speak | spoke | spoken |
| speed | sped | sped |
| spell | spelt | spelt |
| spend | spent | spent |
| spill | spilt or spilled | |
| spit | spat | spat |
| split | split | split |
| spoilt | spoilt or spoiled | |
| spread | spread | spread |
| spring | sprang | sprung |
| stand | stood | stood |
| steal | stole | stolen |
| stick | stuck | stuck |
| sting | stung | stung |
| strive | strove | striven |
| swear | swore | sworn |
| sweep | swept | swept |
| swim | swam | swum |
| swing | swung | swung |
| take | took | taken |
| teach | taught | taught |
| tear | tore | torn |
| tell | told | told |
| think | thought | thought |
| throw | threw | thrown |
| tread | trod | trodden |
| understand | understood | understood |
| wake | woke | woken |
| wear | wore | worn |

| Infinitive | Simple Past | Past participle |
|---|---|---|
| weave | wove | woven |
| weep | wept | wept |
| wet | wet | wet |
| win | won | won |
| wind | wound | wound |
| write | wrote | written |

# Appendix 4: Glossary of Language Words

**Adjective**

An **adjective** describes (or gives information about) a noun or pronoun. It can come before a noun (a **tall** man) or after the verb 'to be' (He is **tall**.). In a few cases, an adjective can come *after* a noun (We painted the wall **white**.)

An **adjectival phrase** has two or more words. It gives us information about a person or thing. It does *not* have its own subject and verb: The man **in the back seat** is Kwesi's uncle.

An **adjectival clause** has a subject ('who', 'that', 'which') with its verb: The girl **who is talking to Paul** is Errol's sister.

**Adverb**

An **adverb** gives us information about an action. It can tell us *how* something is done: Miss Dionne walks **slowly**. It can show *when* something was done: Uncle arrived **yesterday**.

An **adverbial phrase** does not contain a subject and verb: Paul left **in a hurry.**

An **adverbial clause** contains its own subject and verb: The game was postponed **because the field was flooded after the heavy rain**.

**Affix**

An **affix** is a letter (or more than one letter) which we can add to a word to make a new word. If letters are added to the front of a word, we call them a **prefix**: 'sub' + 'way' = 'subway'. If the letters are added to the end of a word, we call them a **suffix**: 'run' + 'er' = 'runner'.

**Agreement**

In English (and in many other languages), the form of a verb depends on which subject we use with it. For example, we say 'He is' but not 'He am'. We say 'She walks' but not 'She walk'. We call this **agreement of the subject and verb.** Sometimes other words have to agree with a word, e.g. 'this book' but 'these books', 'that woman' but 'those women'. Similarly, a pronoun must agree with the word to which it refers: Look at this watch. **It** is very cheap. Look at these shoes. **They** are very good.

**Antonym**

An **antonym** is a word which is opposite in meaning to another word, e.g. 'hot—cold', 'rich—poor', 'valuable—worthless'.

**Articles**

We call the words 'a' and 'an' **indefinite articles** (because they do not refer to a definite person or thing.) We call 'the' the **definite article** because it refers to a definite person or thing. Some writers call 'a', 'an' and 'the' 'determiners'. It does not matter whether you call them articles or determiners.

### Auxiliary verbs
The word 'auxiliary' means 'helping'. Examples of auxiliary verbs include 'am', 'is', 'are' (Uncle **is** coming), 'do', 'does', 'did' (What **did** she say?), 'has', 'have' (**Have** you finished your work?), 'shall', 'will', 'may', 'might', etc.

### Clause
A clause is a group of words with a subject and a verb:
> The man stopped.
> The old man with a paper bag full of ragged clothes stopped for a moment to rest and recover from the long walk.

In both cases, the subject is 'man', and the verb is 'stopped'. A clause can be an **adjectival clause**, an **adverbial clause** or a **noun clause**. It can be the **main clause** of a sentence or it can be a **subordinate clause**:
> *main clause:* The man stopped to rest in the shade of a tree.
> *main + subordinate clause*: The man stopped to rest in the shade of a tree **because he was very tired.**

### Complement
These sentences make sense by themselves:
> The bus stopped.
> Stephanie woke up.

Some verbs need other words added to make complete sentences:
> Kingston is **in Jamaica**.
> Anna looks **much better now**.

The words in bold are called the **complement** of the sentence. Verbs which require a complement include 'be', 'look', 'appear', 'seem', 'become', etc.

### Conjunction
We often use **conjunctions** (joining words) such as 'and', 'but' and 'or' to link words, phrases or clauses. They are also called **connectives**.

### Contractions
A **contraction** is a short form used in speech, e.g. don't = do not; it's = it is *or* it has. If you use dialogue in a story, remember to use contractions and not the full form of some words.

### Dialect
A **dialect** is a type of language spoken mainly in one town, district, region, etc. or by certain groups of people only. The dialect of Jamaica is not exactly the same as the dialect of Guyana or Trinidad. The dialect of London is not the same as that of Liverpool, Glasgow or Tobago. One problem with most dialects is that if you use a dialect, you may not be able to communicate efficiently with people outside your own group.

### Dialogue
**Dialogue** is conversation written down. It can be in playscript form or be part of a short story or a novel. Inverted commas are not needed for playscript but they *are* needed when dialogue is part of a printed story or novel.

### Exclamation
An **exclamation** shows strong emotion: joy, pain, disgust, fear, etc.: Ow!, Oh! and Bah! Short sentences can also be exclamations: Get lost! Help! Sit down!

### Finite and non-finite verbs
A **finite verb** is a working verb with a subject. A **non-finite** (or infinite) **verb** is a verb which does not have a subject and is not used in any tense. A verb can be finite in one sentence but infinite in another sentence, e.g.
- *finite:* Paul **is swimming** to the beach.
- *non-finite:* Paul likes **to swim.**

### Gerund
A **gerund** is a noun made from a verb. It often ends in '-ing'. It is different from other nouns because it can have an object: Birds like **eating** seeds. **Eating** vegetables is good for you.

### Idiom
An **idiom** is a popular expression in which words are often used with a special meaning, e.g. to bury the hatchet (meaning 'make peace').

### Infinitive
An **infinitive** is the (base) form of a verb before we add any endings or change it into a tense. An infinitive starts with 'to' but we can omit 'to' when necessary:
- *with 'to':* All cars ought **to stop** when the lights are red.
- *without 'to':* All cars must **stop** when the lights are red.

### Literal language
When we use a word literally, it means what it says. Consider the word 'comb':
- *literally true:* Use a brush and comb to make your hair tidy.
- *figurative (not literally true):* The police will comb the forest in their search for the escaped men.

In the figurative example, 'comb' means 'search very thoroughly'. The police will not use a comb and brush.

### Noun
A **noun** is the name of something. We often use **common nouns** (tree, girl, shoe), **proper nouns** (Barbados, Sharon, Amazon), **collective nouns** (herd, team, flock) and **abstract nouns** (ambition, kindness, bravery, wisdom). We can count many things, so we call them **countable nouns** and can form their plural. We cannot count such things as 'dust', 'mud' and 'hatred', so we call them **uncountable nouns** and use them in the singular only.

### Object
In a sentence, the **object** is the person or thing *to whom* the action of an active verb is done: We repaired the **pipe**. Mr Harris thanked **us**. Sometimes there is an **indirect object** in a sentence. It often follows 'for' or 'to': Miss Smith made this dress for **me**. Please give this letter to **your mother**.

### Participles
**Participles** are formed from verbs. They are used to make tenses but they are often used as adjectives. A **present participle** usually ends in '-ing.' Many **past participles** end in '-ed', but the past participle of an irregular verb may end in '-n', '-t' or another letter.

### Parts of speech
**Parts of speech** are the names we use to show the work which a word does in a sentence. You can say that they are the names for the tools we use in a language. In English, we say that the parts of speech are nouns, adjectives, pronouns, verbs, adverbs, prepositions, conjunctions and exclamations.

### Person
In grammar, **person** is used in this way:

|  | Singular | Plural |
|---|---|---|
| 1st person | I | we |
| 2nd person | you | you |
| 3rd person | he, she, it | they |

### Phrase
A **phrase** is an expression of two or more words which does *not* contain a finite verb. Many phrases start with a preposition or a participle, e.g.

> The girl **with long hair** is Paul's sister.
> I can see a boy **climbing up a tree**.
> The men cleared away the tree **knocked down by the storm**.

### Prefix
A **prefix** consists of one or more letters added to the beginning of a word to form a new word:

> **sub** + marine = submarine
> **tri** + angle = triangle

### Preposition
A **preposition** is a word put before a noun or pronoun to show its relation with an earlier word. Common prepositions include 'at', 'by', 'in', 'on', 'for', 'above', 'below', 'into', 'under' and 'through': We got **off** the bus **at** the market. Prepositions are often used at the start of a phrase showing when or where an action happened.

### Pronoun
A **pronoun** is a word used to replace a noun. Then we do not have to repeat the noun. Examples of pronouns include:

| | |
|---|---|
| *personal:* | I, me, she, her, he, him, it, we, us, you, they |
| *possessive:* | mine, yours, hers, his, ours, theirs |
| *reflexive:* | myself, yourself, herself, themselves |
| *relative:* | who, that, which, whom, whose |
| *demonstrative:* | this, these, that, those |
| *interrogative:* | Who, What, Which |
| *indefinite:* | anybody, everyone, nothing, somebody |

### Proverb
A **proverb** is a short traditional saying which makes sense by itself and often gives advice, e.g. Look before you leap.

### Sentence
A **sentence** is a word or group of words which makes complete sense by itself. It contains a finite verb and a subject which is mentioned or understood:
   Stop! = (You) stop.
   St Lucia is an island.

### Subject
When we use an active verb, the **subject** is the person or thing that *does* the action shown by the verb: **That bus** goes to Ocho Rios. When we use a passive verb, the subject *receives* the action of the verb: Has **the computer** been repaired yet?

### Suffix
A **suffix** is a letter or group of letters added to the end of a word to make a new word:
   -ly: quick + ly = quickly
   -er: swim + er = swimmer

### Synonym
A **synonym** is a word which is similar in meaning to another word: small—little, false—untrue. Synonyms are similar in meaning but usually not exactly the same in meaning and/or usage.

### Tense
A **tense** is a form of a verb used to show the time of an action, e.g. whether it happened in the **past**, is happening at **present** or will happen in the **future**. Most western languages have tenses. Some African and Asian languages do not have tenses. They use time words to show when an action happened.

### Transitive
The word 'transitive' tells us that a verb has a direct object: Our cat caught a mouse. If a verb is intransitive, it does *not* have an object. Some verbs are always intransitive: Grandma **seems** much better today.

### Verb

A **verb** is usually a word which shows an action. Some verbs can show a state or a relationship:

| | |
|---|---|
| *an action:* | My aunt **works** in a shop. |
| *a state:* | Our car **is** very old. |
| *a relationship:* | This key **is** yours. |

### Voice

In grammar, we use the word 'voice' to show whether the subject *does* an action or *receives* the action. A verb can be used in the **active voice** or **passive voice**:

| | |
|---|---|
| *active:* | Tom **kicked** Paul accidentally. |
| *passive:* | Paul **was kicked** accidentally. |

# Appendix 5: Glossary of Literary Terms

Terms marked with an asterisk are included in the syllabus for the CSEC examination.

**Allegory**
An **allegory** is an account or story with a hidden meaning. For example, a story about animals may really be a criticism of politicians because each animal is meant to be one of the politicians criticised.

***Alliteration**
**Alliteration** is the repetition of the same letter or sound at the beginning of (or in) words which are close together, e.g.
    We went **s**liding down the **s**lippery **s**lope.

**Antithesis**
**Antithesis** is the arrangement of words to obtain a contrast, e.g.
    Give me liberty or give me death.
    To err is human; to forgive divine.

**Aposiopesis**
**Aposiopesis** is suddenly failing to finish a statement, e.g.
    Oh, tell him to go to …!
This device is often used to leave a reader to use his or her imagination.

**Apostrophe**
This involves making an appeal to a person or thing (usually in a poem or speech) that is not present, e.g.
    Oh, Nanny, if only you were with us now!

***Assonance**
**Assonance** is the use of the same or similar vowel sounds in words which occur close together, e.g.
    Get to bed, you sleepy head!

**Climax**
A **climax** is the most dramatic, exciting or intense point in a narrative or an event.

***Connotation, denotation**
Many words can have at least two meanings: a primary or basic meaning and a secondary (often emotional) meaning. For example, the primary meaning of 'home' is 'a place where a person or animal lives'. Its secondary meaning can imply shelter, comfort

and affection. The primary meaning is the **denotation** of the word, i.e. what it denotes. The secondary meaning is the **connotation** of the word, i.e. what it may imply to some people.

### *Couplet
In poetry, a **couplet** is a pair of lines which come together, especially a pair which rhyme.

### Didactic
**Didactic** means 'intending to teach'. A poem can be didactic if the poet seeks to teach or give advice. This word is sometimes used to contrast with 'amusing' or 'entertaining', and it implies that a poet has a serious purpose.

### *Ellipsis
**Ellipsis** has two meanings. It can mean the use of … to show that something has been left out. Then a reader has to use his or imagination to complete a sentence. It can also refer to words left out (especially in poetry) but which we can easily guess, e.g. in this sentence the second 'was' has been omitted:
> The man was arrested and sent to prison.

### Euphemism
A **euphemism** is deliberate understatement. If a man is evil and/or corrupt, we can use euphemism by saying that he 'has flexible principles'. Similarly, 'passing away' is a euphemism for 'dying'. A writer might not want to admit that the slavery of children is widespread in some parts of the world. He or she may avoid an unpleasant truth by saying that it is 'not unknown'.

### Explicit/implicit
We use **explicit** when something is clearly stated and is obvious, and we use **implicit** for something that is not stated openly but is implied or can be deduced.

### Fiction/non-fiction
Works of **fiction** are ones which are not true. The events have been made up by a writer. **Non-fiction** is used for works which are true.

### *Figurative language
Figurative language involves the use of words which may not be literally true. In a wider sense, figurative language is simply language which uses figures of speech such as **metaphors**, **similes**, etc. If somebody is in trouble, we can say: 'Figuratively speaking, his world has collapsed about him.' The figures of speech are sometimes called 'devices', especially in an examination, where you might come across a question like this: What devices does the poet use to …?

**Hyperbole** (pronounced: (high) (**per**) (b*li), stress 'per'. The sound * comes after 'th' in 'the game'.)
This is the use of obvious and deliberate exaggeration, e.g.
> There were millions of spectators at the football game last Saturday.

### Implied
Meanings which are **implied** are those which we can deduce from a statement but which are not stated openly.

### Infer
This means to deduce, to conclude by looking at a statement. We can say that somebody 'would be better employed in a position which does not involve handling money'. We can **infer** from the statement that the person is dishonest. The statement **implies** that the person may be dishonest.

### *Innuendo
An **innuendo** is a statement (often bad or critical) implied about somebody but not stated openly.

### *Irony
**Irony** is an outcome which is mainly the opposite of what is expected, e.g.
> Mrs X attended the funeral of her husband whom she disliked. While taking part in the ceremony, she had a heart attack and died. It is **ironic** that she should have died in this way. She was going out of her way to show respect for somebody she did not respect — but the only reward she got was her own death.

### *Limerick
A **limerick** is a short humorous poem of five lines. Lines 1, 2 and 5 rhyme. Lines 3 and 4 are a rhyming couplet. Many limericks start with the words:
> There was a … from ….

### *Litotes
**Litotes** is a type of understatement, and sometimes involves using a negative, e.g.
> Winning a gold medal at the Olympics is not bad at all.

Here 'not bad at all' is used for 'extremely good'.

### *Metaphor
A **metaphor** is a word used for something which it does not denote literally, often to make a striking comparison, e.g.
> That shopkeeper is a real **shark**.
> Lara is a **tower** of strength in the team.

### Metre
**Metre** is the way in which words are arranged to obtain rhythm, especially in a line of poetry.

### *Mood
**Mood** can refer to the state of mind of a writer, especially a poet, or to the impression of a poet which we get from reading a poem. A poet's mood can be reflective, pensive, joyful, resentful, cheerful, etc.

### *Onomatopoeia
This is forming or using words which imitate the sound of something to which they refer, e.g.
> playing **ping-pong**
> waves **smashing** and **crashing** and **slashing** the rocks.

### Oxymoron
**Oxymoron** involves using two contradictory or contrasting words together, e.g.
> a deafening silence
> with cruel kindness

### Parenthesis
Words in **parenthesis** are in brackets or marked off from the rest of a sentence by commas.

### Personification
To **personify** something is to give life to something which is lifeless, e.g. by writing about a tree or mountain as if it is a living person, able to think and perhaps speak.

### Plot
The **plot** is the storyline in a film, novel or story; information about the actions in the story.

### *Pun
A **pun** is a humorous play on words.

### *Rhyme scheme
A **rhyme scheme** is the pattern of same or similar sounds in words (usually at the end of lines in poetry). When rhyming **couplets** are used, the rhyme scheme may be *a, a, b, b, c, c, d, d*, etc. If alternate lines rhyme, the scheme may be *a, b, a, b; c, d, c, d*. In a **limerick**, the rhyme scheme is usually *a, a, b, b, a*.

### *Rhythm
The **rhythm** in a poem is the (often regular) beat in a line somewhat like waves breaking regularly on a beach. Sometimes poets will change the rhythm within a poem to suit whatever it is that they are writing about in different parts of the poem.

### Run-on line
In a poem, a **run-on line** occurs when part of a sentence is on one line and the rest of the sentence is on the next line.

### *Sarcasm
**Sarcasm** is intending to cause pain or embarrassment by using bitter words or by making a statement that you and another person know is false, e.g.
> A student may have written a composition with very poor handwriting. A teacher may hold it up, show it to the class and say (sarcastically): 'Now here is a *fine* example of handwriting. Yes, a fine example of what *not* to do.'

### *Simile
A **simile** is a comparison which is made by using 'like' or 'as'. Similes can make a description more vivid or striking, e.g.
> He sings **like** a frog with a sore throat.
> Joe shuffled to the front of the class **like** an old man awaiting execution.

### Style
**Style** is the way in which something is written, spoken or sung. People may have different opinions of a writer's style. Words which may sometimes be used to describe the style of a writer include 'dull', 'boring', 'monotonous', 'hesitant', 'inconsistent', 'laboured', 'polished', 'fascinating', 'engrossing', 'effective', etc.
In an examination, if you write about a poet's style, you should try to quote words or lines from the poem as evidence in support of your opinion.

### Suspense
**Suspense** involves keeping a reader (or viewer) interested by presenting him or her with a problem and then by not revealing the solution immediately. In a play or film, the suspense often increases steadily until we reach a **climax**. Then comes the denouement when the plot is finally resolved.

### Syllable stress
**Stress** is the amount of emphasis which we put on (parts of) words when we read a poem. Dictionaries normally put ´ before or after a stressed syllable to show the pronunciation of a word. On some English words, the first syllable is stressed if the word is used as a noun; the second syllable is stressed if the word is used as a verb, e.g.
> To black people, Paul Bogle was a hero and a patriot. To the British he was a **reb**el.
> People will re**bel** if they are treated badly.

### Tautology
**Tautology** is when we use more words than we need to, e.g.
> The referee added on **an additional** five minutes for injuries.
> The injured man died as a result of **fatal** injuries received in the accident.

In the first example, we do not need 'an additional' because this idea has already been expressed by 'added on'. In the second example, we can omit 'fatal' because we already know that the man died.

### *Tone
Like **mood**, the **tone** of a poem can be almost anything: cheerful, happy, one of rejoicing and celebration, or it can be grim, showing bitterness and resentment. Most poems are the result of some strong emotion which the poet feels. When we want to discuss the tone of a poem, we can start by considering the emotions felt by the poet.

# Index

a, an 130
accompany 21
adapt, adopt 156
adjective
   adj or adv 214
   clauses 39, 76, 232
   comparison 175
   compound 126
   forming 138
   possessive 161
   too + adj 10
   using 171
adverbs 214, 232
advice/se 156
affect, effect 156
affixes 157, 232
afraid 145
agreement 23, 51, 75, 79, 232
allegory 238
alliteration 238
alternately 156
antithesis 238
antonyms 5, 74, 232
answer 21
aposiopesis 238
apostrophe (punctuation) 52
apostrophe (fig device) 238
arrive 21
articles 130, 232
as 197
asking questions 135
assonance 238
assure, ensure 156
attend 21
auxiliary verbs 221, 233

because 132
books, parts of 24
busy 145

cable, sending 154
capital letters 80–1
ce/se 107
characterisation 56–7, 210
clauses, main & subord 11, 233
climax 238

cloze passage 196
common errors 91, 211
complaints 119
complement 233
comprehension: see 'reading comprehension'
comprehension/ive 155
conditional tenses 219
conflict & plot 56, 172, 190–1
connectives 40, 233
connotation 238
construction shift 39
continue 145
contractions 52, 233
couplet 239

demand 21, 145
denotation 238
despite 145
dialect 49, 210, 233
dialogue 56, 58, 234
dictionary 48
didactic 239
discovery, invention 156
discuss 21, 145
discussion 62, 67, 210

economic(al) 155
ed (final) 226
ed/ing 139
ei/ie 12
eligible 155
ellipsis 239
emotive values 87
emphatic pronouns 127, 236
enter 21
envelope, addressing 94
epitaphs 148
euphemism 3, 239
exceed 145
exclamation mark 209, 234
explain 145
explicit, implicit 239

fear 145
fiction 239
figurative language 35, 65, 239

(non) finite verbs 218, 220, 234
formally, formerly 156
full stop 11, 41, 47
future tenses 219, 225

gerund 218, 234
grateful, thankful 156

handwriting 6
help, asking for 34
homophones 102
hyperbole 239

idioms 36, 72, 169, 185, 234
illegal 155
illegible 155
imperative mood 221
implications 240
indirect questions 198–9, 201
indirect speech 160–3, 185–6
inferences 240
infinite verbs 218, 220, 234
infinitive 10, 187, 218, 234
innuendo 240
inverted commas 174
irony 240
irregular verbs 228–232

lack 145
letter 94, 178
licence/se 107
limericks 95, 240
listening 65, 147, 175
literal language 234
litotes 240
logical thinking 7
looking ahead 6
loose, lose 155
lower 145

many, much 205
map 65–6
metaphors 35, 240
metre 240
mood 220, 240

news report 44
non-fiction 239
nouns 34, 205, 234

object 235
occupations 140

omit 145
onomatopoeia 241
orders, reporting 160
oxymoron 241

paragraphing 3, 62
parenthesis 241
participles 218, 235
parts of speech 235
past continuous 50, 219, 223
past, simple 20, 22, 92, 219, 223
perfect, past 142–4, 219, 225
perfect, present 89–91, 219, 224
person 235
personification 241
phrase 235
pie charts 213
plot 56, 172, 241
poetry 25, 54, 81, 93, 95, 108, 111–15, 133, 148, 163, 177, 188, 203, 216
precede, proceed 156
prefixes 157, 158, 235
prepositions 21, 128, 145, 215, 235
present continuous 36–8, 219, 223
present, simple 8, 9, 219, 222
principal, principle 155
principal parts of verbs 227–31
problem words 155
pronouns 235
    demonstrative 236
    interrogative 236
    personal 106, 236
    possessive 236
    reflexive 127, 236
    relative 39, 76–8, 236
proverbs 170, 236
pun 241
punctuation
    apostrophe 52
    capital letters 80–1
    comma 150
    exclamation mark 209
    full stop 11, 41, 47, 80, 131
    hyphen 126
    inverted commas 174
    question mark 159, 187
purpose 187

question mark 159, 187
questions, asking 125, 135
questions with tags 104–6

reach 21
reading comprehension 2, 16, 32, 46, 61, 71, 85, 99, 117, 124, 137, 152, 167, 181, 193, 208
re-expression 39
reference sources 25, 48
refrain 155
reply 21
reports 44, 64
request 145
restrain 155
rhyme scheme 241
rhythm 241
run-on-line 241

sarcasm 241
semaphore 154
sentence 236
setting 56
simile 242
so as to 187
so that 187
speaking 19, 34, 62, 67, 124
   letter 'h' 200
   final -ed 226
   syllable stress 200
   'th' 24
spelling
   ce/se 107
   ei/ie 12
   final consonant 13
   ing/ed 13
   problem words 13, 119
in spite of 145
starting a story 60, 134, 172–4
statistics 213
stories
   characters 56, 172, 210
   dialogue and language 56, 172
   ending 172
   plot 56, 172, 190–1
   setting 56, 172
   starting 60, 134, 172–4
   writing 56–8, 171–4, 190–1
study skills 24, 25, 74
style 242
subject 236
subjunctive mood 221
suffixes 157, 236
summary 27–9, 30, 44, 68, 93, 118, 124, 134, 184
suspense 242

syllable stress 200, 242
synonyms 74, 102, 236
synthesis 188

tautology 242
telegram 154
tenses 219, 222–6, 236
then 40
there is/are 79–80
therefore 40
thesaurus 74
thinking skills 7
time, it's 92
tone 242
too + adj 10
transitive verbs 219, 236

used to 202

verb forms 218–21
verbs, principal parts 227–31
visit 21
vocabulary
   affixes 157
   antonyms 5, 74
   cloze passage 196
   dialect 49
   emotive values 87
   expansion of 5, 18, 63
   homophones 102
   idioms 36, 72, 169, 185
   meaning in context 4, 17, 33, 61, 71, 86, 101, 117, 125, 137, 153, 168, 182, 194, 208
   occupations 140
   prefixes 158
   problem words 155
   proverbs 170
   synonyms 74, 102
voice 220, 237

who/that 76
whose 39
writing
   Argumentative 55, 62, 165
   Descriptive 150, 165, 178, 217
   Factual 14, 55, 68, 97, 110, 121
   Imaginative 97, 121, 178, 217
   Letter 94, 178
   Narrative 13, 62, 97, 150, 191
   Pictures 13, 97, 110, 141, 179
   Story 13, 68, 83, 110, 121, 134

# Acknowledgements

The author and publishers are grateful to all the staff and students involved in sampling *English Alive!*, in particular Dianne Boyd at the Convent of Mercy Academy 'Alpha', Merlyn Taylor-Cox at Haile Selassie High School and Shawna Henry at St Hugh's High School, Kingston, Jamaica.

The author and publishers would like to thank the following for permission to reproduce copyright material:

Photos:

- Corel 38 (NT) p179
- Corel 286 (NT) p14
- Corel 448 (NT) p30
- Corel 541 (NT) p141 (top)
- Hulton Deutsch/Corbis p112
- Paul Velasco; Gallo Images/Corbis p141 (bottom).

Extracts and poems:

- *A Brighter Sun* by Sam Sevlon pp15–16 and pp45–46
- *Colonisation in Reverse* by Louise Bennett p111. With thanks to Sangster Bookstores Ltd, Jamaica
- *If* by Rudyard Kipling pp25–26. By permission of A.P. Watt Ltd on behalf of the National Trust for Places of Historic Interest or Natural Beauty
- *On an Afternoon Train from Purley to Victoria, 1955* by James Berry pp93–94. Reprinted by permission of PFD on behalf of: James Berry. © James Berry
- *The Emigrants* from *The Arrivants* by Edward Braithwaite p113. By permission of OUP.

Every effort has been made to contact copyright holders and the publishers apologise to anyone whose rights have been inadvertently overlooked and will be happy to rectify any errors or omissions. We have been unable to trace the copyright holders of the following extracts and poems:

- *If* by Una Marson
- *The Precious Corn* by Michael Anthony
- *Dawn* by Raymond Barrow
- *The Village* by William S. Arthur
- *I Look into my Glass* by Thomas Hardy
- *Limbo Dancer in Dark Glasses* by John Agard.